ANNIHILATOR OF INNOCENCE

TAHIERA MONIQUE BROWN

Pg. 27.
Sgt. major.

Pg. 200

❋

We welcome your comments about this book.
Please send us an email with your comments, or write to us at the address below.

Tavine'ra Publishing, LLC
Birmingham, Alabama 35242 USA
www.annihilatorofinnocence.com

Annihilator of Innocence

Requests for information should be addressed to:

Tavine'ra Publishing, 270 Doug Baker Blvd., Suite 700 – 316, Birmingham, AL 35242
tahiera.316east@earthlink.net

Brown, Tahiera Monique, 1956-

ISBN: 0-971-39530-6
1. Non-Fiction Drama. 2. True Crime. 3. Women's Interest. 4. Memoir. 5. Biography.

Cover Artwork by Wendy Lovoy,
Design by Mike Hawkins
Editors: Kathy Ptacek, Betsy Stokes, and Vickii Howell

2006908867

Printed in the United States of America

❀

The Table Of Contents

❖

Imagine living two years in hell
without the hope of ever getting out.

•

Imagine walking the line to meet death
to save the lives of others.

•

Imagine a veil over your eyes
shielding you from
the love of your children . . .
and your children from you.

•

Imagine someone else
bathing you,
dressing you,
watching you
when you use the restroom.

•

Imagine sleepless nights being
trained to be someone else . . .
someone you didn't choose to be.

•

Imagine a gun on you every hour,
every morning . . . evening . . . night.

•

Imagine not knowing if your
children are dead or alive,
or if you are allowed to live
the next 24 hours.

This is my story,
the story of Barbara Clark.

❧

ANNIHILATOR OF INNOCENCE:
I've Been Dead for Two Years

The Barbara Clark Story

"The eyes of the Lord watch
over those who love him
he is their powerful protection
and their strong support,
their screen from the desert wind,
their shelter from the midday sun,
a guard against stumbling,
and assurance against a fall.
He revives the spirit,
and brightens the eyes,
he gives healing,
life and blessing."

Ecclesiasticus 34:19-20,
JERUSALEM BIBLE

❧

Dedication

⍥

This book is for all of the individuals who looked after my children while I inhabited the corridors of Grady Memorial Hospital in Atlanta, Georgia, struggling to regain my memory and learning to survive in a world that had become foreign to me.

To DeKalb County District Attorney J. Tom Morgan and his staff for representing my daughter, and for their outstanding dedication to victims of abuse. You were incredible and loyal.

To the Grady Memorial hospital staff. You were very careful and understanding of the nature of my condition. You did not promise me miracles. You made me understand that surviving amnesia and the circumstances that I would face; after I left, was up to me.

To my brother, James, who did not throw stones but stood by my side through the times when I was homeless. You were like the net that caught me whenever I felt the world was tossing me about.

To Margaret, my best friend for more than 25 years, and counting.

To Lottie, who became the other mother to my children . . . with out any questions.

To Marty Polak, Anthony Lloyd, and Bobby White for being my three buddies who were always there in the lean years. When all I knew was poverty, you treated me as if I was the richest person on earth . . . I truly thank you guys.

To Dee Voight, who gave me the opportunity to work in the film business and to show that I can do anything.

To Dana Weed, the rock that stood before me and encouraged me to be who I was meant to be . . . always with a comforting voice.

To the honor of all children of physical and sexual abuse, battered women, and disabled children and adults, a percentage of proceeds from this book will go to an organization called "The Gussie Grant Foundation." This non-profit corporation that I am organizing supports the needs of the physically and mentally disabled, sexually abused, and battered women and children.

❧

Introduction

❧

In 1988, I wrote a script, while we were still in trial called, "Too Scared To Scream." I had been out of the hospital only a few weeks when I realized that having a life would require living every day with two children who had endured the unthinkable.

I sat at the computer in September 1996, trying to get up the courage to write the story of my life. I was so depressed, because I had no idea how to use the machine that seemed to gaze at my trembling fingers. There were so many words in my mind; I somehow hoped that the keypad would jump to my touch the way a regular typewriter used to do for me. I just could not work the thing properly. I was sitting at a real computer for the first time and I was afraid of it.

One night there was an electrical storm in which a surge ran through the computer and erased my whole book. I broke down and cried. It was very difficult for me to trust the computer after that.

My struggle with this machine took control of me until the last two days of 1999, coming into the new millennium. I heard my name on the television. A man had killed his family and his wife's name was the same as mine, Barbara Clark. I was in shock, but I worked to keep a clear head. I cannot forget the pain and terror that still leaps into me in my dreams. Just to think that this man killed his family while they were sleeping.

Oh, the many nights the Old Man had tried to choke me to death in my sleep. Oh, the nights that he dragged me down the hall screaming with a snarl in his voice, "Do you know if your kids are dead or alive?"

Honestly, I am still afraid to tell the story of my life. It's as if I would like to separate myself from it all together…change my name and move to another city.

❖

It's now 2006. As I read the newspapers, I realize how so many people are suffering. I searched for the courage within to tell people who have suffered that I, too, have suffered, and that I am truly a survivor. The only way to get through the pain is to live true and truly live.

Living True and Truly Living is an inspirational book that I hope to publish next year. I could not be true to you without being true to myself to live free in spite of fear. I wrote this book so that my story could show others how to move past the fear and on with their lives.

*Some names in this book have been changed to protect the innocent, and there will be some obscene language to accurately portray reality.

❖

Prologue:

⍨

The Story Begins Where It All Ended

It has been a treacherous journey, digging into the crevices of the darkness. The pain is like having cancer in its advanced stages, without the morphine. It is April of 1988, and I have awakened from a coma. Or perhaps I continue to sleep among what appears to be the living. I have amnesia.

It has taken me many agonizing years to adjust to life outside of the walls of Grady Hospital. The people who get to know me also get to know what I do not know. It's simple things to them, but it is a feat of great difficulty for me when I am not sure how to open a bottle cap or operate a radio or a television set. Sometimes I sit at home all day without watching TV or listening to the radio because I am just too confused about how to turn either on. I am sometimes afraid to walk down the streets, because people might speak to me, and I do not recall their faces. It seems as if a shadow is always lurking over my shoulder. I was afraid of my own fears and the shadows of the past chasing behind me.

These fears were keeping me from grasping the whole glory of the now, which I must overcome in order to face the future.

I wrote one last poem before making a decision that almost ended my life.

❉

Please Help Me Somebody

Please help me somebody

Can you not see me out here

Can you not see my tears falling

I'm crying in the wilderness

Bitter, stinging, ringing pains

Cluttering the closets of my soul

How do I stop the pain . . . the pain . . .

The pain . . .

Deep within the corners of my mind, I have searched for a way to put together the words that would express to you the conditions that my children and I had to endure during the two years that we were held hostage by a heartless, tormenting Old Man. No one ever knows what might come along in life that might change them forever.

�֍

Chapter 1.

✄

I Was Born In the Country

I was born in Albany, Georgia, in 1956. My mother was a beautiful woman who was well built and well defined. Her name was Jessica. My daddy was tall and very dark skinned and he called me "Happy Jack." His name was Donald.

My father was an alcoholic and he became verbally abusive. He did not trust my mother, and life became much more difficult with the birth of his two other children by her.

I lived where I had several grandmothers and three granddaddies. My mother's mother, Ellen Jackson, was living, as were her daddy, her grandfather, and her husband. We called my mother's father Granddad Jackson.

On my daddy's side, his mother, Bertha Wilson, was living. So was her husband, Granddad Wilson. Also, Grandma Bertha's mother was living, and we called her Great Grandma Peaches. We also had a host of aunts and uncles.

Grandma Bertha Wilson had 17 children, and five died. Grandma Ellen Jackson had, I think, 12 children, with nine surviving.

I was raised deep in the country sometimes with my daddy's mother or my mother's mother. Having a lot of relatives had its disadvantages when it comes to anyone getting

❄

enough attention or enough direction in life. I can assume that people saw my brother, James, and me as the grandchildren, or the niece and nephew. So we were treated as if we would soon be going home to our parents.

My parents divorced and my mother remarried, leaving James and me behind to be raised by our relatives. We had no real authority figures, and we seemed to float with the days like an ocean current that had no ending. We kind of melted into nothingness, with no real values or place to call our true home. We felt as if we were always visiting.

Mommy, Where Are You?

On the day that I remember most about my mother leaving – I believe I was four or five years old – she was taking me to some kind of school. She took me into a room with some small children and a tall lady who took my hand. My mother kissed me on the cheek and promised to pick me up after the bell rang. But she didn't.

At the end of the day, I sat on a stoop looking down the alleyway. I saw all the children leave, some with parents, while others skipped off down the alleyway. I watched a little girl and a boy playing on the swing and decided to join them. But as soon as I sat on the swing, their parents came. It was not unusual for a small child to be walking from school alone in the country, so the other parents did not feel it was necessary to help me. I did not look concerned, because I truly believed my mother was coming for me.

I played alone for a while, and then I went and sat back down on the stoop. I heard a loud clap of thunder as heavy winds began to blow. As the rain started falling, I ran down the alley. The thunder became louder, and darkness was settling over the city. I was scared to death and screamed, "Mommy, where are you?"

Tears flowed with the rain as I climbed into some tall grass to hide. It was so dark when I heard the sounds of footsteps coming toward me. I was hoping it was my Mommy as I came out of the bushes soaked in tears and rain. But it wasn't. It was Mrs. Molly, the old lady who lived down the street from my grandmother. She tried to comfort me to take me home, but I resisted, because I was terrified of my mommy missing me. I screamed as she took hold of my hand and wrestled with me. She was very strong, so I gave in and followed her.

It seemed like forever as we walked down the dirt road to my Grandma Ellen's house. When my grandmother saw us and heard my cry, the first thing she said was, "Child, hush your mouth and get in this house!"

For days after that I watched for my Mommy. I used to wake before daybreak as my grandmother began making biscuits. She would send me outside to get the firewood for the pot-bellied stove. I would look up the dirt road where the darkness and the shadows danced together, and I'd envision my mother coming down the road singing one of her songs. Just then, a hand would reach out to me. It would be James grabbing the hem of my old gown telling me that grandma said, "Bring in the firewood!"

I would come back into reality, with the load of wood that I hadn't realized I picked up. In the midst of my fantasy, tears would stream down my face. As always, like a set alarm clock, my grandma would tell me to shut my mouth as she took the wood from me. Her voice was never harsh … just firm.

No More Pickin' Cotton

Although I was very young, I knew how to cook and light the fire. And I'd help little James get dressed for the long journey that we took during the hot summer months.

I would hear the old pick up truck coming down the road. Then it would stop, and the old white man, Mr. Sims, would yell, "Come on, old lady. Cotton pickin' time."

❧

Grandma Ellen always made bologna and fatback sandwiches with big hunks of cheese. We would eat biscuits with thick homemade syrup. I can remember the syrup dripping through my little fingers. I could see the dust billow from behind the truck as we made our way to the cotton fields. The truck would be loaded down with black folks looking tired and somber. I longed for my mother every day. As we traveled through the fields, the truck passed endless aisles of cotton. The fields went on forever.

I used to look for the field master's house. It was the house with huge red brick and beautiful flowers and little white children playing in the yard. I used to say that one day I was gonna live like that.

My Grandma Ellen was always so silent. She taught by example, and I learned by watching her. She was fussy in the fields, though. I used to get pinched a lot as Grandma Ellen would try to make me stop complaining about the heat and the critters. I was scared to death of the boll weevils. And just about everyday, somebody would holler, "Snake!" James and I used to sing a little cotton pickin' song to help make the day go by faster:

I'm gonna jump down turn around,

pick a bail of cotton.

I'm gonna jump down turn around

pick a bail a day.

O, Lawdy, pick a bail of cotton.

O, Lawdy, pick a bail a day.

Folks also sang old spirituals as we worked. Somebody would holler, and another person would add a tune, and the next thing you know, the whole field would be alive with song. It didn't matter what we were pickin.' Whether it was peas, pecans, or corn, the workers still sang those hymns.

Back at home, we ate a lot of our food from the garden,

and there was a little grocery store down the street. There were rows of wooden houses and the dirt road that seemed to my eyes to go on forever. Sometimes, we stayed at my Grandma Bertha's house way out in the country. Her mother, Great-Grandma Peaches, lived down the street, as did other relatives.

They all had farms and outhouses that were way out in the back of their homes. Grandma Peaches' outhouse had a path that led from the back porch with tall grass on either side. To me, it was a forest. I was scared to death to go back there.

Everybody had pee pots made out of old paint cans or buckets that they either kept on the back porch or somewhere near at night. It was always fun in the country, because there was so much to do and see. There was a pecan field across the way where cattle grazed.

We had to pump water at my Great-Grandma Peaches, but my Grandma Bertha got hers from a spigot on the front porch, which had a rag tied around the base. I used to slide across the wooden floor into the puddle around it, and many times I landed on the ground below. And just like clockwork, she would tell me over and over again, "Child, you goin' to hurt yo sef."

Sometimes the men killed a hog, and that would be a day for a feast as the women cut up the meat. They roasted pecans over a fire. Or sometimes it would be peanuts, depending on the season.

My Grandma Ellen loved boiled peanuts. We ate a lot of sugarcane, watermelon, various vegetables, and fish caught fresh from the creek, chickens and eggs hand-picked from the farm.

I didn't have any little girls to play with, but I always had dreams of being rich, with a mansion and lots of friends. I always wondered if there were people of other colors besides the white people that I saw at the fields. I had never seen a

Mexican or a Japanese or a . . . you know what I mean, don't
you?   I wondered, "Why did we always have to get out of
the white folks way?"   My Grandma Ellen never told me
verbally; she would just nudge us away as we passed them.

I always wanted to sing and be a great speaker. I tried
to sing to the sounds of the water flowing in the creek, or to
the sounds of the crickets at night. I liked skipping down the
alley behind the shack houses and creating the sound of song
to the tapping of my shoes on the ground. Sounds were my
universe to escape the loneliness.

My cousins and uncles used to play tricks on me all the
time. Of course, I heard a lot of words about me being a girl.
Yes, I was the only girl. And my mother had left me behind.
So my playmates were my uncles and cousins. Other girls
were either grown, gone away, or too young.

We walked everywhere around Albany, and James was
always by my side. We used to go by the funeral home to
view the dead people who were displayed in the window.
We would create all kinds of games using old cardboard
boxes and old tires. Even trees were great places to play.
One evening as it was getting dark, we went down to a very
old graveyard. When we got there, my uncles scattered,
leaving James and me scared in our tracks. Our uncles made
sounds to further the intimidation. We heard one of the guys
call us all to a very old grave where the top looked as though
it was going to cave in. We all joined him and began to peer
closely at it. And sure enough, it fell with a loud bang. I've
never seen black children run that fast ever since.

Over time, Grandma Ellen started to buy more foods
from the store, and it took a while for me to realize why.
My granddaddy had left, and I soon came to know that he
would leave for months at a time. She did not talk much
any more. Mr. Sims stopped coming, and there was no more
cotton pickin' for us. Even as a young child, I realized that
pickin' cotton was a way of survival for many of the black
folks, and the poor white folks, too.

❊

I began to look at the house in a new way. I noticed the wooden steps in need of repair, and we did not have grass, much less a green lawn like the white folks did. I could see Grandma Ellen's heart breaking whenever the horse and buggy came around with the old iceman, Mr. Rogers, and my grandma could not afford to buy. The iceman told her, "Since the cotton man ain't comin,' the gov'ment will start providin' pretty soon. You can have some ice on credit."

I guess the old iceman was right, because one day the gov'ment sent us a lot of rations. It was some good eatin' then. They sent us cartons of canned meat, macaroni, eggs, milk, cheese, oats, butter and much more. The rations came twice a month.

One night I was in a deep sleep when a bunch of men broke down our door looking for a "nigger." They sounded white even though their heads were covered with white hoods. When they called out the name of someone unknown to us, my grandma shook her head no. The men pointed guns at the covers, and one of them pulled the covers off of us. We did not make a sound. They were gone in a flash when they were satisfied that the man they were looking for was not there. No one talked to me about the white men, ever. I just wanted to know what a nigger was. I never heard that word in that house again.

I looked out for my mother for so long until I started to believe she had died. I did see my Daddy occasionally. He was a big-rig driver, and would be gone for long periods of time. I soon realized my parents did not want James and me.

No adults would discuss my mother and father with us. So I made James my main concern. James just went along with the program. He never asked any questions, and we never ever discussed our parents. I was so lonely, but no one noticed, or else they were so busy with their own lives that they did not see the pain of loneliness on our little faces. I guess my Grandma Ellen was depressed, because she seemed unaware of a lot of things going on around her. I would just get up in the morning after a while and start the fire and wake up my brother. Many days James and I went outside without our hair combed or our bodies washed. I was never embarrassed by our condition, because it was all we knew. I wanted to see the inside of other folks' lives and homes far away from the country. I was just a child with dreams . . . just a dreamer. I created games in my head that I was a dancer or a great opera singer. But reality quickly awakened me when my Mommy and a stranger came to visit.

A Brief Visit from Mommy

One day I was playing with the tadpoles, in a puddle under the porch where the spigot leaked, when a big car drove up. I saw a beautiful woman get out, while a pretty little girl with long pressed hair loaded down with ribbons came out of the back seat. A little light-skinned boy came out, too. I didn't recognize the lady as she ran up to me crying and picking me up. A very tall, handsome man pulled me by my arm away from her and told her that I was ugly and needed a bath. James ran out of the house, and he too was pushed away.

The man was my stepfather, wearing a U.S. Marine uniform with a lot of medals. His name was Mr. Darryl McArthur. He told the pretty little girl to stand near us and told her that I was her ugly sister. He told her to look at what my brother James and I looked like. I did not have sense enough to take it offensively. He looked down at my muddy feet and said, "Jess, get those children in a tub, before they can talk to me or play with their brother and sister!"

When he said that, I knew that this beautiful woman was my mother. There was something terribly wrong. I felt so abandoned, even though she bathed me and put new clothes on me.

❊

I could never measure up to these children who were strangers to me. They seemed to be rich by nature. Everything they wore was pressed and creased. They spoke differently, and they did not play with us at all. I could not connect with this woman, my mother. Even though she was finally near, she seemed so far away.

After two days, she was gone again. I started looking for her, and many days my Grandma Ellen would make me get away from the door. I cried a lot, seemingly for nothing. I just wanted to understand why James and I were left behind, and why our parents didn't want us. As time went on, I realized that it was really just James and me among a host of relatives.

❊

Chapter 2

⚝

The Visitor of Pain

Sometimes James and I spent time with other relatives, but we were always sent back to live with Grandma Ellen in Albany. One evening, when we came back home, Grandpa Jackson was back home with a man named Mr. Johnson. Mr. Johnson was kind of a lady's man. I used to watch him take women to an old junk car in the backyard, near the alley.

My Grandpa Jackson fixed cars in a makeshift garage, where he had a large metal drum that he used as a furnace. The men put wood and coal in it in the wintertime to keep warm, and stood around it, telling stories and talking about the fights or the games.

I was around five or six years old when I was skipping home from the playground, and I was all dirty. Albany is a red-dirt town, and as a child I loved to make mud cakes. I would take leaves from trees and pretend they were collard greens. I had gotten red, wet clay all over me, including my hair. I decided that it was time to head back home to play with James and the tadpoles.

I came near an old shack and stopped because I saw coins on the ground. I began to pick them up, one at a time because they were spaced apart. Just as I came to the steps, I saw a shadow of someone lurking behind the creepy door. I

�֎

looked down again and saw that the coins stopped just at the door. I dropped the coins and ran home, scared to death. A few minutes later, Mr. Johnson walked in smiling at me with an eerie smile.

My Grandpa Jackson adored Mr. Johnson. They used to talk a long time about their friendship.

Mr. Johnson began to stay over a lot, and eventually, he became our baby-sitter.

Whenever Grandma Ellen was away, she left me with Mr. Johnson. I'd cry and she would tell me she would be right back. Then Mr. Johnson would give James a dime and send him to the store or over to a friend's house. I was only around five or six years old. I knew I would be forced to play "the game" with him.

I'd sit in the middle of the floor by the pot-bellied stove and pray in my own little way. Sure enough, he would pick me up and carry me into another room and take my clothes off. He would get on top of me and hurt me with his toy between his legs. He would say, "Just let me put the tip in, and I won't hurt you!"

But he did hurt me, every time. I tried not to show just how much I was hurting, but my grandmother noticed me walking differently. She would always ask me in front of Mr. Johnson, "What's wrong with you, child?"

I would look at Mr. Johnson and ball up in a knot. As a child, I had no voice. Mr. Johnson would look at me with evil eyes to intimidate me, slyly rise to his feet, and walk towards his room.

One day he got too excited and hurt me pretty bad. The blood was warm and I did not know it had seeped through my clothes. Grandma Ellen noticed the blood, and she pulled up my dress, revealing my bloody underwear. She asked me if anyone had touched me. I pointed to the room where Mr. Johnson slept, and she told my grandfather. I heard Grandpa

✻

Jackson screaming at Mr. Johnson. I crawled on the bed in my grandmother's room, and curled up into a little knot in the dark. I felt my grandmother's warm hand as she patted me on the back to comfort me.

Back in those days, family took care of matters like these, not the law. I do not know what happened to Mr. Johnson, or if he put up a fight.

The next day, I overheard my Aunt Betty telling Mrs. Molly, the old lady next door, about Mr. Johnson and me. Soon afterwards, Aunt Betty moved to New York.

Even after Mr. Johnson was gone, I was a changed person. I was afraid to be left alone. My grandmother began to send me over next door to help Mrs. Molly with some of her chores. James spent the night sometimes over at the home of a little boy named Joshua.

Mrs. Molly was the oldest person that I knew. Her husband had taken ill, so I would always see him asleep in her small living room. There was a small bed in there and a nice sofa and chair. She had a very small kitchen with a few cast-iron pots and pans. She and her husband, before he took ill, slept in a bedroom behind the kitchen. She slept there alone, except for when I spent the night.

I had to go over most mornings before daybreak to help get the eggs out of the chicken coop. I would also sweep the backyard and help hang clothes on the line.

I loved to help her make soap. She would start a fire in the backyard and sit a huge, black cast-iron pot on it. Then she would have me mash up flowers for their oil. Some were purple and yellow; they smelled beautiful. I did not know all of her ingredients, but I would just stir them together with a long wooden paddle in the big, hot pot. We would dip out the boiling mixture and pour it into greased trays, and when it had cooled, we cut it into squares. Mrs. Molly used that same pot to wash sheets and white clothes.

❧

One night a storm roared in, and Mrs. Molly battened down the chickens and her other animals. The wind howled in the dark skies, and from all over the neighborhood, folks were screaming out orders from their homes. There was a tornado nearby.

Mrs. Molly was strong and swift as she worked, and I watched her in awe. My eyes were like moons of terror as a whirling wind almost picked me up and carried me away. She grabbed me, and we pulled and tugged our way back into her little shack. I was thinking about my brother, who had spent the night at Joshua's.

Mrs. Molly took off my wet clothes and put me on a gown. She also began to change her clothes. I had never paid attention to nudity before, but I noticed her pubic hairs and wondered if I had any. So I innocently lifted up my little gown and tried to check and see.

Mrs. Molly laughed at me and asked me just what was I checking for. She pulled down my gown and told me that one day I would have titties and hair down there, too. I just could not wait to have hair down there. I thought that when I got hair down there, then I would be all grown up. She put me in the bed and went to tend to her ailing husband.

What's Wrong, Grandma?

Soon my Grandpa Jackson was away for a long time again, and Grandma Ellen was even more silent. She baby-sat a couple of very young children. I did not know how to relate to them, even though I changed their diapers and helped feed them. I hardly ever saw the parents of these children, because they brought them so early in the morning. The children were picked up at different times in the evening, and sometimes I would be at Mrs. Molly's until after supper.

James played with one of the little boys called Bro' and

every now and then we would go to his house. His mother, Mrs. Sallie Mae, kept her house so clean, with furniture like nothing I had never seen before. It was all matching, with marble-topped tables, and lamps with glass crystals hanging around the shades. She had electricity and also a small piano. There was a music box that played records. For the first time, I was beginning to realize the differences between the poor and those with a little bit more. My brother, however, paid no attention to the differences. He simply enjoyed Bro's company.

I used to run my hands along the sofa's fabric and smell the beautiful aroma of the flowers in her house. I could hear the echoes of laughter as the young boys played. Mrs. Sallie Mae had carpet on her floor, and she even had a bathroom on the back porch, with a toilet that flushed. And a bathtub was in there, too. She had an electric stove as well as a fireplace that seemed to be there just for decoration. She had family portraits that hung all over the living room. I was so impressed! I thought that this lady was *rich*. She liked to tell me about pretty things in her house. She would tell me about people that made all kinds of furniture and thought that I had an eye for quality. But all too soon, the dream would end when Mrs. Sallie Mae would tell us it was time to go home.

I had to go to work for Mrs. Molly a lot. While I was there, I missed my brother. But my grandmother depended on me to be there.

One day I was sent over, and the preacher man was there. Mrs. Molly's husband had died, but she was not crying. She was bathing him, and she had already picked out a suit for him to be buried in. I was scared to death of dead folks. I saw her kiss him tenderly on the face and tell him good-bye. Then the funeral people drove him away in a big black car.

Back in those days, they brought the dead family member home, on the day before burial, so that family and friends could come and give their respects. The funeral car arrived to place Mrs. Molly's husband's body for viewing. While the funeral people put flowers near the body, I spied him through the open front door. I looked at the old man lying there so peaceful. I had never really looked at him before.

My eyes were bucked wide with curiosity as Mrs. Molly kissed him gently, once again, on the lips. I swore that he would get up. People began to arrive to say their good-byes. They went around the body, like a ritual, singing sad songs. They did not acknowledge me at all. It was as though I were invisible; I automatically moved out of the way. An old lady they called Miss Will Lou sang a sweet gospel spiritual. When she had finished, weeping and wailing filled the tiny house as Mrs. Molly finally screamed from the pain of her loss.

A Family Secret

Soon after that, James and I were sent to live with my Aunt Carla and Uncle Mike by the railroad tracks, although we stayed there only a very short time. She had an electric stove and lots of beautiful furniture, too, just like Bro's mama had.

Her sheets were so soft and smelled so good. Every day she cooked. There was the smell of fresh biscuits and bacon in the morning and the aroma of chicken or steak in the evening. This was the *life*, I thought.

One night, James got very sick coughing. Aunt Carla rubbed him down with some menthol and put a pot of boiling water on a dresser near the bed. She made a tent over his head and put some of the menthol in the hot water. The scent filled the air, and I was curious. She caught me peeping under the makeshift tent and gave me a tongue-lashing. I was not the one sick; James was.

James and I helped Uncle Mike clean buildings. One night, he took us with him to clean a building downtown, and the place had a funny smell. There was a pharmacy

❈

near the doctors' offices, and the mixture of chemicals was nauseating. On this night something familiar happened. He sent James away and asked me to come into another room. It was an office with an examination table in it. Uncle Mike sat me on the table and took down my panties. He wanted me to play with him, just like Mr. Johnson had. He sat me on a table, spread my legs and played between them with his toy. I was scared to tell anybody, because this was my Uncle Mike. I was afraid that my Aunt Betty, or Aunt Carla would talk to Mrs. Molly about me again. I was afraid, and I felt as though I could not trust anyone. I was just six years old, and I didn't understand why men were hurting me like this.

Soon I began to withdraw. I did not care about anything, as to whether it was day, night, or if I was here or there. I seemed to exist just for James. Days came and went. During the hot months of summer, I continued to be molested. Soon afterwards we went to live with Grandma Bertha, our father's mother, in the country.

Praying Grandma

Grandma Bertha used to sing and pray a lot, and I loved her soothing voice when she sang Christmas carols. We had often gone to the country to stay with her, but this time we were to stay for a while longer. I guess the family was deciding where they were sending us next.

There was a hallway between her bedroom and the front room. I used to peep through the small hallway late at night while she read her Bible by candlelight. The wooden shack was laden with the sounds from outside: the crickets chirping, the wind whistling by. I was in another world then, as I watched her read and the candlelight glow was radiant upon her face. Shadows danced vividly across the room as I would hear her say, "Uh huh," to the words jumping from the pages. It was as if she was talking to someone hidden in the glow. She seemed to read for hours. I guess I must have dozed off, listening to her humming, "Uh huh" to her imaginary friend who beckoned to her every night from the big black book. I always woke up the next morning in bed, not remembering how I got there. To this day, I still remember Grandma Bertha Wilson when I read the Bible and a passage makes me moan, "Uh huh."

I always found an excuse to run across the dirt road to look beyond the fence toward the pecan fields. That winding fence would stir up visions in me of some place beyond the country. I saw stages with people dancing and singing. I saw cheering crowds, and I saw my big beautiful house. I saw myself singing gospel hymns and people enjoying my words. I would remember the way my Grandma Bertha sang, and I could hear the wind, and I would sing the songs I heard her sang. Oh, how I loved the way sounds felt! I would listen to a bird chirping or a rooster crowing in the morning. I could hear the sound of a dog barking far away. I would listen to the sound of the train whistling early in the morning, and the sound of the coffee perking, and even the sound of footsteps as other children played around me. Perhaps I was weird to others, because I would hear my Grandma Bertha say that I was different from everyone else. She would point me out if she caught me daydreaming and tell those standing near, "Will you just look at that child? There she goes, dreaming again!"

One morning I got up thinking it would be a usual day, but my Grandma Bertha was packing things, and she was removing her big Bible from the table. I saw the tears in her eyes as she placed it into a box. She told me that we would not be visiting her in the country any more. Things were changing so fast for my little mind. The white folks were moving all of the black folks around in Albany, including Lee County, where Grandma Bertha lived. Because of modern technology, the farmers were not needed anymore. Although slavery was over, many black folks still lived on their past slave masters' land, as tenders of the farmland to

❁

provide food for their families. But they weren't needed anymore. Many of these black folks were uneducated and had no financial security.

I watched times change; I paid attention to everything. My Grandma Ellen finally got a gov'ment house, too. And my Uncle Tad and his wife, Gena, got one right next door; they used to fight all of the time. I began to see more cars and fewer people walking. I thought that maybe us poor folks were beginning to get rich, too. The folks around me were changing and listening to the radio. Some richer folks had a television set. Soon we got one, too.

There was a war going on, and the people in the city were listening to singers named Aretha Franklin and Diana Ross. The people were listening to the fights with Mohammed Ali and the talk about the marches against segregation. I liked Frank Sinatra, Dean Martin, and Elvis Presley. Was I different or what? I was called a nerd a lot and picked on for being absent-minded. People were doing dances like the twist and the mashed potato and the swim. I knew all of the dances, but how could I show off when I didn't fit in anywhere and older folks were always telling me to sit down? I was to be seen and not heard. James and I just blended in with the new growing city of Albany until I turned about nine years old.

The Trip to Paradise

Grandma Ellen seemed to waken up from a deep sleep one day when Granddaddy Jackson came home, driving an old station wagon. She cooked delicious meals again. I would smell bacon in the morning, and roast in the evening; we were in heaven.

I got up very early one morning to go get some firewood. When I went outside, I saw that the station wagon was packed with some of Grandma Ellen's things. I was afraid that we

❧

were going to be left behind again.

There were no words said as my Grandpa Jackson walked past me with my meager box of clothes. I smiled so big, and my heart was beating so fast I had to hold my chest. When he came back toward me, and I heard the car door slam, he looked at me with a crooked smile. He sensed my thoughts. I ran into the house and helped Grandma Ellen take vittles to the car. James was running ahead of us. This was the first time that I really looked at Grandpa's face. He was very dark with sharp features, and at that moment, he looked like a giant to me. We were going to Florida.

I have very little memory of Florida, except for the long trip. It seemed to me that we were there a short while before my grandmother started complaining about me getting too mature. I already needed bras, and I'd started on my monthly. She seemed afraid that I might end up getting in trouble in Florida.

After a while, my Aunt Betty came to Florida. She was a grown woman now and so pretty; she loved to put on makeup and do her hair. I longed to wear makeup and pretty clothes. My aunt talked about New York all of the time. That was where she was living with my mother to help care for my brother and sister.

We're Going to See Mama

My mother sent a letter to Grandma Ellen, asking her to send my brother and me to live in South Carolina. My grandmother said nothing to James and me that I can remember, until the day she put together a paper bag full of vittles for us. But we already knew where we were going, because a few days before, Aunt Betty had said that my mother was sending for us. Of course we were used to the old folks not telling us anything.

On the day of the trip, James and I dressed in our best

❀

clothes, and my Grandpa Jackson put our little suitcases in the old station wagon. As we drove down the street to the bus station, I looked back, just knowing that we would be coming back soon. At the station, Grandma Ellen hugged us very tight; this was the first time I had ever seen her show any emotions. She waved goodbye to us and stepped away from the bus.

It was dark and the loneliest night of my life. My brother slept, oblivious to where we were going. I watched the night sky through the bus window, and I tried to understand what was going on. Every now and then, the bus driver would stop at a small town, and I would think that it was time to go. He would look back at me and shake his head.

I held my brother close and vowed never to forget the country. We could not be sure that we were going to live with our mother. I could only be sure of what we were leaving behind. Where we were going would be foreign to us. We were strangers in the land we knew; how could we be anything more in a land we didn't know? I had always wanted to see what was beyond the picket fence. Here it was, about to happen. And I was scared to death.

❊

Chapter 3

⌀

Paradise Left Behind

It was daybreak when we arrived in South Carolina. I had not slept a wink, and I watched as the sun rose, and we pulled into a bus station. The bus driver reached to shake my brother awake, but I would not let him touch him. I grabbed our leftover vittles, and the man handed me my little bag of clothes. I gently woke up James.

The driver was white, but he was very nice to us as he took hold of my brother and carried him down the steps. He told me where we should go to sit inside the bus depot.

As we stepped off of the bus, a woman came out of nowhere and hugged us tightly. The driver released us to the woman and went into the depot. The tall man from long ago told her to turn us loose and get into the car.

He said, "I told you I was going to send for them and now they are here. Now come on and get your ass in the car!"

I was angry with this man. He seemed to cuss nonstop. The pretty girl and the light-skinned boy were in the car, and they were completely silent. My mother was crying so much. I wanted so badly to comfort her, but there was one problem: I wasn't sure that we were going to stay.

The little girl was my sister, Trina. When my mother

❀

had left us years ago, Trina had been such a little girl. The light-skinned boy was my brother Sandford, who was just beginning to walk back then. James sat snuggled close to me. The girl sat as close to the car door as possible, so as not to touch me or James.

After we began the ride, the tall man told us to call him either Sergeant Major or Daddy. He turned to us and asked, "Which will it be?" I stuttered, "Sergeant Major." He liked that, and he laughed until his nose turned red. I thought he was a white man. His eyes were green, and he had slick black hair. He was so light skinned that I wondered if he would catch a tan in the sun.

As we drove home, he constantly made references to my brother and me as country bumpkins and low-class niggers. I didn't know what a nigger was, and I had never heard the word said by a black man before. (Quite frankly, I did not believe that he *was* black). I didn't know it was aimed at us as an insult. He looked back at us with flared nostrils as if he wished we had never been born. My mama only wept and looked back at us pitifully. The ride was long and – when he stopped talking – silent.

I thought, 'We might be there just a day or two. Everything was happening too fast. Who are these people? I can't let that man hurt James.' I watched his little body as he curled up as much as he could to caress his pain.

Beautiful Misery

When we arrived at their house, I thought it was a mansion, just like the white rich people's in the cotton fields. It was red brick with a screened in porch, and a lush green lawn. I had never before seen grass so green.

Inside was furniture more beautiful than anything I had ever seen. The kitchen had all modern appliances, none of which I knew how to work. As we went down the hall, we found out that the girls had their own room, my brothers had their own room, and my mama and stepfather had their own room. There were two bathrooms. It was a palace!

And my mother cooked a meal for a king. As we sat down to dinner, I noticed Trina and Sandford shaking. The Sergeant Major sat at the table with a mouth full of Copenhagen chewing tobacco, and he leaned over and spit into a can. He reached across the table and slapped Sandford hard across the face and told him to stop shaking so much.

My eyes almost popped out of my head. He turned to me and told me that I was nothing but a country bumpkin and uneducated. He pointed to James and called him a nappy-headed nigger. I was not used to language like this.

One thing about the country, we were never hollered at or hardly ever whipped without a reason. My Grandma Ellen might pinch you for discipline. And if my Grandma Bertha found out that somebody had lied about something, although she had a brood of children, she would whip every last one. By the time she got to me, I would be crying and tired from watching her whip everybody else. I would get a couple of licks and it would be over with. But I'd cry ever so much more just because my grandma had hit me. Her whippings were child's play compared to what I saw living with my stepfather.

That first night we also discovered that my mother was expecting another child. I do not remember much more about South Carolina except the birth of my baby brother, Devon. He was such a beautiful baby. But there was one thing that my stepfather used to joke about all of the time, and that was the fact that my infant brother looked like a little white baby. He used to tell my mother how lucky she was to have a baby born with light skin and hazel eyes. His hair was a mass of blond curls, and his red lips looked like a valentine heart when he slept. He was such a smart child who developed language skills at an incredible rate. He was smart with numbers, too. We used to spell words so that

❊

Devon would not always know what we were talking about. But in no time, this became a game to him, and soon he began telling us what we were spelling. Devon could curse like a sailor, too. The Sergeant Major loved to show him off to the other officers.

When it was time to move back to Georgia, a few of his Marine buddies threw the Sergeant Major a big going-away celebration, giving him a Medal of Honor and a Bronze Star. One day he handed me a suitcase and told me to guard it with my life. He opened it, and it was full of money and important papers.

Not long after Robert Kennedy was assassinated, a moving truck came to our house and packed up everything. My mama cried about going back to Georgia, but these were happy tears. It was a very hot day, and the neighbors were stopping by to say their tearful good-byes.

Scattered Pieces

We moved from South Carolina on a beautiful clear day. I don't know why I remember what the weather was like. I was not sure of anything as we drove down the dusty highway. A few miles out, my stepfather told us to put our heads down because he needed to piss and get some damn beer, as he worded it. He took off his hat, and once more, I was awestruck by his amazing blue-green eyes. He got out of the car, and my mother began to pray. I was wondering why she was praying now.

A few minutes later, I heard laughter as the Sergeant Major and some white men walked up to the car. A man in his fifties peered in and he turned blistering mad. He screamed obscenities at the Sergeant Major, calling him a nigger-lover, while the other one called him a nigger, too, and that he was passin' for white.

❊

It was a silence like none I had ever known as the fat white man pointed a gun at the Sergeant Major's back. He told my stepfather that he had believed that he was a white man. The man stared through the barrel of his shotgun and told the Sergeant Major to walk, but instead, the Sergeant Major stared him down. He slowly opened the car door on the passenger's side and sat inside as my mother slid over to the steering wheel. He told my mother to drive off slowly. The white man pointed the gun at us until we were out of sight.

The silence continued for miles. After a while, my mother pulled over and my stepfather took over the driving. I didn't know it then, but I believe that my parents were afraid. The Sergeant Major appeared to have a flashback of some kind. He was shaking as he held the steering wheel. I was so ignorant about me being a black girl and him being a black man passin'. I still didn't understand the full scope of racism.

When we arrived in Georgia, I was a little disappointed. This most certainly was not Albany. This place was just as foreign to me as South Carolina had been. We moved into an Atlanta apartment where everybody was discussing Martin Luther King, Jr. The big talk was about moving his body to a new burial place, which was to be called the King Center.

People were protesting bussing and race riots were buzzing all over the city. For the first time, I really listened to the news. I had never realized how under-exposed I had been to racism. I was sent to a school where the students were always fighting each other, and there were no white students there. These children were different from what I knew; they were tough and angry all of the time. I lost myself in the midst of a crowd, vanishing into a void. I removed myself from the students the same way I always did, by being silent and almost invisible.

One day some students were tossing a midget boy around like a football. I stood against a locker, terrified. A pretty

❦

young girl grabbed my hand and led me away, and she talked to me in a soft voice. "I live across the hall from you, and I heard that your dad had been a soldier." I softened up to her as she led me away from the commotion.

Her clothes were mature for her age. She wore a huge Afro wig and a mini skirt with tight white boots that came up to her knees. And her makeup was pretty heavy for a young girl. Trina and I were not allowed to dress like that or wear makeup. All of the Sergeant Major's children were not allowed to wear Afros, either.

When we rounded a corner, she stopped off at a restroom to change her clothes. She put on a pair of jeans and a tie-up shirt. She talked about having to survive in the streets as a hooker to help support her family. Her mother did drugs and drank a lot of alcohol, and I never saw her sober.

I didn't understand her way of life. In the country, I was so shielded from this sort of life. I could not comprehend this new place in Georgia. The way that I was being raised had left no room for things outside of my home life. This young lady had to be wise beyond her years, and I was protected from her kind because of my strict stepfather. Still, this girl watched out for me until we moved. I do not remember anything more about the school or the girl. We did not stay in that apartment long. Come winter, we were preparing to move again into a house. Mama began to sing a song as she packed. I was in awe because this was the first time I had ever heard her sing a whole song. She noticed my surprise and told me of the times that she used to sing on the radio. She had a robust, spiritual voice. It was sultry, but not too sexy. I had never heard singing like hers before. From then on I tried to imitate her, and Mahalia Jackson and Aretha Franklin, and especially my Grandma Bertha. She had that old spiritual tone in her voice, and she sang in a beautiful soprano, with an almost opera-like quality.

❖

"I Will Not Move. I am Not a Part of White Flight."

A few days before Christmas, we drove up to our new home. The neighborhood was full of red brick houses with beautiful Christmas decorations and flashing Christmas lights on every street.

The neighbor next door, Mr. O'Neil, walked up to the car to greet my father. His face turned as red as a beet as his eyes took a scan of the rest of us. He stared at my mother and mustered a half-smile.

Mrs. O'Neil walked up to the car with a pie, and her tone never changed. She walked over to my mother's side of the car and opened it. The lady was so welcoming, but the quiet that set in the moment my mother stepped out of the car was deafening. The Sergeant Major stepped out of his side of the car with a smoothness that I had never seen in him before. He never took his eyes off of the eyes of the white man. His stare was intense and serious.

Mr. O'Neil said with a shiver due to the cold, "That's why you're a Sergeant Major – old soldiers never die!" The man grabbed my stepfather's hand and shook it like they were old friends. The couple came into our home and gave us the full welcoming address. Mrs. O'Neil said, "We get together as a community every other week and work to keep the homes here beautiful. The men work outside and gossip about sports, and the women talk about the men." True to the times of that day, as the group of adults chatted, I melted into the background.

The two men started talking about the war and why white folks were running from their neighborhoods. Mr. O'Neil welcomed my mother as the first black woman in the neighborhood.

The Sergeant Major laughed as the couple left. He turned to us and told us how we were to act, and that we were not to wear Afros or Afro picks in our hair. My parents took the rest of the children with them back to the apartment, and

❀

they left me behind with the briefcase full of cash to man the house. My mother had turned on the stove and sat a pot of water on top for heat. There was a paper fireplace in a box of Christmas decorations that I assume my mother had brought earlier. I put the fireplace up and sang Christmas carols and gospel songs. I listened to my voice echo through the empty house. It was the biggest house I had ever lived in.

I was so hungry because there was no food in the house. As it grew dark, I became afraid, just like the time of the storm when I was a little girl. I curled up in a knot in front of the fake fireplace. I must have fallen asleep, because the next thing I knew, I smelled chicken and my mother was standing over me. The Sergeant Major told us to get the blankets out of the car, and we ate that night as if we were on a picnic. On this night, the Sergeant Major was nice. Early the next morning the gas man came and we had heat. A couple of hours later, the furniture movers arrived.

The house was so clean, and it smelled so good. But it wasn't long before the Sergeant Major began beating on Trina and my brothers again. Not his baby boy, Devon, though.

It was pure hell behind those walls. It didn't take much to make my stepfather angry, especially when he got drunk, and that was almost daily. Sometimes his antics spilled into the yard. Those were the days when it seemed proper for a man to beat his family. People called it "keeping them in line." My life was torn between discipline and hopelessness.

A few months later, my mother took me shopping at South DeKalb Mall. I immediately found a job at J.C. Penney's restaurant. I wanted something to do to make my own money. The manager told my mother that if she signed for me, I could start that day. My mother was happy that I had the courage to seek out a job. She told the manager that she would have to buy me a pair of black shoes. My mother got the black work shoes and signed the papers for me to start working the following day. Of course, the Sergeant Major made an example of the country bumpkin getting a job. But

❧

I looked forward to working and being with other people besides my family.

I'm not sure where it was, but I think I began attending high school, and I do not know where Trina, Sandford, and James went to school. School? Who went for me? I'm still trying to remember, hoping that some recollections would come back to me before I finish this book. There are spots of memory that elude me like a phantom in my dreams.

I have tried to remember more, but I cannot. I wish that I could remember days at school. I can't remember the halls, cafeteria, or teachers. I have a vague memory of my music teacher. He overheard me singing one evening after class, and he wanted me to join a singing club. It seems like a fog, because I cannot make out the faces of other students. I sang with the youth group that met after school, and I looked forward to going.

There were a couple of other black students, and I was always the last child picked up from events. My stepfather believed that I needed to wait, just to be waiting, because he said so. It was just fine with me. I took the opportunity to be one with nature. I would sit out on the steps and sing as the sounds of the night filled the air. I was never afraid as long as I had my voice and the sounds of nature to keep me company. I had grown used to being last.

The Confession

On a hot summer night, the Sergeant Major was drunk and he was teasing Trina in the bedroom. I ran into the room and started grabbing him away from her. He hollered for my mama. When she came into the room, she was surprised to see such a stone look on his face. He told us all to come into the living room and sit down for a family conference. Every child was present, including Devon.

When we sat down he began a discussion about good

❧

and bad sex. He looked very serious at my mother and then back at me. Then he asked in a very compassionate voice, "Barbara, did anybody ever touch you in a bad way?"

I nodded yes. I told them about my Uncle Mike. His reaction was pure anger. I was surprised, and I was afraid to tell him about the others. There was no comfort from my mother. She did not move a muscle as the Sergeant Major raised hell. I believe that he blamed himself for taking so long to send for the little country bumpkin.

A few days later, my mother and stepfather went to Albany and stirred up a lot family confusion about the child molestation. My Aunt Carla was devastated and left Uncle Mike, temporarily. But soon they were back together, they still are today, and life continues.

Two Plus Two

I do not remember my prom or my graduation. But I do remember my boyfriend, Jim. I can't say much about the actual dating, except that Trina and I dated brothers. I guess we were two plus two. I truly admired the way my sister was treated. Trina's boyfriend gave her a lot of respect and treated her like a queen. He bought matching clothes for them and he always said nice things about Trina. I admired that about her boyfriend. He was light-skinned, and mine was dark and muscular. My stepfather did not at all like Jim, who was dark-skinned; he wanted me to date a light-skinned black or a white man.

One day my stepfather brought a white man home with him to see if I would interested in dating him. The man was an officer from Fort McPherson, and my father introduced the man to me. But the guy got very drunk that night and fell asleep on the sofa. I guess when my stepfather sobered up, he realized that he had made a fool of himself. I never saw the man again.

❊

My boyfriend was quiet and somewhat too attentive. He watched my every move and he dared anyone to look at me when I was out with him. I thought he was being protective. I was considered such a nerd and practically overlooked most of the time.

When James became a teenager, he got a job, and he has worked ever since. Most of the time, he worked two jobs. Work for him was a kind of escape from the chaos at home. I tried to stay to myself as much as possible. My sister was angry all of the time, and she spent a lot of it writing letters about how she felt. I guess she did not know any other way to escape the pain. She chose to be a pain to someone she saw to be beneath her – me. I was always patient with her, because my stepfather had chosen to try to create what he considered to be perfection through Trina. She was groomed to hate the country bumpkin.

Country Bumpkins

My stepfather had never hit me, until one day when I overheard him talking to my mother about what James and I meant to him. He said that we would never be more than country bumpkins, and that I did not have the sense of a turnip. I started screaming, and the next thing I knew, he was hugging me. He took me outside alone to talk. I only wanted to know why, if he hated James and me, did he even send for us? He had humiliated us for years. He cried and dropped his shoulders. He told me that he did not express himself well, and he walked away.

But I wanted to know, so I followed him. I was talking loud about how we were never beaten in Albany and at least my real daddy loved me. Well, before I could finish another sentence, he slapped me across my face. That totally brought me to my senses. Some kind of coldness came over me that, to this day, I can't explain. From then on, there was a change

❅

in him toward me. I did not cry nor did I talk much for a long time afterwards.

A few weeks into our silence toward each other, we went to downtown Atlanta as a family. All of us were walking, and I could hear the voices of my sister and brothers. My parents were discussing the downtown stores, like Macy's and Woolworth's. I vaguely remember the car coming. I only knew that at that moment, I saw a way to never return to the house of hell again. I heard the horn blow, and I felt a strong tug. The Sergeant Major spoke soft and firm in my ear, "Barbara what is wrong with you? You need to be careful." I heard my Mama screaming out my name, "Barbara!" The next thing I knew we were on our way home.

As we drove home that day, everything was a fog to me. The voices of my parents meant nothing to me. When we got home, I was told to fix the Sergeant Major a drink. As I prepared it, he constantly cursed at me. He called me "stupid nigger" and "country bumpkin," saying that I would never amount to anything. The next thing I knew, I felt him gently holding my hand. I had squeezed the glass, shattering it with my hand from pure pain deep somewhere inside of my heart. It is pain in its most agonizing form. 'How could he think it is OK to talk to us like we were nothing? Nothing. Nothing!'

I could only hear the sounds of my own mind as the Sergeant Major's words blended in as if from an echo. He kept saying my name as I stared into space, only hearing the painful words, over and over again.

My Mama came to me with tears in her eyes as the Sergeant Major slowly released my grip on the broken glass. I felt a scream echo from deep within me, but I would not dare let him hear my deep-rooted pain. The scream was planted deep within me. I could hear it, but not my parents. I wondered if they'd ever heard my crying. My Mama led me to my bed as liquor dripped through my fingers. Ironically, I did not cut myself.

✳

I stayed to myself most of the time after that. I became a loner of sorts in my own home. The other children never questioned anything within those walls. We were all just waiting on adulthood. When we talked to each other, most of the conversations began with, "When I grow up I'm gonna..." In my mind, I knew I did not want to commit suicide. I just wanted a voice, a right to life, a right to be recognized as a person with a soul. When was that suppose to happen? I wanted some kind of structure. No one could learn right from wrong amidst the screaming, the alcohol, and no hugs. Drip, drip, drip. I heard the tears fall upon my pillow at night.

Unto Us a Special Child Is Born

Soon my mother was pregnant again. She had a little girl named Justice. She was special, and she needed a lot of attention. And I was the one to give it to her. I sang to her constantly, and I loved to admire her when she slept. I was always left to baby-sit her.

Justice was truly special because she was diagnosed with cerebral palsy. My stepfather blamed my mother. I loved Justice with all of my heart, and Justice adored me. I sang to her and dressed her real pretty. I had a purpose now. She had dark curly hair and a beautiful smile. She lit up like a Christmas light and her eyes would crinkle with glee whenever she was with me, which was a lot. She dragged her legs behind her when she tried to crawl. I knew something was wrong, but yet again, I was forbidden to ask. My mother waited until Justice was almost a year old before she told us about Justice's condition. She was afraid that the rest of the children would reject the new baby.

Justice was almost like a rag doll, a little too fragile. She loved to watch your face, and try to play with your eyelashes. She was a very precious child with hands that were so tiny, and she had my heart. I promised to always take care of her, and I do to this day.

Another Tragedy Follows

One day my stepfather was mowing the lawn on a steep hill and cut one of his toes off. He showed no fear as my mother searched for his toe. He just kept drinking from a liquor bottle and saying, "Come on, Jess, and take me to the hospital."

My mother cried as we drove to the hospital. I could see the love that she had for this man, and I saw her age a few years that day. For some reason, a police officer stopped us. But when he recognized my stepfather as Sergeant Major Darryl McArthur, he jumped on his motorcycle and sped off down the street with us in tow.

The Sergeant Major stayed in the hospital for a few days, and I never heard him complain about the discomfort. He grew dependent on me. He held on to my shoulder as he learned to walk with the missing big toe. When he came home, I took care of signing all of the business papers, including his checks.

I was hardly ever out of the range of his voice demanding me to do something. He had a peculiar way of saying my name. He had only hit me that one time, and I could never understand why. Ever since that time, I had become less affected by his outbursts. He was no longer sure of me. I guess he was trying to show me that he could truly be a nice person.

Jealousy Stirs

I believe that it was during this time I saw a jealousy develop in Trina that became a wedge between us. Trina began to do little vindictive things to get attention. I used to tell her to be careful. I knew that she was missing the closeness that she and my parents had shared, even though my stepfather was a bit overpowering. When these are the only people that you have known all of your life, how dare a country nigger come along and get so much attention? To Trina, all of the responsibilities that were being placed upon me were a sign of power. She felt that all power belonged to her. How could they feel that a country nigger like me could handle the family's legal affairs? For some reason, the Sergeant Major always trusted me with his financial responsibilities.

During this time, I knew that Trina would never want me to have more or be more than she. Who could blame her? It became a ritual for her to find ways to cut me down. I just sat back and let her berate me in front of people as if I was not around.

I believe that I was around 16 years old when my mother accused me of having sex with my boyfriend Jim, but it was Trina and her boyfriend who were actually having sex. I used to hide the evidence of my sister's episodes. If I confronted her about them, she would say that I was just jealous. I was getting tired of being accused of what she was doing. I just wanted to grow up and get out of that sad house where it seemed I would never be believed.

One evening I came home from work, and there was a family discussion. My mother told my stepfather that Jim and I were having sex. The plan was for me to go to the hospital for birth control. I was devastated because I was not having sex, yet. Sometimes, if you are accused of something so much, it crosses your mind to prove them right. The doctor told my mother he did not believe I was sexually active, but he put me on birth control anyway. My mother was concerned about the wrong daughter, I thought. In her eyes, my sister could do no wrong.

So You Have the Pill

A couple of months after I was accused of having sex, Jim and I went on a little romantic joyride late one evening.

The conversation turned to making love. I told him that I was on birth control, and I was very curious about the experience after a time of abstinence. Soon we were making love in the back seat, parked in a dark alley.

On the way home from our little fling, he hit the side of a ditch and slammed on the brakes. My head went into the windshield and the glass cracked. We came up with an elaborate excuse as to how the break in the glass happened.

I was scared to death, and from then on I would be concerned about my boyfriend coming around. In no time, I realized that I was expecting a child. I was just a child myself, and a very unprepared one at that. I believe Jim talked to my mother about marrying me, because one evening she approached me about it. I didn't know what to say, and I felt that I had no way out. Although I had been on birth control, I still got pregnant. I had not taken the pills long enough for them to protect me. I didn't know that the only way not to get pregnant was to use a condom. At that time, I had never seen a condom before. I had no idea what one was.

It was a sad time for my mother as we discussed my pregnancy. She told me not to tell my stepfather because he would be upset with us all if he knew. We were sworn to secrecy. I did not want it kept secret, but as before, I did not know how to defend myself. I became very depressed living in secrecy. I suppose you can say I had no choice but to marry this man.

One evening the Sergeant Major approached me again, asking me to compare my life with him in the city to my life in the country. I truthfully told him that I didn't believe he really loved me. Though my real father abandoned James and me, he never hit us, called us niggers or other ugly words. I guess that was too much for Sergeant Major, because the next thing I knew, I felt a whack across my face. The Sergeant Major hit me in the face with the butt of his shotgun. It knocked my front teeth loose. You can believe this: just like in the cartoons, you do see stars. He did not know that I was pregnant.

❧

The Wedding

In June of 1974, Jim and I were married. The Sergeant Major sat on the porch with a shotgun to mimic a shotgun wedding. He meant it as a joke, but he still had no idea about the pregnancy. My stepfather was so happy for me, or at least, tried to be happy for me. I cried all day, but no one seemed concerned about me. It was so easy for my mother to get me out of the house this way. I know that she was trying to spare me a lot of pain. If she only knew the pain that I was about to endure.

On my wedding night as I was walking through my parents' house, when I caught Jim and Trina in a sexually inappropriate moment together. I told Mama about it, but she said it was harmless. Jim and I left my parents' house and went to our new apartment, where I continued to confront him about what I saw. Rather than giving me a reason why Trina and he were together on my wedding day, Jim beat me. This was his way to avoid facing up to the pain he was causing me. I lived a life of deceit and terrible misery as an abused wife.

A few months later, Mama brought my stepfather over to my home and told him about the baby I was carrying. Sergeant Major cried and held my stomach tenderly. The following day, he took me to the farmers' market, and bragged to the cashier about becoming a grandfather. He called me to the counter and grabbed my stomach. He was very much looking forward to being a granddaddy.

Silent Weeper

To call out a man's name with so much love

To hold one so near who has uttered words so painful

He now caters to you as if you are a beautiful dove

❀

I weep a silent weep 'though a smile hides the tears

O', what joy we've missed through the years

I've always been the silent weeper

With no one to be my gatekeeper

So here you are, this great man who shows tears openly

I am too afraid to wipe them away

For I hope to remember this moment every day

So long old Soldier

So long

Good-bye, Sgt. Major

A few days later, the Sergeant Major died in a six-car pile up on Glenwood Road in Decatur, Georgia. My mother lost an ear in the accident, and a plastic surgeon replaced it before she came home. The Sergeant Major was dead, and my mother never was the same again. I got married and turned eighteen that June, and my stepfather was dead in August.

My baby was born severely underweight, and I had no support from Jim. I named her Tisha. She weighed a little over two pounds, and she had to remain in the hospital. Jim was in no way supportive of me, and the beatings continued up until the baby came home.

One day I was holding little Tisha in my arms and someone knocked on the door. It was my mother with a U-Haul truck, Jim and I were being evicted. As we were taking things out of the house, we discovered bills hidden everywhere and the eviction letter hidden under the bed. It all seemed like a dream.

Jim followed me to my Mama's and begged her to let him stay with us. I did not want him anywhere near me.

❀

My Mama had a talk with me and told me to let my husband come with me. She told me that he was my husband, and she truly believed that I needed to stay with him.

Soon she became a witness to the beatings and his quick temper. He was always chasing after other women, but of course I was not supposed to say anything. I always caught him staring at Trina, and I would walk away, laughing under my breath at how much of a fool he was. "Desire of the untouchable" is what I used to call it. When a man looks at a woman, I guess it appears complimentary, but it's downright nasty when it's a married man, and especially so if it's your sister's man.

A couple of times, Jim and I tried to make a go of it on our own, but each time we got evicted, so we would move back home. No one respected me.

Good-bye, Mama

About the time that I was considering a divorce from Jim, I became pregnant with my son, Jimmy III, whom we called Junior because he was named after his father. My mother was looking forward to another grandchild, but she became very ill. She went into the hospital the first of April, and she died the first day of June, 1978. I had a quest to bring my mother home and care for three children, plus the one growing within me. While in the hospital, Mama had begged me not to let Jim drive her brand new car she had bought just a few weeks before she became deathly ill. I tried, but as I visited my mother in the hospital, Jim kept stealing the car anyway.

I did not have time to cry when Mama died, and Trina was very angry with me. All I could think about was that Mama would suffer no more. I had so many responsibilities to deal with, and I'd watched Mama suffer so much. I just could not cry any more when the doctor said, "She's gone."

❧

Trina felt that I should have cried at Mama's funeral and she told me so.

And Then There Were Four

During the months before my mother passed, I had never questioned myself about the time of day or night. I had so many responsibilities every minute. Justice had many allergies, and I was having a difficult pregnancy. Jim did not seem to care about anything that was going on.

When Junior was born by cesarean section, I was still struggling in probate court with legal issues surrounding my mother's death. She did not leave a will, and I was in the process of selling all of her possessions so that my sisters and brothers could have the money divided. But this was not enough for Trina. She had other plans, which will come to light later.

Even though I was in a lot of pain on the day that I got out of the hospital, I still had to go grocery shopping and cook. I had become accustomed to making time out of no time. When I'd go to sleep at night and rise in the morning, there was no time for me. I had had no opportunity in all of my life just to be me, and now there were four little ones depending on me. I was just like a shadow. Wherever there was the slightest chance of a twinkling of a little light, there was the shadow of my spirit. The shadow of me followed me everywhere, even in my dreams. The spirit within me carried me through.

In the meantime, my marriage grew worse. Jim was into drugs, cursing, and name- calling. He would always steal money from James and me, always promising to pay it back. Jim also had the luxury of being able to borrow money from work. One pay period, I discovered that he had a check for 69 cents. When I got through crying, I called an attorney and began divorce proceedings for the second time.

❖

This time there was no turning back. I discussed my decision with Jim a few days later and I promised to work with him on temporary separation for 90 days. I promised not to tell anyone, so that he could have time to get himself together. But he became more aggressive towards me and seemed to beat me every chance he got.

A few weeks had gone by when one evening, Jim stood in the living room threatening me, and he had no concern for the children. My brother James came into the living room complaining about missing 50 dollars. Jim told James that he would pay him back as soon as he got his paycheck. James looked at me, hurt and disappointed. That was the night that I told Jim he needed to leave the house. He went to his mother's house and she called me saying, "Y'all can work through these problems. Think about the children." If only she had known everything about her son.

Jim refused to move out simply because the judge ordered him to, even though the judge had granted me a divorce. One night, Jim and I had a terrible fight, and I put him out of the house. But I still kept the divorce a secret.

One evening I went out with a male friend, and Jim accused me of messing around with the man. Jim approached the car and demanded that I get out. The gentleman got out of the car with me, and refused to leave me alone with Jim. For the first time in my life, someone was really standing up for me. And for the first time, I saw that Jim would not stand up to strength. So I decided to use my own. I stood up to Jim and told him that the man was just a friend. After a lot of cursing and threats Jim finally left the property, but threatened to take my children. I called the police, but they told me that even though my husband and I were divorced, they could not keep him from coming to my home.

For months Jim stalked me. I would catch him lurking around the house. He would call me threatening to take the children. In the meantime, Sandford, who was now in the Navy, was calling me about selling the house, because Trina

❃

had been talking to him and Jim. Trina was also calling family members without my knowledge about taking Devon and Justice away from me. It was impossible for me to keep up with Trina's trickery. She called in people who had never endured the hardships that we shared. Everyone that I tried to talk to about Trina's true intentions was already entangled in her schemes. I realized how much my stepfather had influenced her greed. Her heart ached at the thought that James and I, the country bumpkins, were staying in *her* house. She resented us so much that she wanted us removed at any cost.

During the planned meetings for the siblings, Trina was trying to take possession of the house. I was willing to give it to her, but she did not want to have to deal with us coming to stay on her, as she put it.

Trina took control of everything. To others who listened to her, it seemed as if she was taking pressure off of me by reducing some of my responsibilities. Even James believed Trina's intentions were well-meaning, until the day he realized that she was getting rid of him, too. He was heartbroken.

Trina had been raised to believe that I was beneath her, and she let it be known. But I was stronger than she could ever imagine. I knew time would be on my side. I tried hard not to do any of my siblings wrong, no matter what they did to me. I figured that if I stayed faithful to what was just, by law, justice would be my defense some day. I was not angry about not having control of my life at that time, because everything was moving so fast. I only wanted to have a voice.

Remembering Mom and The Sergeant Major

I was walking through the living room late one night, trying to plan my future, and I bumped into my stepfather's military trunk. I knew that James and I would have to leave the house soon, so with trembling hands, I opened the trunk and started crying. I took out a few articles: a large battle knife, a few medals, some clothes and pictures. I also found a letter from the President that was sent to my mother for the Sergeant Major's funeral. I found discharge papers dated September 1, 1966, USMC, which read "Reason for Discharge: Expiration of Enlistment." At the bottom of the papers, he had re-enlisted for two more years, ending April 1968. Then I saw the marriage certificate. There were two photos of my Mama and him celebrating their wedding day. I fell to the floor crying. After what seemed like hours, I pulled myself together, and read a listing of medals he had received. But a letter stood out among the pile. It referred to his second Bronze Star. It read:

"For meritorious service in connection with operations against the enemy in the Republic of Vietnam while serving in various capacities with the Third Marine Division from 30 April 1967 to 8 May 1968. Throughout this period, Sergeant Major McArthur performed his myriad, demanding duties in an exemplary and highly professional manner. As Sergeant Major of the Second Battalion, Ninth Marines, he skillfully assisted the commanding officer in supervising the myriad functions of his command. Working tirelessly and with meticulous attention to detail, he consistently provided superb guidance and professional advice to young Marines, thereby greatly enhancing the efficiency and effectiveness of his unit. On 29 July 1967, the Second Battalion was returning from an operation near the Ben Hai River when the Marines were suddenly attacked by a numerically superior North Vietnamese Army force. Alertly observing four enemy soldiers concealed near his location, Sergeant Major unhesitatingly maneuvered toward the hostile emplacement and directed accurate rifle fire into the position, killing all four enemy soldiers. Throughout the remainder of the engagement, he fearlessly moved about the fire-swept area, shouting words of encouragement to his Marines and ren-

❧

dering aid to casualties. Reassigned as Sergeant Major of the Ninth Motor Transport Battalion on 17, November 1967, he continued to distinguish himself in the performance of his duties. Largely due to his sincere concern for the welfare of his comrades, he contributed immeasurably to the high level of morale within the command and won the respect and admiration of all who observed him. Sergeant Major's superb leadership, outstanding professionalism and unwavering devotion to duty throughout contributed significantly to the accomplishment of his unit's mission and were in keeping with the highest traditions of the Marine Corps and the United States Naval Service."

Sergeant Major is authorized to wear the Combat "V"

FOR THE PRESIDENT . . .

BANG! BANG! BANG! Trina was knocking at the door before daybreak. She came to tell me that she had talked to a realtor about helping her take the house. I didn't mind it anymore. I was tired, but in no way was I defeated. She scurried through the house, telling me how she was going to put James and me out. She was taking possession of Devon. I maintained my composure, because I trusted God, and I knew that He was my strength. So whatever happened, I knew that He would take care of me. I watched as she fussed and pointed contemptuously at me. I could hear her belittling me, but stop short of calling me names. It was as if the Sergeant Major had stepped out of his grave. I watched Trina slam the front door as she left. I watched her from the kitchen window until I saw the tail end of her car turn out of the driveway. I went outside and watched her as she turned into her mother-in-law's driveway a few doors down. I went back to the memories in the trunk. The smile on my mother's face in the photo told the whole story. I held the pictures to my chest and cried out.

It was a terrible time, and I was so alone again without my Mama. I had four young children to care for, including

*

Justice and Devon. I never complained or considered my responsibilities burdens.

A couple of weeks later, I received a call from an aunt in Rhode Island asking me to allow her to keep Justice for the summer. I truly thought that she was trying to be helpful. I put Justice on a plane not realizing that my aunt was in on a scheme against me. As soon as Justice got to Rhode Island, my aunt called me to tell me that she was not sending her back. I was devastated. This was the worst blow to me. I didn't really know this aunt well, and I was scared to death. I called my sister and as soon as she heard my voice she started screaming at me: "Yeah, it was me! I told her to help me take Justice from you, and I'm taking Devon!"

I put the phone down. Deep inside, I truly wanted to hate her. I took all of the anger and worked to prepare for what might happen next.

❋

Chapter 4.

ᶻ

My New Life

I got a job working for a child development center, and James and I began to look for an apartment together. We found a new subdivision that my boss told me about the resident manager gave me an application to fill out. I was so happy when he called to come inspect my parent's house to see if I would keep up my new place. It was part of the requirements if I was to receive one of these beautiful units.

Trina had got the house with the intent of throwing James and me out with nowhere to go. She already had possession of Devon and Justice was away. Sandford was calling for his money from the sale of the house. All that was left for her to do was to get James, me and my children out of the house and on the street. But she was in for a surprise.

James called me at work. "Barbara, don't go to the house tonight. I have taken everything to the new apartment, and Trina is taking possession of the house today."

I could hear him crying on the phone, and the tremble in his voice broke me down. I hung up the phone and went into my boss' office and told her everything that was happening.

When I arrived at the apartment Trina and her husband had already walked through it. Trina told me that I should

❀

give James the master bedroom since he made more money than I did. I told her that this was not her place, and the decision as to where anyone slept would be between James and me. She and her husband left, and James and I began to decorate. My children had a safe place to play at our gorgeous new home. God had surely taken good care of us.

My husband was not around to steal all of my money, and I was able to buy lots of clothes for my children. I bought new furniture. I began to sing at churches and started feeling that I mattered to someone. The people at the churches made me feel like family. Maybe I felt too important, until I forgot that I was serving God. My head got a little big when I saw the people react to my voice. One day I sang at a church where I was the last singer, and the people who were leaving turned back to hear me. I loved the attention.

I felt invincible, until one day, I took the stage, all puffed up and ready to sing, when I forgot the words, and lost my voice. I was devastated as I stepped down from the stage that I left my voice there that day. My wounded pride opened up doors that led me to try things that I knew were wrong.

A few days later, a friend offered me a glass of wine. I thought it would ease my wounded ego. Then as night fell, she offered me marijuana. Jim had on many occasions tried to get me to smoke, but I would hide the joints. Jim would always find them and make jokes about me. I did smoke with him sometimes, but it felt so wrong. But this time, I wanted to ease my selfish pain. I guess that this is how some people end up as drug addicts. I was tipsy from the wine as I took a puff from the joint. I took one puff, and my head began to spin. She laughed at me, and called me a cheap, easy drunk. For a while, when I wanted to ease my discomfort, I would go to her house. It became easy to associate myself with others who smoked, because now that they knew I would too, they did not mind letting me know their vices. Smoking marijuana was not fun for me. I just wanted the company and to be accepted by someone.

Sometimes, after the children were asleep, I would tell James that I was going to visit my friend. He didn't mind, because he could then have some quiet time for himself. The ladies would get together after the kids were sleeping and we would talk about our day. It was an easy way to escape reality. With poverty always staring you in the face, nothing seemed wrong about a few friends getting together to drink wine and complain about the harsh realities of life, right?

I had stopped going to the church so much and began to loose hope. It wasn't long before I began to see previously hidden vices revealed to me. I looked around a church one Sunday and noticed so many eyes that were red and swollen from drunken stupors and remnants of marijuana smoke. I decided to stop my new life with drugs, and I began to drift away from my old friends.

I wanted to find God again. I guess that I was afraid of loosing my soul after all that I had been through. When I began to pray again, I began to see my faults. I also began to have female problems, though they seemed to come and go.

I really began to search for answers, but I stepped on a few toes in the process. I was confused about my life and I felt completely alone. I shared a secret with a friend and I almost lost another friend in the process. I had betrayed a trust, because it seemed a heavy burden for me. I knew I had made a mistake when I saw this woman walk out of the other woman's door, with a glare of, "I told on you!" look on her face. I could never fix the wrong. I felt so humiliated and decided not to visit either friend for a while.

That's when I learned that a secret is best not shared with anyone, even your best friend. This became my personal credo: "Secrets are like stolen moments of peace. When you are pulled in, you end up looking over your shoulders."

❊

He's Back

One day I went to the hospital with a lot of pain in my stomach and was told I would need to have a hysterectomy. As I went into the hospital for the procedure, Jim convinced me that he would be able to help me with the children. So while I was hospitalized, he moved in. He would cook and care for the children. But he would not move out, and almost immediately, the beatings and the drugs started. He began to steal again, and one of his uncles came to live with us. My brother moved into his own apartment when he could not take it any more. My life went downhill from there. I could no longer work at the childcare center. One of the complex's apartment buildings where a family of six lived caught on fire. I had to let that family have my beautiful four-bedroom apartment. I moved across the street into a less desirable apartment that was roach infested, and the beatings became worse.

I finally got the courage to get another job, working for the Marriott. I constantly fought with Jim because he constantly stole my money. The final straw came when one evening all of the utilities, including the phone, were shut off on the same day.

Trina just so happened to be at my place. I took my children and left with her, leaving him in the dark. I stayed with her for a couple of weeks. Although Trina and I had our differences, she did not want to see my children in the dark. She did not ask me to come with her; she only wanted to take the children. But when I thought back on what had happened with Justice and Devon, I knew I had to go along with her. I stayed with her for about two weeks.

I had a hard time maintaining my job at the Marriott because Junior was often sick. He had a severe form of asthma that had me running him to the hospital a lot. I went back to my apartment one day to drown in my tears. The place was dank and smelly, and no one had been there for some time.

❖

I discovered that Jim had been locked up while I was living at Trina's. I moved back into my apartment. Life at Trina's wasn't terrible, but I knew my place.

I was fighting for my job, and at the same time I got all of my utilities back on. But soon I was fired, and I had to report my situation to my apartment manager. He directed me to agencies that helped me. I was surprised that there was other help besides welfare.

The Marriott Corporation had just built a new facility a few blocks down the street, and I got a job there as a house-keeper. Soon I was transferred to concierge area. I loved my job. I was a trusted employee and worked as if I were always being observed. I was proud to be employed at one of the most elegant and beautiful hotels in Atlanta.

I loved the hotel guests and my fellow workers. I took special care of my appearance and the way I carried myself. I tried to avoid trouble as much as possible. Although I liked people, I spent a lot of quality time alone as I went about my job. I loved to go into the stairwells to walk the many flights down or to just meditate. It was wonderful to run into some-one else singing a song; many employees were entertainers. I started singing again with a gospel group, and I was more creative than ever.

I made one mistake that haunted me. I had a friend at work who ate a lot of candy that guests left for her. She would store what she could not eat in her locker. Guests would leave me stuff, too. I was leaving one day and forgot I had left some candy in my pocket. I simply did not bring chocolate home around my sickly son, so I always left it in my locker. I also kept all my notes from my guests, in which they thanked me for my great service. As I walked through the security stalls, the candy set off an alarm, and it almost scared me to death. The security guard had me remove ev-erything from my pockets. The 10-cent piece of candy was his target. I was shocked. He took the candy, telling me to see my supervisor the next day.

❧

I arrived at work the next day feeling like I had done something terribly wrong. I was not a thief. The supervisor told me that the candy was hotel property; she said that I could have even taken a flowerpot if a guest left one for me, but I needed to let her know. She told me that she needed to suspend me for three days. She sent me off to work for that day, but midway through, she sent for me. She said she would forfeit the suspension if I admitted in writing on the blue sheet that I had stolen the candy and I would not do it again. (The blue sheet was a form that employees signed for job offenses.) I refused to admit any wrongdoing, but I did want to answer the charges on the blue sheet.

I answered by stating that the candy had been left as a gift to me and that neither the guest nor myself knew that it was hotel property. I chose to take the three-day suspension and receive training when I returned on what was proper to take and what was not. When I returned, I was given a special pass as a trusted employee. I had an access key to every room or office where my services were needed. I was sent on special errands. I adored my new responsibilities. I tried to dress, even in uniform, with style and I walked with grace. I tried to always be a model employee.

Diary--Must Continue To Write

Diary

Nov. 4th, 1996

Hello my little diary,

I had to pull away from writing on this book for a few days, because I could not bear to write the rest of the story without feeling the terror of the past creep back up on me. Actually, a few days became several months. I still tremble at the thought of the terrors that we endured. I will not fail. I will finish this book

✿

for the sake of all children of incest, battered women, handicapped individuals and rape victims. I still cannot believe that this many years of my life has been taken away from me. I can't ever go back ... I just pray that the words in this book will save someone else from the same kind of hell!

[Second Entry]

Today is November 4th, 1996. I went to see a friend of mine, Jeremiah, who had been bedridden for several years. We talked about God and trust of people. I told him that even though many people walk around without the aid of a wheelchair, they are just as handicapped as he is, but in their spiritual health. He talked about how he once felt sorry for himself and how he used to feel ashamed to pray for himself, until a woman of God told him that it was all right to pray for himself.

So, he unselfishly decided to pray for others. I said a prayer for him, and I realized how sad a person I was, holding onto this terror within. I wondered if I was holding onto the fear just so that I would be on guard against the past catching up to me. But how could something catch up with you when you never let it go? It has been there all along. I found a new kind of courage, or maybe I actually found courage for the first time after I realized that I was wheelchair-bound to this thing that feels hopeless, empty, inconsolable, and at times pathetic, pitifully pathetic.

❀

The past few days I was seriously considering a ghostwriter so that I could escape the pain of the spear in my side. If Jeremiah could give me a piece of his deepest emotions without flinching, why can't I be of good courage and help someone else like he helped me, without shame and without looking for pity from anyone?

Diary

November 13th, 1996

Hello my little diary,

I have come to realize that everything my friend said to me was right. I needed the courage to do the will of God. I know that my children and I did not suffer for nothing.

Diary

August 23rd, 1998

Hello my little diary,

I am asking you, God, to help me write this story in a way that will tell other women not to let this happen to them or their children.

How do I keep a mother and her child safe through my words? Please guide my words and my strength. Help me to be able to give the life back to myself so that I can give life to those who are still trapped like I once was. Amen.

❧

Chapter 5.

ℒ

That Old Man

On March 24, 1986, I was working on the ninth floor of the Marriott, and I saw an old man – he appeared to be around 60 – working on a conference room door. He looked comical, because he kept spilling some of the paint. His clothes were wrinkled, and his hair stuck out from under a dirty cap. He was short, stocky, and had a protruding stomach. He looked a lot like a leprechaun. I continued my work, hoping to never have to come close to the old man.

On the second day, it seemed inevitable that our paths would cross. The man stood at a door attempting to paint once again. Only this time we were in speaking distance. I nodded my head hello. What a big mistake that was! He began to speak a mile a minute.

The Old Man was full of it and so much of a talker that I gave him a poem to read, since he claimed to be a producer of some kind. He said his name was Charles Johnson. He claimed that he knew James Brown, Quincy Jones, and a host of famous people. He apologized for the way that he looked and said that he had been robbed of his nice clothes. He grabbed the poem and shuffled away. I was in the habit of giving poems to people. Some were inspirational or comical. This one was a song, but I had many more in my head.

❧

I did not feel a sense of loss giving one to this old man.

Early the next morning, when I walked around the corridor at work to clock in, I saw Mr. Johnson standing by the clock, but he did not see me. I slowly backed away, never taking my eyes off of him. He had shaved and cut his hair. He had taken the hat off, and his clothes now looked as if he had washed and ironed them. I must say that I thought this man to be kind of strange.

I took a real hard look at the Old Man. I had no idea who he was and why he was following me throughout that day. This was no coincidence. Mr. Charles Johnson seemed to be everywhere. I was afraid of him, but who would believe me? This was just the third day of my being this aware of him. In my mind, I referred to him as that "Old Man." His name did not mean anything to me, except this weird feeling called fear. I did not want to acknowledge his name or even his presence. I truly wanted the Old Man to simply go away.

On the fourth day, I had loaded a cart of goodies that I was taking on the employee elevator when the Old Man, Mr. Johnson, forced his way inside with me. He gave me a half grin that seemed to tremble on one side of his face. A slither of drool ran down that side as he stared menacingly at me. He reached into his pocket and pulled out a military knife, flipped it open, grabbed me, and held me hostage on the elevator for nearly an hour. I even asked myself, "Why did the third day mean so much to him?" In time, I realized that numbers carried significant meanings to him, such as the number three. It was my fourth day seeing him, but his third day of talking to me.

I could not believe this was happening to me. Mr. Johnson insanely persisted in calling me his wife and said he was not going to let me go. He asked me over and over again, "Why do you want to leave me alone?"

I tried to make Mr. Johnson understand that we had only spoken two days ago. But he did not hear a word that I

❖

was saying. He was determined to either kill me or take me home with him until I said this one thing: "What about my children?"

Mr. Johnson looked confused and told me that we had no children because he wanted to wait a while. We stared at each other as he pondered what to do next. I kept on praying as the blade of his knife rubbed my throat. I wondered where everybody was; no one came to use the elevator. Finally, I felt his grasp loosen, and he pressed the elevator button. As soon as the doors opened, I ran. At every turn, there was the Old Man, just enough that he was always in my line of vision as he followed me.

When I finally lost sight of Mr. Johnson, I ran into my boss's office and asked to leave. This was a new boss. He was not very fond of blacks, and he had already given me a hard time that day. The boss waved a weary hand at me to leave his office.

Changes were being made at the hotel, and a lot of people were being fired. But at this moment, my only thoughts were about my life and getting home to try to make some sense of what was going on. I went to the small kitchen on my floor to call my sister. Just as she answered, Mr. Johnson grabbed the phone from me, hung it up, and walked swiftly away. I was scared to death.

I Made It Home

I was so scared I constantly looked over my shoulder as I made my way to the train station and then onto the bus. I wanted to go to the police, but I didn't know anything about the Old Man. I stopped at the corner grocery store and picked up a few things for dinner. When I arrived at the projects, I stopped at my girlfriend Cindy's house, which I did often. When I walked into the door she looked at me and said, "The kids are at your house playing checkers with an old man."

I dropped everything, and as oranges and apples fell to the ground. All I could envision was my children's faces. As I approached my apartment and started walking up the steps, I felt as if everything was in slow motion. Junior came running to me, asking me if the Old Man was really going to make me a star. I grabbed him and held him close as I saw Tisha and my friend's son, Jackie, looking up at me as if I had a bag of gold.

I slowly made my way up the steps as Mr. Johnson stood up and purposefully nodded toward the front door. Then he pulled back his jacket just enough for me to see he had a gun. I knew what I needed to do. I saw a black briefcase blocking the entranceway, and my first instinct told me that something dangerous lurked there. I stepped inside the front door around the briefcase, and he slid it with his foot through the door. Mr. Johnson gently closed the door behind us, leaving my excited children on the porch playing checkers. I could hear their laughter.

After he closed the door behind me, he picked up the briefcase and slammed it on a table. Mr. Johnson had a large white gift box under his arm; he gave it to me and watched me open it. Inside were a pink dress, pink shoes, pink stockings, pink earrings, and a little blue velvet bag.

Mr. Johnson grabbed my left arm and twisted it hard behind my back. I started to yell out in pain, but he covered my mouth. With his free hand, he popped open the case and revealed a machine gun and a box of bullets. I immediately stopped struggling. He turned me loose and began that sinister grin, allowing drool to run from his mouth. His eyes were pure evil as he picked up the gun and placed the nozzle of it to my temple.

Mr. Johnson took the white box, and I noticed the word "BARBY" written on it. He handed me the little blue velvet bag, and it had a gold string on it. When I opened it I saw a solitaire ring. The man was ecstatic as he grabbed the ring from me and got down on his knees before me.

❧

"Barby, you are my wife now," he said.

Mr. Johnson put the ring on my finger and stood to his feet as I tried to look as happy as possible under the circumstances. I knew that I was dealing with a crazy man. Looking angry or disappointed was not an option. I had quickly learned from my experience in the elevator that this man was quick and very strong.

Just then, Junior burst through the door. Mr. Johnson quickly hid the big gun and slyly let me see the gun in his side pocket again. I had overheard Jim talking to my children from outside. Junior looked back and shouted to his father who was coming up the front steps.

Mr. Johnson swiftly closed the case and placed some extra bullets in his pocket. He walked quickly to the dining table. As Jim walked into the room, he made a comment about the Old Man having a crush. Jim stared at the white box. Mr. Johnson was as swift as a sly fox as he walked up to Jim and introduced himself as my producer. I was shocked at how quickly the two men clicked. Jim seemed to be impressed with the Old Man.

I took a seat on the sofa and watched the two challenging each other's wit. They talked until the sun went down. The Old Man seemed as if he realized he could not out-sit Jim. Mr. Johnson grabbed his case and bid farewell as I was putting the children to bed. A wave of relief washed over me as Jim came down the hallway asking me if he could sleep on the sofa. I told him he could stay until morning. For the first time in the last few days, I felt safe.

Some might wonder why I did not immediately call the police. My phone was still disconnected and a pay phone had not yet been installed at the apartment complex. The only pay phone was at the bus station almost a mile away. Neither my girlfriend Cindy nor Jim knew the danger that I was in. To them, the Old Man seemed to be, well, just an old man.

❧

Just as Jim got comfortable, I heard someone knocking at the door. When I asked who was it, the Old Man spoke, claiming to have left something behind. Jim nodded for me to go ahead and open the door. When I opened the door Mr. Johnson sat his case close to the entrance. He looked down towards his case, stepped his foot in the doorway, and leaned his body forward. I didn't have a phone to call for help, and Jim did not think that the Old Man was dangerous. But I knew instinctively that my family was in real danger. For some reason, I knew that the Old Man had never left.

As he walked across the threshold, he told Jim that I was his old lady now. He also told him that he did not want to deny him the right to see his children, but I was off limits. Jim stood to his feet and told me he would come and see the children the following weekend. I was terrified of Jim leaving and just as terrified of him staying.

I sat on the sofa as the two men stepped outside. They must have talked for hours, because I fell asleep from exhaustion. I'll never forget what happened next. I felt pressure around my throat that kept getting tighter and tighter. I thought that I was dreaming until I felt his hot breath close to my ear. It was Mr. Johnson. He was trying to choke me to death in my sleep. I pretended that I wasn't breathing, and I felt a wave of relief as he loosened his grip on my throat. Air was forced deep down into my lungs. I was dizzy, and I just knew he was going to kill me. I was scared to death and couldn't think. Everything was happening so fast.

Mr. Johnson said, "That motherfucker is gone. If he comes back I'm going to kill everybody!!"

I couldn't believe what I was hearing. Mr. Johnson grabbed me from the sofa as if I were a rag doll and dragged me down the hallway to my bedroom. He made me take off all of my clothes as he pointed his big gun at me in the darkness. As the last piece of clothing fell to the floor, he began to run the gun all over my body. He smelled awful as he lay his fat, sweaty body on me in an attempt to seduce me. I refused him, but he forced himself on me, calling me Barby throughout the horrible next few moments as he tried to please himself. Death at that time would have truly been merciful.

From that moment, my life – as I had known it – was truly over.

Mr. Johnson stood by the bed and he could see his shadow on the wall. He made a comment about being fat and how the children used to pick at him when he was a little boy. He claimed that he was a stud, and he could make a woman have thirty orgasms. He looked like a big, fat leprechaun to me.

Insanity must have gripped him again as he jumped on the bed like a cat and grabbed me around the throat and again began choking me. I must have blacked out, because the next thing I knew he was standing over me with the lights on calling out "Barby" over and over again. To this day, I hate to be called Barby or Barbara.

It was difficult for my children to wake up and see Mr. Johnson still there. They were hoping to wake up to see their father. I dressed them and told them to go over to Cindy's.

Mr. Johnson and I left as if we were going to work, and we ran into a minister that I knew who had a street ministry. He offered us two tickets to a play at the Civic Center for that Sunday, which was March 30, 1986. Mr. Johnson and the minister instantly became buddies, or so the minister thought. As soon as the minister walked away, Mr. Johnson began accusing him of looking at me in a romantic way. He was threatening the minister under his breath, so only I could hear him. Mr. Johnson decided we should follow him to his office.

The Old Man watched from a block away as the minister entered his office. We walked up to the door, then he knocked on it. The minister looked surprised to see us. Mr. Johnson claimed that we just happened to be coming that

❧

way. The Old Man felt so important after the minister offered us a seat. Mr. Johnson began to squeeze my hand under the table, causing me considerable pain. I knew he had
a gun, and he had a con game going on. It was up to me to
keep the minister alive. Somehow, I knew this was what my
role would be.

This was another nail in my coffin, another life that I
must try to save. Once you are a victim, it doesn't take long
for you to know what your victimizer is up to. The problem
is that other people who might get involved are unaware of
the danger. To the Old Man, tricking people out of anything
that he thought was important to them was a reward to him.
It could be important documents, money, property or a title
that could possibly open doors for him. I was in a fog as the
two men talked, trying to figure out how I was going to get
out of this horrible situation. After a few hours with the minister, Mr. Johnson and I left, greeted by the darkness.

"Do You Know If Your Children Are Dead Or Alive?"

As soon as we arrived at my apartment, Mr. Johnson began issuing threats. My children came home about an hour
later. Mr. Johnson had put his case in the living room closet.
Later, I put the children to bed.

When I walked back into the living room Mr. Johnson
had one of his guns in his lap. He pointed it at me with a big
grin drooling again. He tormented me with threats for hours,
and he led me down the hall into my bedroom. I was told
to get into the bed. He held the gun on me the entire time it
took for me to put on pajamas. He left the room as I lay in
the bed. I must have fallen asleep when I heard, "Tonight
you were supposed to be obedient!"

Mr. Johnson snarled as he stood over me with his hands
around my throat, squeezing. To me he was a big blur as he
straddled me and pulled me to my feet. It was almost 5:30

❧

in the morning. He told me to wake up my children. I was gasping for air as I struggled down the hall, with him following close behind me. Junior was about 7 years old, and Trina was about 11 and so innocent. When I opened my son's door, he was not in his bed.

Mr. Johnson laughed insanely, and in a demonic voice asked, "Do you know if your children are dead or alive!?"

My legs involuntarily carried me to my daughter's room, and as I opened the door, I saw both of my children lying close together in a fetal position, clinging tightly to each other. They looked up to see Mr. Johnson standing with me, holding a machine gun in his hand. They begin to scream.

Mr. Johnson did not expect them to scream. Somewhat startled, he put the gun down next to the bed and grabbed my son. In a sly tone, he told them that when they go to school they were not to say anything about him. He told the children that he would kill me if the police came.

We stayed up through twilight, listening to Mr. Johnson's antics. When it got close to time for the children to go to school, I dressed them and sent them out the door without breakfast. As they were leaving, Mr. Johnson let them see the weapon again. As soon as they walked out the door, I looked into their souls and promised them that Mommy will make all of the evil go away. Mr. Johnson yanked me into the house and slammed the door in my children's faces. He warned me never to look my children in the eyes again; he accused me of warning them with my eyes.

Mr. Johnson dressed me that morning his own way. From that day on, for two years, I was not allowed to dress myself or fix my own food. The life that I knew was over. That is why I say that during this time, I was dead for two years.

�֍

Chapter 6.

ॐ

The Odyssey of Darkness Begins

I was argumentative and difficult to control that first morning as Mr. Johnson began his task of molding me into the Barby that he wanted me to be. He ran my bath water. He personally bathed me. He combed my hair and put on my makeup. He talked constantly as he directed me on how I should walk, talk, and act in public.

I began to write poems or short stories that I called The Vineyards. As time went on, the Old Man assumed they were preludes to sermons. Mr. Johnson transformed himself into the Reverend Charles Johnson, a self-appointed minister. I was to be called Sister Johnson. I had to change certain aspects of my poems and stories so that he would not know my writings were actually prayers, because I was not allowed to pray. I would write these stories sometimes when I was locked up in darkness for days at a time.

I also wrote a horror script that seemed to fill the quiet in the apartment whenever I was locked up for many hours. Mr. Johnson encouraged my writing of the script, because he thought it would help us get to Hollywood. I wrote constantly, because he approved, and he allowed me no choice. I took to the writings as if I were Job. I looked to the heavens and I constantly would hold my thoughts on "The Shroud

✤

of Turin." Writing separated me from the terror. But the Old Man was also curious to see how long that I would hold out.

There was an exhibit of the Shroud of Turin at the CNN building, and we went to see it. The features of the Shroud, apparently the face of Jesus, frightened the Old Man so much at first. A priest who was there gave me a large poster copy of the Shroud and a lot of reading material. Of course, Mr. Johnson felt that we had to bring my children to see the exhibit. We brought them the next day. Another priest led us inside the exhibit and gave us some documents about the cloth. A few slides were included. I carry one of them with me everywhere to this day. The Old Man felt compelled to be a priest. He claimed that he was filled with the spirit, and was ready to preach.

"The Seedling of Triumph: The Vineyard"

The Vineyard

Placed beside a bush of great size and vigor was a tiny seedling whose tender faith seemed to be sealed in doom. The Great Bush constantly made the seedling bow so low it stunted its growth. Not far away was the Master's house, and every day He came down to check the fields, but the little seedling was always overlooked. Every time He walked by, the Great Bush would ridicule the Seedling, and the Seedling would bow even lower and pray. One day while the Master was walking in the field, He became distraught about the huge bush. He noticed that it was covered with thorns, and a wild, exceedingly great weed had tangled itself throughout the bush. For two days, the Master pulled at the weeds and thorns. The little Seedling saw that the Great Bush was going to be destroyed. The Master was hurt and walked away with deep sorrow. He stayed in the house for three days because of rain. After the rain and very early in the morning, He wanted to feel the wetness of the grass under His feet. He was weeping, and He wanted His tears to be soothed. As He walked, He was very sad. But up ahead, He saw the tiny Seedling standing as tall as it could, and its leaves were a deep green. He ran to it and began to speak, and these are the words that He said: "O, you blessed Seedling, the only one who survived the storm. As I destroyed the Great Bush, I commanded a great storm to destroy the field. But, here you are, the one and only one. Now I can start a new vineyard, all because of you, a most triumphant Seedling. What a joy to see you! What a joy!" He sang. After He finished, the sun rose again, and the destruction of the field was total. The little Seedling was standing tall to reach the rising sun, and the Master blessed that day forever.

"You Are My Woman!"

Whenever we arrived at work, I could see the shocked expressions of my coworkers. Mr. Johnson huffed as he walked alongside me, giving every man an evil stare. Every now and then, he would whisper close to me saying, "You are my woman, and if I catch one of them with you, I will kill you and your fucked up children. Do you hear me, bitch?" Although Mr. Johnson worked in another department, he seemed to be everywhere.

I saw some people snicker at the Old Man and some spoke out loud about the odd couple. He hated to be called old, and he constantly turned to me to ask if he looked old. I would always know to shake my head no. As we made our way to the time clock, he constantly complained about the rooming house that he used to live in. I didn't understand until later.

One day as we approached the cafeteria for breakfast, a young woman was sitting a few tables away. As we received our breakfast, the Old Man and she kept staring at each other. Then she looked at me with a warning stare. It was as if she was scared to death of him. It was a stare that I would never forget. He grabbed my arm and gave me a painful squeeze and claimed that he and the young lady dated once, but he had dropped her because she thought she was too good for him.

Throughout the morning I kept seeing the young lady, but the Old Man was always there to make sure we did not talk to each other. I know that she knew that I was in trouble, and there was nothing that she could do. I know she could see the terror in my eyes.

That same evening, we attended a play at the Civic Center. It was a gospel play written by a friend of mine. The Old Man and I had run into him on the way to work that morning, and he had given us tickets. The Old Man took his number and kept calling him every moment he got. The man had to keep reassuring him that he would get in After the play was over, my friend and the Old Man talked about my being ordained as a minister of songs. The Old Man questioned him about starting a ministry in Georgia. My friend gave him his address and told Mr. Johnson to stop by his office. I saw a light bulb go on in the Old Man's head.

Mr. Johnson shuffled away with a grip on my arm so painful I could not help but flinch. He turned to see if my friend had noticed, then he looked at me with drool running down the side of his lip. "I'm going to kill him one of these days. I saw the way he looked at you. No man messes with my woman. I'm going to kill him. Do you hear me, Bitch?"

For some reason I did not flinch. I guess that there is only so much fear that you can take at a time, and then you just kind of shut down. Little did I know what he had in store for me.

"The Big Gun"

Mr. Johnson was not letting me go home on this evening. He had me call my best friend from a pay phone on a street corner. She agreed to keep my children overnight. Before I could say good-bye to her, the Old Man slammed the phone on the hook. He told me that I was going to get to see where he lived. When we arrived at his apartment, I was shocked to see that they were the same ones that my stepfather had rented for us to live in when we first arrived in Atlanta. As the Old Man walked up the walkway, I could tell that his mind was racing.

When we arrived at his door, he pulled a radio out of his briefcase. He kept turning buttons on it to hear police calls. He opened the door as if he were expecting a bomb to go off. When the door swung open, his two roommates were sitting at a table eating. They seemed accustomed to this kind of behavior.

I was surprised to see these two men, because they worked at the hotel. One worked in the kitchen, and the other man was a housekeeper. The housekeeper had a look of fear on his face. He nodded at me and quickly left the apartment. The Old Man claimed that the housekeeper had left, because he had a history of stealing. He motioned with his head for me to go down the hallway.

The apartment was small, but it seemed like an eternity for us to reach the end of the hallway. His room was at the very end, and I had the impression of walking my last few steps to Doomsville. I could actually hear my own heart pounding to the rhythm of absolute fear. There were locks on the outside of the door, and a small wire stuck out just a little over the top of the door. The Old Man had to jimmy one of the locks open, and when he did, a piercing siren shattered the silence. I was in a state of shock as he grabbed the radio and said something into it. He reached his arm behind

❧

the door and I heard him pressing some buttons. The siren stopped. He again said something into the radio and listened to it. I was literally about to pee on myself.

As the darkness cleared, I saw a weird array of wires crisscrossing the room. They seemed to be suspended by tiny thumbtacks. Cigarette butts were everywhere. Dirty clothes were strewn about, and there were no sheets on the bed. An old rag of a curtain hung about the window which was nailed shut. At the top at the rod, I saw the beginning of the wire. As my eyes traveled along its trail, I saw that it was attached to a dresser-drawer knob, then a small table, and then finally the trigger of a huge machine gun. I started to scream, but he held my mouth with his fat hand, nearly suffocating me. Tears flowed from my eyes like a river. I could not control my trembling, and I literally wet my clothes. A look of joy crossed the slobbering Old Man's eyes.

He jumped like a kitten at the machine gun weapon and began cocking it in my direction. He pointed the gun at me and motioned with a grunt and a nod for me to sit on the bed, which had no sheets; it was just covered in plastic. He closed the bedroom door with his foot and put the huge gun in a black sling. He hung it in a corner next to an outfit that looked like something from the military or the secret police.

He started taking off my clothes and indulged himself while I cried. He was getting such a rush from my fear that he responded sexually towards me. As he undressed me, I told him that I knew that someday, God would set me free. He did not speak a word until he had me completely naked. Then he talked for several hours, telling me about all the men he had killed. I told him that I liked to spend time with God. He forced me into his closet and shut the door. A few minutes later, he opened the door and threw in my pocketbook. My heart pounded in the quiet. This was when writing in the darkness became a ritual.

❧

The Closet

I was held hostage in his closet for three nights. He would make me get out of the closet at 5:30 every morning, and he would dress me for work. No one ever questioned my weird appearance on the job or on the streets. During those three nights locked away in the Old Man's closet, I would pray and scribble on little pieces of paper, feeling the words deep in my soul. There was no light, so my hands had to remember the movements I needed to create words. This routine became the norm for the next two years. If he ever found one of my scribblings, I told him I was creating a sermon. One night I wrote the following:

The Vine Has Fallen

High up on the hill stands

a pitiful vine

lost and condemned to die.

No one heard it,

no one saw it,

no one knew when

it shouted from the hilltops.

"Here I Am!

Here I Am!

There It Goes!

There It Goes!

It shall be no more!!!

❧

So, Who's The Star?"

I was looking ragged and somewhat ill on the fourth day, and as we walked to work that morning, I was thinking of a way to protect my boss. As I approached concierge area, with the Old Man in tow, my boss beckoned me into his office. He told me that the Old Man had been threatening him and that it was up to me to keep him under control. My boss was obviously very shaken. When the meeting was over I walked out of the office towards the service area. My boss shouted for me to take a tray of snacks to a female guest who was a well-known star. I looked around for the Old Man, but I did not see him anywhere.

I was surprised by the reactions of the people I knew and spoke to every day; their attitude toward me changed. They said nothing about my weird appearance with the wig and the makeup, not to mention the two gold crosses the Old Man had placed on my lapels. He encouraged people to call me "Reverend." He wanted me to have a look that represented some image that was in his mind. He had developed a custom look for the woman of his imagination, and he was trying to bring her to life through me.

As I carried the tray to the famous guest, I trembled all over. I licked my lips, trying to remove some of the heavy lipstick the Old Man made me wear, and I constantly looked behind and around me. I kept praying in silence that he would not bother me at that moment. My daily walks down the hotel hallways felt like an eternity. It was so astounding to me, in that moment, how sensitive my hearing was becoming. I could hear the inner workings of the elevator cables far away. I could hear my own heartbeat sounding like a bass drum. Remember when you were a child, how afraid you were of the boogie man? This Old Man was truly the boogie man.

When I arrived at the star's door, the tray shook in my hands. I still did not see the Old Man anywhere. I was absolutely sure that he was watching me, though. I knocked, then the door swung open, and there stood the actress from "Good Times." She looked tired as she beckoned for me to place the tray on the table. She was talking on the telephone and obviously had been crying. She hung up, and she wanted to talk for a few minutes. She asked me if I knew where she could find a condo, and I told her about the one across the street from the hotel. She asked me to pray for her. We prayed that morning, and I left, knowing that God heard my prayer, too.

As I stepped outside her door, a strong arm pulled me by my waist, lifted me from where I was standing, and dragged me around a corner. The Old Man breathed down my back as he dragged me to the service elevator quarters. This was truly the boogie man. He turned me toward him. Spit was running down his jaw, and his eyes were ablaze with anger. I wanted to scream, but he had placed a gun between my eyes. He was such a sight, and I was so frightened that I started laughing hysterically. He put his gun in his pocket and started shaking me, trying to bring me to my senses.

"Barby! Shhh. Look honey, don't fall apart on me." He tried to sound as calm and as reassuring as possible. "I'll take you home today to see your kids. Just tell me who was in the room!"

I was giggling, and I just could not stop. He slapped me hard across the face, and I started to scream, but he put his hands around my throat in a death grip. He wanted me alive, but I wanted to die rather than leave that place with him. He realized that I was not struggling, and he turned me away from him, forcing me against the wall.

"Listen to me. I'm going to take you home, OK?" He sounded like a bad little boy, but I believed he was really taking me home, so I nodded yes. I envisioned my children running to me and calling out to me.

The Old Man had temporarily forgotten about the guest in the room. He looked at me with lust in his eyes. He took

❋

my hand and made me feel his hard-on. His skewed view of life bewildered me. Looking at the Old Man, he seemed incapable of picking me up like a rag doll or doing the kinds of physical things he was doing to me. He was a sexual predator and a pervert. His craving for sex and control were high. He loved to attack me, terrorize me, and then force himself on me, all the time calling it love. I prayed to survive each episode; some of them took place several times a day.

When he turned me back around to face him, his eyes were full of crocodile tears. He poked me in the side with his gun. I told him that the guest in the room was the star of a play in Atlanta at the time called Dreamgirls. His eyes lit up, and he wiped my tears away and began to make his plans. He led me to the door and nodded for me to knock. He tried to look as important as he possibly could. He slid his hands over his clothes trying to remove wrinkles and he took off his hat and brushed his hairs back. He placed the hat back on his head as if it was a crown.

With trembling hands I raised my fist to the door.

He grabbed it down and looked at me closely and said, "You must not look afraid!" These were words that I would constantly hear from then on through the two years that my family and I were held hostage. Instead, he knocked for me.

I heard the woman say, "Who is it?"

I told her that I had someone with me who wanted to meet her. She wanted to know who it was.

The Old Man grabbed me and whispered in my ear, "Say, 'Reverend Johnson'!" I did so, and thus began my new life's odyssey as the holier-than-thou Reverend Johnson.

When the door opened and the Old Man saw the celebrity, I knew instantly that he was star struck. The smiling Old Man greeted her, saying, "I see that you've already met Mrs. Reverend Johnson. Well I'm Mr. Reverend Johnson!"

I stood there like a statue as the two of them spoke. He mesmerized her. She told him all about her reason for doing the show in Atlanta and asked again about the condo across from the hotel. After about 15 minutes, her phone rang and she answered it, asking us to pull the door closed as we left.

The Old Man was ecstatic as he chased after me down the hall. My feet had a mind of their own as I tried to run away. To my astonishment, he caught me; he was much faster than I thought. As if nothing had happened, the Old Man started talking busily about his plans to present a tape of me singing to the star and how he was going to finally take me to Hollywood. He looked as if he had found a million dollars and bounced around like a little child. I was thinking, 'How was I going to warn this woman?'

Just as I was leaving for the day, my boss called me into his office. I could see the Old Man from afar. My boss did not like my talking to the "Good Times" star, because he did not care for her much. She had called to thank me for suggesting the condo. I felt terrible for her, because I knew the Old Man would never leave her alone. I headed to the service area, my eyes full of tears.

Mr. Johnson came into the service corridor, his eyes lit up with anger. Of course, he wanted to know what my boss was talking about with me. He told me that he had confronted my boss, who walked away from Mr. Johnson a bit frightened. The Old Man did one of the jolly-green-giant laughs as we walked into the full service elevator.

All Hell Breaks Loose

When we arrived at my home that evening, there was a note on my door from Trina, who had come to take my children. She accused me of being a bad mother who put a man above everything else. I was happy, but Mr. Johnson was pissed, to say the least. I was happy because – at least for now – my children were safe. As we opened the door, a music representative who had heard me sing before was coming up my steps. He was dark-skinned, well-built and carrying a case. The Old Man looked nervous as I quickly asked the music rep into the house. The Old Man swung his case on the table loudly. The man did not catch his hint and sat at the table. The Old Man grabbed his case and went into the bedroom with a huff. I could imagine him putting a smaller gun into his waist as he left the big gun exposed for easy access.

When the Old Man came back down the hall, the producer was talking about starting me on a singing career. He said he had a band; this excited Mr. Johnson as he pulled a chair to the table. I watched the two men as Mr. Johnson began to brag.

The Old Man started the story that I had heard over and over again. He claimed to have played for James Brown and that he was a good friend of Quincy Jones. Mr. Johnson had brought his musical stuff into my home, and he wanted to demonstrate a piano run on the keyboard. The producer was cordial, but his attention was on me. This made Mr. Johnson angry, so he told the rep that I was his woman, and that if he wanted to do anything with me, he had to go through him. And so the two men began to plan my career as a singer. So this next phase in my odyssey of prison life was now in session, as another innocent became entangled in this insane web of deceit.

As soon as the rep left, Mr. Johnson grabbed me and put his gun to my head. Since my children were away, I took this opportunity to be bold. I told him to go ahead and shoot me. Just as I was feeling comfortable with my bold move, a knock came to the door. It was my children. The Old Man put the little gun away and ran into the bedroom to get his machine gun, because he thought Jim would be with them. When he came back down the hall, he sat on the sofa, hiding the gun, and beckoned me to open the door.

❧

There stood Trina and my smiling babies. I still had my uniform on with the crosses on the lapels, and I felt so silly. I thought Trina was going to scream about my children, but instead she walked in ranting and raving about social security checks for Justice and Devon.

During her tirade, I was looking around my house. I noticed the musical equipment as I walked down the hall with her and the children in tow. I was about to pass my son's room when I noticed the Old Man's bed in there. I tried not to look panicky when I heard another knock at the door. When I opened the door, my girlfriend Cindy was standing there.

Cindy was sympathetic, but asked me to please let her know when I would need her to keep my children for more that one day. Trina interrupted, accusing me of being a bad mother. Yet another knock sounded at the door; it was the rep who returned, promising to get back with me. He handed me his business card as he pushed passed Trina, who had never stopped talking.

As I started to close the door, Jim drove up and stood outside by his car. But then another car drove up, and it was Jim's uncle. I went down the steps to find out what was going on.

Trina followed after me, saying, "I called Jim and there is nothing that you can do about it!" Like a zombie, I reached into my pocket and gave Trina what she really wanted: the checks. She left in a huff.

Jim said, "If you can't take care of the children, then give them to me. You shouldn't let an old man come between you and the children, Barbara."

I was totally in shock as Cindy came down the steps and hugged me. I heard Mr. Johnson call my name. His voice caused a terrible chill to go down my spine. I only knew one thing: My children were alone with Mr. Johnson.

I bolted up the steps, and just as I reached the top, Jim's

mother drove up. The Old Man let the children and me see the gun behind his back; we knew that we were not to act afraid. The children's grandmother, Mrs. McArthur, was the boldest person of them all. She ran up the steps, pointed her finger in the Old Man's face, and accused him of holding me against my will.

She said, "I know that Barbara would never leave these children alone, and I know it's because of you!"

Mr. Johnson was sitting comfortably when he coolly said, "I have nine children."

Mrs. McArthur cut him off before he could finish his sentence. "You're a liar! I don't believe that you have ever had any children. If you did, you wouldn't keep Barbara way from hers for days at a time without even a phone call!"

Mrs. McArthur had a gun in her pocketbook; she adjusted it to expose the gun's outline.

She told the Old Man, "If you ever hurt one of my grandchildren, the world will not be big enough for you to hide in!"

Then she pointed her finger at me and said, "That old man better not hurt Jim!"

During all of this, I was wondering, Just when, and how, did the Old Man begin moving his things into my house?

When my children's grandmother turned to go down the steps, Trina had returned. She was having a conversation Jim. As the group stood together talking about me, I was consumed with fear. Cindy had left and I was not even aware of it.

Trina went up the steps, entered the apartment, and took a seat. I followed close behind as Jim's family drove away. Trina began to tell the Old Man about Justice and Devon. She also told him about our deceased parents. The next thing I knew, Trina was telling the Mr. Johnson all about me. Trina must have thought she was putting fear in the Old Man when

❈

she told him how dangerous Jim was. It had always been easy for Trina to think that she had all of the answers for others' lives. But she had no idea that these little information nuggets she was giving the Old Man only fed his demons.

I was overwhelmed with how easy it had gotten for people to discuss me as if I were a piece of furniture; none of them realized how many nails they were driving into my coffin.

And so their discussion continued until Trina concluded, "She is stupid to let everybody else make decisions for her. She's never going to amount to more than this!" She let her eyes roam around the room in disgust. She felt that as long as I lived in the projects, I could in no way compare to her middle-class existence.

At that moment the Old Man felt vindicated, as if my sister agreed with his controlling my life.

After Trina left, Mr. Johnson summed her up: "She's a bitch, isn't she? She's greedy, and she's stupid to think that she can outsmart me. But she's the one I'm going to show just how much I'll take."

Everything happened so fast and so unexpectedly. In spite of all of this, I still didn't blame Trina for the way that she thought of me. From childhood on, my stepfather trained her to believe that James and I were country bumpkins, niggers from the fields. It was difficult for her to see beyond how she was raised. I understood. I myself was raised by older people who didn't prepare me for the cruel world that lay ahead. I believed that my sister loved me, but she didn't know how to show it. At this point of my life, I really needed to believe that. Trina was so immature about life, thinking there was no other truth but hers. Every time Trina did anything for anyone, she felt as if she were saving the world.

Trina had a tendency to point the finger and place blame, then walk away thinking everything was all right. She used to always say that people thought that she had it together

❧

when in reality, people who knew her just refused to argue with her. She felt superior when she had the floor. Trina would say to me sometimes that I was going to be the death of her, and here she sat, putting her life in jeopardy by talking to this deranged man.

Mr. Johnson found Trina's antics entertaining. After she left, he leapt from the sofa, took the big gun from behind his back and pretended that he was shooting her. He enjoyed believing that he had so much power over anybody who intimidated him. I was so glad that the children were in their bedrooms.

Mr. Johnson made jokes about what Trina would do if she ever saw the machine gun. He swung it about and was almost in tears with laughter. I had to control what I said and how I sat through his fits. I began to quickly learn how to seem in total control of my emotions.

That day, a song kept ringing in my ears; I called it "Satan's Bars And Chains." The words were a reflection of the opinions that people thought were just absolutely OK to say around me, because I did not have a voice.

Satan's Bars and Chains

Satan's bars and chains are not made of metal
the bars can't be grasped by hands
and the chains don't go a-clank-ka-de-clank
but heartache, humiliation, jealousy, and pain
are Satan's bars and chains
are Satan's bars and chains
loose me, please loose me
from Satan's bars and chains
from Satan's bars and chains
Satan, what's the reason

❀

for these bars that the mouths

of man has put around me?

They have closed the books to my case and scream,

"Hang him! Hang him! Hang him!"

"Hang him" was my sentence, as if I had gone to the trial of my life, and judgment had been found against me. I felt like my life was an open book to anyone who was interested in reading it.

The next day, Trina returned, demanding that I go with her to the bank to cash one of the social security checks. When I started for the door, so did Mr. Johnson. Trina protested his coming along, but the Old Man told her that I was not going anywhere without him.

After we left the bank, Trina took us to her brand new house. Her new attitude toward him surprised the Old Man. He thought that on the last evening, they had an understanding. Now Trina was rejecting him. She did not want him to come inside her home, but he got out of the car to come in anyway. He was getting paranoid. He grabbed my hand and squeezed it as hard as he possibly could, pulling me out of the car.

When we got inside, Trina went to another room. The Old Man grabbed me by the hand, squeezing my knuckles together again and threatening to kill Trina. I wanted to cry out in pain. He whispered in my ear for me to call Trina back into the living room, and he showed me the gun he had hidden inside a pocket of his jacket. I called out for Trina. When she returned, she began berating us about the children. She so infuriated the Old Man that he stood up. She took this as a sign that we were ready to leave, so she drove us home. She babbled on and on until we arrived home. The Old Man got out of the car in a huff and grabbed me, trying not to seem angry. He gave her a sinister grin and asked her inside.

❋

Once inside the apartment, Mr. Johnson began to tell Trina wild tales about the two of us being ministers, and that the children were part of our calling. I could not believe my ears. Trina was ready to add her two cents about my lifestyle. But she did realize the Old Man was only sizing her up.

After Trina left, the Old Man went into his game. He laughed at her and wondered if she just wanted to show him how well off she was. He warned that she'd best be careful, because now he knew where she lived. He told me that she liked to brag around me to show me how superior she was to me. He said that he would fix that, because he was going to make me a star. I didn't care about being a star; I just wanted him to go away.

To the outside world, I might appear to be a weakling by allowing Trina to talk about me this way. Some might think that I had no guts to allow the Old Man to treat me the way he did. There was a lot going on, and I was in no way prepared to deal with it all. I wasn't prepared in life, even as a child, to defend myself. I wrestled in this pitiful state of existence without any idea as to how to get out. I was scared to death when more people got involved. What is a mother suppose to do when her children are the target of a mad man? I thought that I was finally free from the abuse of my children's father, but lurking in the shadows was something much worse.

Mr. Johnson had put an alarm on my back door and a large piece of wood wedged under the doorknob. He put furniture in front of the back window and placed knives in the jams of the door. It would have been impossible to break the back door in. He slept in the living room on the sofa surrounded by his guns and knives.

I didn't have a phone in my apartment and the Old Man took advantage of that. Mr. Johnson would tell me he was leaving, but most of the time he was lying. When he stepped out the door I would run to the window to look out. He'd be sitting on the porch with his gun in his lap or pointing it at in-

❖

nocent passersby who had no idea the Old Man was watching them. He would be looking in the window back at me with a suspicious stare. Sometimes he would turn right back around and throw the door open like a crazed man, allowing the alarm to go off. Then he would grab his CB radio, pretending he was talking to the police, and would turn the alarm off.

Many nights, he would turn on a tape recorder and hold mock trials until daybreak. Some nights he'd be the judge, another night, the attorney. The trial would always be against Jim, and the theme was always the same: he came home to find Jim inside the apartment, and the Old Man had to kill him. He was his own defense attorney. He chose the jury and he controlled the judge. These episodes never lasted less than four or five hours, no matter what time he played them out.

❊

Chapter 7.

ᔕ

The Burning Rooming House

That same night after Trina left, Mr. Johnson put on a black outfit that kind of reminded me of a ninja. He had been talking about the rooming house he once lived in, and he kept babbling about them putting him out. He was vowing to get even with them. He grabbed another briefcase that was hidden in the closet and gave me a warning as he set the alarm on the back door and walked out.

"Barby, I'll be back in a few minutes. Don't let anybody bother you. If you try to leave, I will kill Trina. Remember, I know where she lives!"

I was getting use to him doing this. I was told to talk on the tape recorder about my life. I sat down and placed the recorder in front of me and started talking as the Old Man set the alarm. He was gone in a flash. His warning was still ringing over and over again in my mind. I was happy that the children were at Cindy's. I quickly grew tired of talking and began to play the keyboard.

A few hours later, the Old Man pushed open the back door with a bang. He quickly turned off the alarm. I was still seated at the keyboard, but he grabbed me by the throat and forced me to the sofa. I fell over books and papers along the way. He turned on the television and took a seat next to me.

❀

The news was just beginning, and the Old Man was grinning as if possessed. The announcer began telling the story of a rooming house fire near the Martin Luther King Center area. The Old Man laughed out loud. He held my throat tight and my muscles ached. He began to take off his Rambo outfit, and placing his knives on the television, he crossed over me to put the guns into the closet. As he did all of these things, he somehow maintained his grip on me.

He told me that he would do the same thing to me if I ever left him. Then he confessed to me that he had set the building on fire, because the owner had put him out months before. He explained that he always waited a while to give his victims time to forget. He talked as if he was obsessed with the thought of bombing the Marriott Hotel.

He was very bizarre this night, and then he raped me as he had done so many other nights. He did not see these violations as rape, because I was his wife in his mind.

Unfortunately, I survived this episode like so many others. Thank God my children were over at Cindy's. The Old Man did not have them on his mind after the fire, because he was rejoicing.

"I'm Going to Make You a Minister of the Gospel"

That night, the Old Man began a mission. He made me take out the typewriter to create a 501(C)3 organization. He discussed a church and how he would use my voice as the instrument to draw a congregation. He pulled out his keyboard and played a few amateur cords. I had to stand on a stool and sing as if I were on a church platform. He acted as if ministers were in the room, and I was to preach and sing a gospel song. He had strung a microphone over the light fixture and wanted me to act as if I were performing for a large audience. We were up all night long. I stood on that stool until I saw the shadows from the sunlight filter into the living room curtains. I was exhausted. He yanked me down off of the stool and began his plans to start a church at the apartment, hoping to make a lot of money.

I had to go to work with puffy, tired eyes and the way that he dressed me. The Old Man dressed me like a doll. He had bought me a wig, glitter nail polish and makeup a few days earlier. The makeup was heavy, and he even painted my nails. He made me up in the image he envisioned in his twisted mind. I didn't know this Barby that the Old Man fantasized about.

When I got on my floor, my boss stood in the doorway to the concierge lounge. He was beet-red, and I did not know why. He led me to the little kitchen and began to say something to me, but just then Mr. Johnson walked up. I swear I saw my boss tremble with fear. I found out later that the Old Man was constantly reporting the young boss to his boss and then to the general manager about all kinds of things. The Old Man was covering his bases like the pro that he was. By this time, I was praying for the young prejudiced boss, because I could understand his fear. I did not know exactly what else the Old Man was doing to the boss, because Mr. Johnson was like a thief in the night, silently stealing the man's peace of mind.

I wearily made it through the day. On the way home, we stopped at a cheap jewelry store, and he bought a cross for himself and two lapel crosses for me for about six dollars. Then we stopped by a religious store where he asked about robes and relics. After that, we visited a small church near my home while the members were still in service. The Old Man decided that we would join them.

After the service was over, Mr. Johnson told the minister that he used to preach in Ohio. The minister asked us to meet him in his office after everyone left. As we sat in his office, I noticed some certificates that weren't framed. The Old Man asked about them. The minister told him that if he took a few of his classes, he could get one of the pre-signed

❧

certificates to become a deacon. The Old Man held onto the minister's every word, and when we arrived home, he pulled several of the certificates from his jacket. He cursed the minister for telling him that he needed to take a class. He made me sit at the typewriter and type out "Ordained Minister." He signed the second signature with some fake name on the witness line. He then taped the forged documents to the living room wall.

That night the Old Man forced me to write about the kind of organizations that we would be starting. He wanted me to sing songs into a cheap tape recorder, and he had a reverb box and drumbeat box going all night long. I alternated between writing and singing until the sun rose. When the Old Man dressed me for work that morning, my feet were so swollen he could hardly put my shoes on. I was losing weight and my dress hung loosely from my frame. My eyes were so dark that the Old Man cringed at the sight of me. He pushed me down the hallway and began to lay down the law about me not looking ill. He heavily applied makeup on my face, all the time cursing and spitting out insults to me. My children were still at Cindy's, so on this day, they did not get to see me this way.

When I got to work that day, my boss called me into his office for a meeting to fire me. I felt relief, but Mr. Johnson stood at the door and over heard the discussion. The boss turned away, satisfied that he was about to get rid of me, and I was satisfied that I could leave before anyone got killed by a deranged Mr. Johnson. Fewer lives for me to try to save, I thought. My boss was frightened out of his wits when he stepped out of the door and the Old Man was there.

I don't know to this day why things were happening the way they were. I don't know how Mr. Johnson was able to manipulate people's minds. It seemed so easy for him to deceive people, because he looked grandfatherly. People were looking at him as if his actions could be dealt with rationally, but this Old Man did not live by rational laws or rules. Mr. Johnson was the type of man who appeared to be weak and

❋

predictable, and he expected people to believe that. Where people thought his age was his weakness, it was actually his strength. He constantly bragged about the way people responded to his gray hair.

Mr. Johnson led me away from the hotel threatening to blow up the Marriott Marquis. He followed me, planning everything as to how he would kill everybody there. His voice grew tired as he repeated his ideas over and over again, as if he were talking to an imaginary double of himself.

It was weird watching this man's personality transform from one kind of person to another. He fluctuated between a spoiled child to the tormented spirit of an old man.

My children were confused by the changes around them. But they somehow seemed to grasp the danger we were all in. Junior was so young, and he could not understand why his father was always calling him a sissy. He cried a lot when his daddy teased him. I wondered if Jim had some idea about what was going on with his children, but was just not man enough to do anything about it. Jim would tell Mr. Johnson about Junior's crying episodes. The Old Man would agree with Jim that Junior was a sissy. So he began a 50 pushup regiment for my son every time his father brought him back from a visit, all the time referring to Junior as a sissy.

The Old Man was quick-witted towards Jim. If Jim ever challenged him, he would stroke Jim's ego. Jim enjoyed the Old Man's long-winded conversations about being the master of his home. The two always ended up in these man-to-man talks, about Junior crying all the time, and how they must always have control of their households.

Where was Junior to go to escape being referred to as a sissy by his father figures? He was only 7 years old at the time. Before the Old Man came, Junior was looking forward to his eighth birthday that September of 1986. And Tisha was looking forward to turning 12 in October. Finally, Jim stopped coming by so often, and Junior felt abandoned.

❀

Devon was a grown man now, and he was very concerned about me. He came by one evening, asking me if I was alright. Mr. Johnson was not expecting anyone, and he was surprised at the way that Devon ignored him. The Old Man sat on the sofa, trying to think of something to say to this new face. He had heard of Devon, but the last thing he expected to see was a strong young adult. I believe he assumed that Devon was still very young, considering how forceful Trina was about receiving his Social Security checks each month. Devon was just about to celebrate his eighteenth birthday.

Mr. Johnson stood to his feet and said, "I'm the man of this house and I will be respected. I've killed nine men; killing one more won't hurt me none. You tell Jim that if he come around here again, I've got something for him."

He went to the closet where he kept his weapons and took out one of his guns. He showed Devon that it was loaded.

Devon did not budge. Instead he said, "Barbara is my sister, and I have the right to see her whenever I want to. I'll tell Jim what you said, but I will be back."

Devon walked over to me and kissed me on the cheek, and the Old Man walked him to the door. I could tell that Devon really scared him, because he was the first person who did not show signs of panic when he saw his gun. Everybody else that the Old Man wanted to frighten never saw the gun. I believe that he sized Devon up, and he did not believe that the brave young man would go to the police. Maybe the Old Man had to show him that he had some kind of backup for his show of strength, not in words, but through his big gun. Mr. Johnson sat up all night on the sofa with several weapons close to his side, expecting combat. Combat never came. Devon did not go to the police.

After that night, Mr. Johnson turned to using more severe tactics to punish me where it concerned my children. He began to talk about Tisha being ready for sex. He began to lock them out of the house, almost three to four days out of the week, whenever they were brought home. He would

❧

make me watch them come across the street through a small opening in a curtain and then drag me to the door to look at them crying as they left looking for shelter. I knew that they were hungry and tired. I knew that the neighbors were getting tired of watching out for my children. When I was locked away in the darkness, listening to their cries at the door, I would curse the Old Man. He would sit at the door with the machine gun, laughing at them.

Cindy would come by and knock, and the Old Man would have me looking at her frustrated face. She would wait a couple of minutes, and I would see Junior running towards the apartment. Cindy would tell him to go back because she didn't think that we were at home.

Trina came to the neighborhood a few weeks later and went by Cindy's house. I don't know to this day if she'd called Cindy before going there. Afterwards, Trina came across the street with my children in her car. She knocked, but I could not answer. I could only watch her through the peep hole with the barrel of the machine gun to my head.

I had been locked in the apartment alone with the Old Man for a few days. Mr. Johnson was holding me hostage, and no one knew I'd been at home all of that time. I'm surprised to this day that no one called children's services on me for child neglect.

Mr. Johnson had just finished raping me, and I was trying to get out of the stained bed when Trina knocked. The Old Man pulled me to the door buck-naked and he grabbed his gun on the way. He was laughing in an eerie way as he forced me to look into the peep-hole to see the angry eyes of my sister. The children sat in her car, looking terrified. I watched Trina as she wrote me a note, slipped it in the door, and ran down the steps. I watched her glance back for one more sign of hope that I might open the door. So here it was, another nail in my coffin. A few minutes later, a neighbor named Lorie came knocking, and she left a note. Cindy did also. I was not allowed to retrieve the notes until early the next morning.

In the note from Cindy, my boss had called telling me to come to a meeting. Trina's note was critical and demoralizing. The Old Man was enjoying this so much that he laughed himself into a coughing fit. I thought that Mr. Johnson truthfully cracked after reading her letter because he felt that her words made him the problem – go figure. Lorie's note begged us to look out for our children.

By the time the Old Man finished her letter, he turned to me with fire in his eyes.

"It's your fault, bitch. Why did you have those motherfuckers by Jim anyhow? I'm going to get rid of them if Trina ever brings them back this way again."

Mr. Johnson's strength was incredible. He had me off the floor by my neck and it was so swift I barely realized it was happening. He dropped me to the floor and straddled me. He put his sweaty face up to mine and just stared at me for about a minute. The lower part of my back hurt and my throat muscles ached. I felt very dizzy, as if I were going to pass out. The Old Man released his grip on my neck, and air flowed into my lungs. Just as I was coming into reality, he grabbed my throat again and began to squeeze.

"Barby! Wake up, Barby!" The Old Man was screaming in my ear, but he did not release his grip.

The next thing I knew, it was the next morning and I was still on the floor. I could hear the Old Man snoring, but he had done this many times when he was faking sleep. I had to go to the bathroom, but I was not allowed to go without asking for permission. My body was in terrible pain. When I stirred the Old Man jumped up, and I realized that he was naked and I was, too. I tried to erase from my mind the possibility of what might have happened during the night while I was out cold.

❧

Without My Children ... Without Hope

Now, we were going somewhere all the time while the children were with Trina. With my battle against the Marriott brewing into overflow, the Old Man wanted me to sue. Despite him, I wanted to fight my legal battle because I had done nothing wrong but be born black and female. I made it clear to everyone that I thought this path my boss was pursuing was based on racism. But now that I look back over everything, the fight was also because of the Old Man's interference.

My birthday was coming in June, so Jim stopped by one night, and the two men went at it again. They were playing word power games. The talks appeared cordial, but anybody listening would know the difference. The Old Man and I were wearing minister's shirts by now, button downs with a white detachable collar that looked as if it belonged to a Catholic priest. Jim joked about us being ministers of the devil. The Old Man held his peace.

The two men went onto the porch and talked for hours. I was so tired I wasn't aware that I had fallen asleep. The next thing I knew, I thought I was dreaming that I was drowning. I heard deep, raspy breathing and tried to open my eyes. Strong hands squeezed around my throat.

Mr. Johnson was whispering in my ear, "I'm going to kill you, bitch!"

I was slipping away as his voice seemed to drift away from me. I felt my body slump to the floor.

After what seemed to be hours, I heard whispering, "Barby . . . Barby."

I opened my eyes and the Old Man was splashing water in my face. He grabbed me by my shoulders, and lifted me to the sofa just long enough for me to catch my breath. Then he dragged me down the hall to the bedroom and raped me, as if nearly killing me had turned him on.

❧

Mr. Johnson was tired of Jim, and he wanted him to go away. He threatened me the rest of the night. Even though this was going on, all I thought about was surviving for the meeting at the hotel in the next couple of days.

The Commission

It took me a couple of days to recover fully. When I went to the meeting, Mr. Johnson went with me, because he wanted the general manager, Mr. Jarvic, to know his face. Mr. Jarvic did not approve of his presence, but the Old Man sat in the meeting, anyway, against everybody's wishes.

Mr. Johnson told Mr. Jarvic, "Barbara Clark Johnson is my wife and I am not leaving her alone. You have witnesses, don't you? Well, I'm Barby's witness."

In reality, Mr. Johnson and I were not married, yet; I don't know why they did not just get security to make him leave. This most certainly would have been an opportunity to let the hotel management know how dangerous he was. But, somehow Mr. Johnson had charmed the staff at the round table, or they thought that the two of us were a bizarre couple.

To this day, I am surprised that they allowed me back on the job. Although I told them the truth about my boss, deep down inside, I was praying that they would honor my boss' wish to fire me. Now I was afraid for the safety of innocent people that might get in the Old Man's way.

From that day on, every time the boss would try to sabotage my job, Mr. Johnson would take me to the general manager's office. Mr. Johnson began to enter the main entrance with me from then on, and he was never checked through security again. He had hidden a gun in his locker, and he carried one in his pants pocket throughout the day. He would laugh every day at the hotel's security system.

I'd secretly kept a diary of the days that my boss would

try to make my job difficult. Mr. Johnson discovered my notes and thought that he should start creating one of his own. He was trying to create a joint effort, using my situation to set up a plan to sue Marriott for 10 million dollars. He decided to make me write a letter to Marriott's corporate office. He also took me to the EEOC (a federal organization that protects employees against workplace discrimination) to file a compliant against the hotel.

We got a response back from the EEOC office and the corporate office of the Marriott chain. Mr. Johnson acted as if he were in a war, and with an answer from these two companies, he thought he was winning. The Old Man became obsessed with the thrill of victory against the Marriott Marquis Hotel.

It became a ritual every day that, when I arrived at work, my boss would confront me with some kind of action. I might get to work and my name would be removed from the schedule. I might be scheduled to work odd hours. I might be given extra floors to deliver supplies to. I might be scheduled to work night shifts. Each day, Mr. Johnson took me off my duty to go make a report to the general manager's office. If Mr. Jarvic was out, the Old Man would leave a note. At the end of each day, we would send a letter to Corporate.

But, there was also something else on Mr. Johnson's mind. He needed to marry me on paper. It was now the middle of May 1986; I'd met the Old Man five months before. Mr. Johnson had discovered, through his conversations with Jim, that we had married as childhood sweethearts just after my birthday in June 1974. Jim and I had married on June 16. And June was a few weeks away. The Old Man wanted to be married to me before my anniversary to Jim. It was absurd, but in his mind, if he did not marry me, Jim would try to take me back. So he secretly married me in June 1986.

Once Mr. Johnson and I arrived at work the next day, he forced me to call my children and tell them about the marriage. Trina raised hell with me and my children were crying

❀

in the background. The Old Man took the phone and told Trina that Quincy Jones wanted to meet me; he was going to make me a star and there was nothing anyone could do about it. I could hear her screaming that I was a fool, and why would I marry a man old enough to be my father. Trina was walking on very thin ice. The Old Man hung up the phone. He took me around my job to get congratulations from the other employees.

Some laughed and hollered, "Congratulations, Old Man!"

Some said, "You've got to be kidding!"

Mr. Johnson walked the halls with his chest puffed out. I felt ridiculously dressed in a 60's dress with pale flowers and high-heeled shoes. My fellow employees looked at me as if I were a joke. I was crying deep inside, but I would not dare show the terror within. Just before time for me to get off of work, another fellow employee called me to the front desk.

"Barbara, Quincy Jones is on the phone!" The concierge receptionist was very excited as she passed the phone to me.

I immediately recognized the voice as Mr. Johnson's. I let him talk to me and I didn't show any sign that I knew it was him. As I hung up the phone, the receptionist was telling other employees that I had received a call from Quincy Jones. The Old Man came around the corner, acting surprised and full of happiness for me. I looked around at the faces and deep inside, secretly, I was falling apart.

That afternoon all of the employees received a flyer from their supervisors stating that there had been secret cameras placed around the hotel to catch thieves. I was holding the letter in my hand when Mr. Johnson grabbed me by the waist to leave for the evening.

Mr. Johnson's voice was cold and calculated when he said, "Barby, that was not me who called you. It really was Quincy Jones. I told him that you are a singer and that you're

※

a writer. We are going to give a tape to him and to the star. He is really interested in you."

I listened to him babble for hours. Time had taught me that he was in another one of his fantasy zones. I knew to acknowledge his every word with the proper nod of approval and to make no sudden movements.

I was also receiving letters from my resident manager requesting me to ask the Old Man to leave my apartment, because he was not on the lease. It was important that he qualified to be on the lease because I was living in subsidized housing. Mr. Johnson began to make it a point to get the resident manager to let him stay. We were going to visit lawyers at the Legal Aid Society. We visited the food stamp offices to add his name to my case. He was always angry when he was turned down.

The Old Man began to blame my resident manager for his failures, so he began to try to build a case against my resident manager for constantly turning against him. The Old Man was determined to be on my lease, so the resident manager told him that only my husband could be on the lease. This is when he took the resident manager the marriage certificate, and he was added to my lease. Afterwards, he was added to my food stamp case, to the utilities bills and on all other necessary legal documents.

With all of these legal issues taken care of, the Old Man was ready to deal with getting rid of Jim. Now it was necessary for Mr. Johnson to make the police believe that Jim was out to harm us. Day after day he would stop by the police department in downtown Atlanta with me in tow. He would tell the police officers that Jim was harassing us. They did not know that the terror on my face was from fear of the Old Man. He loved to go to the Fulton county court house, because at that time, they did not check for weapons.

The first thing that he would say when he left the station was, "See these gray hairs on my head? This makes people believe me. And I know that if you lie long enough, someone will believe you."

Mr. Johnson would say that every time as if he was trying to convince himself that it was true. Each time he wore
a minister's collar with a blue shirt and a pair of black pants.
Some evenings he would stop by a pay phone and call for a
police escort home claiming to be afraid of Jim. The policeman would drive us home, listening to the Old Man, and,
upon our arrival, walk through the apartment to secure our
safety. The Old Man very much enjoyed this attention.

Before I knew it, winter was coming, and the Marriott
had finally fired me, and the unemployment office accepted
the reason for my termination for tardiness. I was torn up
inside to lose my job this way. The Old Man was angry with
the unemployment office for siding with Marriott. We went
to the EEOC, and they too, agreed with Marriott's decision
to fire me. I was inwardly amused by the Old Man's reactions, because he could not see that he was the problem, not
these establishments.

Mr. Johnson discovered that Rev. Hosea Williams, a civil
rights activist that had served with Martin Luther King Jr.,
was preparing for the Feed the Hungry program for Thanksgiving. Rev. Williams was holding a meeting with the media
and financial supporters at the Marriott hotel where he was
speaking. I realized that the Old Man had visions of being a
part of something big like this.

By this time, we had business cards as film producers,
ministers and music producers. I also had a talk show, *A
World of Issues*, on cable TV. We had taken a beginners
course at the cable station on Euclid in an area of Atlanta
called Little Five Points. Most of Atlanta's art, music and
film crowd live and create there, and many reached stardom.
It is the hot spot where many new, talented artists go to get
their start in show business, even today.

When we approached the crowd, Rev. Williams remembered Mr. Johnson from the Feed the Hungry Thanksgiving
dinner the year before. I didn't understand how Rev. Wil-

❧

liams knew the Old Man. Mr. Johnson pushed me up to the podium, but Rev. Williams was not in the mood for another question.

He said angrily to me, "Who are you, and what do you want? If you want to help out, come to my office on the Boulevard tomorrow."

Mr. Johnson was angry with the way Hosea spoke to me. He felt that Rev. Williams should have been inviting, considering that they had served the homeless together before. It did not matter to him that the reverend was angry with me for interrupting his interview.

Mr. Johnson pulled me along as he walked away and threatened to hurt Rev. Williams. In his twisted mind, Rev. Williams had a crush on me. How absurd. Mr. Johnson could not wait until we got home to cause me pain. We rounded a corner near Woolworth's, and he took out a cigarette and lit it. He walked slowly, and burned my hand. I jumped from the pain and the surprise of such a childish prank. It was dark, and no one else was around. He grabbed me around the throat and threatened to kill me if Rev. Williams ever looked at me. I knew his accusations were crazy, but how could I tell him that? All that night he threatened me, unable to decide if he wanted to use a knife or a gun. The burn on my hand was a constant reminder of how impish some of Mr. Johnson's antics were.

The next night, after a long day, Mr. Johnson took me to the train station near home and went to a pay phone to call the police. The cop who arrived was a white woman, with a long blond ponytail. Mr. Johnson told her that my ex was bothering me again. I looked roughed up as she allowed us to get into her patrol car. As she took us home, I knew that the Old Man had a gun. Again, he was able to win people's trust because he wore a collar. To me, he looked like a leprechaun with a new pot of gold.

The policewoman walked through my apartment and came out to tell us that it was safe to enter. She told the Old

❊

Man that if Jim came back, kill him and drag him across the threshold. The cop thought she was talking to a nice man of God who was only protecting his home against evil. The Old Man loved the power that the collar gave him.

The very next morning, we went to the Secretary of the State's office, got the Articles of Incorporation, and applied to incorporate The Great Commission as a home-based church. Mr. Johnson was rushing to make all of the things he was telling people about himself legal. He was now involved in a battle with the Marriott to keep his own job, and he was enjoying it very much.

Mr. Johnson used The Great Commission papers and the papers of another church with 501(c) 3 status to get two very expensive robes on credit at a Christian store. We had been going by the establishment for several weeks, and the owner had developed trust in the Old Man. I could not believe that we were walking out with all that merchandise. Included were two more collared shirts and a few religious lapel pins, a Bible and tapes that cost hundreds of dollars. He walked out of the store laughing.

And so the commission began. On days when I was scheduled off from work, the Old Man made sure he was with me. He constantly called to be off work for no apparent reason.

Mr. Johnson also began a new adventure. He was a hypochondriac. The Old Man would go to an emergency room many nights, pretending to be sick. His plan was to create a history of hospital visits, so that he could win a lawsuit against the hotel.

We started frequenting the King Center, Hosea Williams' office, several churches, and even schools as ministers. He had befriended the "Good Times" star from the hotel by telling her that we would help her get incorporated in Atlanta. We would go downtown to run errands for her. For our efforts, he would get to spend a few minutes with her. Many people came to the projects, seeking religion and information about the music industry. We would go out and feed the homeless and walk with other missionary organizations at night on 5th Street in Atlanta, where well-known musicians came out to give back to the poor.

During our visits to Rev. Hosea Williams' office, we met another self-made minister who wanted to start a store front church. The two men communicated their plans to one another. We also worked at another church, sitting in the pulpit as ministers. We were supposed to have Wednesday night services to try to fill the pews with new members. Of course this did not work, because we had no real members.

Mr. Johnson had a pair of very dark sunglasses that he always wore when he walked the streets or rode the bus. He also began to carry a keyboard around with him in a black case. When he traveled on the bus, he would take the keyboard out and try to play. He enjoyed the attention that he got whenever he did this. His collar, the crosses, and the music equipment actually drew people to him.

One evening when we arrived home, a note was in the door from Lori that read:

"Dear Barbara,

Listen I work seven days a week and I don't want to have to walk in my door and see your children sitting up in my house. I am not your personal babysitter. I have four children of my own, and if I can stay home after work with four, then you can do it with two. I feel so very sorry for your kids out in the rain and it's cold, and you can't even find it in your heart to make sure that if you are going to stay out in the big world, to make sure your children are safe or doing OK. Please don't let this happen again, because the next time this happens, you will hear from me personally. Please try to understand you are not the only one

*who wants to get something out of life, but you are
going about it the wrong way. I am a true believer
that what goes around comes back around. These
are God sent children and without them you have
nothing. They need you so very much and I don't
know if you know that are not. It just breaks my
heart to look up and see them out in the street
almost all the time, Homeless!! Believe it or not,
a friend."*

Mr. Johnson had a temper tantrum like no other
that I had ever seen. We went to the pay phone to
call Trina, and the children were not there. They
were with their father, and Trina was expecting
to get them later that night. The Old Man was so
angry that he sat on the back porch all night long
with his gun by his side.

The March to Forsyth

A well-known karate teacher had marched in Forsyth
County with Rev. Hosea Williams and a few more organizers, and they had been pelted with rocks and bottles. A few
months later, several civil rights organizations began planning a march against Forsyth County, which even in 1986
was still segregated. There were areas where blacks and
other races besides whites were not welcome. January 1987
was a winter for the history books in Atlanta, Georgia. The
story of the snow and the march to Forsyth County were
headline news.

We went to meetings for the march, where Mr. Johnson told the organizers that he was a security guard and had
worked with the CIA. Nobody questioned the Old Man.
Hosea was more focused on the events to come. It was fas-
cinating to watch all the planning and be a part of it despite
the Old Man's involvement. Hosea firmly believed that all

❧

people deserved to be heard. I had the opportunity to hear him talking to a leader of a racist organizer in a cordial and very respectful manner.

Every day, we were going to the King Center, to see the star, to Hosea's office and to town to run errands. Errands consisted of sending letters to the Marriott and to their corporate offices, making telephone calls, going to the cable station to do the show, checking out film equipment, etc. We were doing all of this either riding the bus or walking.

The day of the march was approaching, and times for me were terrible. My body was wearing out. My feet were in horrible shape, and I was so skinny until I had to wear two pairs of pants to appear heavier.

Millions of people converged in the Atlanta area to protest racism in Forsyth County. College students of all races and religions came in droves. Even the homeless were organized, and many created signs and banners that were carried in the march. Many busloads of people of all races and ages, as far as the eyes could see, came organized and peaceful. T-shirts were sold, and children at the King Center prepared boxed meals. Even though it was cold and it had snowed, no one turned around. The Ku Klux Klan and other white supremacists drove beside us with their car tags covered in black tape. Effigies of black people hung from some bridges by nooses.

As we marched through Forsyth, many little white children screamed, "Nigger, go home!" Men stood on the sidelines holding rifles and Confederate flags. Thousands of marchers sang, "We shall Overcome," and "Ain't Gonna Let Nobody Turn Me Around."

Rev. Hosea Williams, Rev. James Orange, Rev. James Taylor, Mrs. Coretta Scott King and so many soldiers of peace came together, as one for all. So many young white children in the march were shocked to see so much hatred march alongside so much peace. Despite the terrorist words that the white racists were screaming, no violence happened on this day, and nothing like it had ever happened.

The ironic thing about it all is, I was a hostage and I was full of terror, but I had to focus on the movement. During all of this, Mr. Johnson used fake police badges and the police radio that he had used to terrify me with. He always had his gun close by.

Now we were everywhere, almost everyday, doing things for the "Good Times" celebrity, Hosea Williams, The King Center, and Feed the Hungry programs.

Trina would show up at the most crucial moments and bring the children home or take them away. If I did not keep my character in line, someone was going to die. Mr. Johnson was totally irrational, and he was eyeing my children even more for sex. He had a daily ritual of discussing my children and sex. I was battling a force that was not of this realm. I had many souls on my mind – the people at the hotel, my sister Trina, my ex Jim, my children, Hosea Williams, Mrs. King, the people at the churches, and the "Good Times" star. All of them were in this Old Man's demented line of vision. I wrote another poem for "The Vineyard."

The Reaching Vine:

The Vineyard

Just the other morning the SON of GOD

walked along the Master's field.

He came upon a lonely vine that seemed beaten

and thrown about by a terrible storm.

He picked up a strong thin pole and gently

wrapped the young vine around it.

Then He took the lace from His sandal

and tied it up to be assured that it would remain

❀

strong throughout the next storm.
Then He tore a piece of white cloth from the skirt of
His garment and tied it around the top of the pole
as a Sign Of Ownership,and He walked away.
The day the vine took a grip of the pole,
it vowed that it would soon reach the
white cloth and that it would grow strong.
It looked to the heavens and began to pray,
"Lord, Lord in heaven, please hear my prayer.
The storm left me ragged and torn.
I was all strewn about and left to die;
But the SON of MAN came and secured me
to a strong pole and afterwards He tied way above
my head a piece of the skirt of His garment.
If I can just reach it,
Lord I know that the SON will shine on me
and all of my stormy days will be over.

No More Light for You

Mr. Johnson would lock me up for days. The children, whenever they were at home, would leave out to go to school, and the Old Man would sometimes go to work, turn right back around and come back to the apartment. He would go back to the hotel later and clock himself out as if he had been there all day. He had a partner that he clocked in and out, also. They had a routine. There were quite a few employees doing this, and I wondered why they never got caught. I saw them dismantle the time clock and set it at will.

❧

With Trina taking the children unexpectedly, it helped me feel that one of these days, I could plan an escape. While Tisha and Junior were away, I was locked away in darkness. I was forced to write . . . write . . . write.

When Mr. Johnson was away, I was forced to tell my life's story over and over again into a tape recorder. I must have told the story of my childhood to the tape recorder at least a thousand times. I was never sure when he would return. He would listen to the tapes, and if it seemed as if I had not told enough of my story, he would conduct another mock trial against Jim; he had a special set of tapes just for that. While cursing and screaming insults at me, the Old Man would go to the pay phone located close to my apartment to call the police, again falsely claiming he was being stalked by Jim. The Old Man loved playing with the cops. He would look so dismayed while they were searching around the house, and when they left, he would yell with laughter.

One evening, he locked me up and he left for hours; I was to never turn the lights on. I began to feel like a robot. I told my story in a solemn voice and I started crying. I forgot to turn off the machine. I dried my eyes and kept talking. I turned off the machine and went into the bathroom. Even if I was home alone, I was not allowed to close the door.

I cried out in deep pain. "Mama, why did you abandon me? I'm so scared here alone. Please help me, Mama!"

The cry came from somewhere so deep down within me that I could never explain it. I finally cried out in abandonment. When I uncovered my eyes, the Old Man was standing right behind me. He did not say anything. He grabbed me and started crying. But anyone could tell it was not sincere. I just stood there with him holding me, and I felt totally humiliated.

On this night, he called himself "praying" for me. I guess he was in a mood relating back to his childhood. With childlike mannerisms, the Old Man said, "The children used to pick on me when I was little, because I was short and fat,

❧

and my father wanted to sleep with my wife, but she said no, because I could give her good sex . . ." And so on and so on.

I was obedient. I was to sit or stand completely still as Mr. Johnson rehearsed these speeches. If I twitched, he would surely shove me, choke me, or rape me. He talked for hours as I tried to maintain a look without blinking or shifting my body in any sudden moves. If I did, he would become a screaming maniac. He would stand in my face and spit and shout.

Everything was so intentional. I stood so still this night until I felt like my knees would buckle. Mr. Johnson became angry, because it did not seem like I was sympathetic. He grabbed my throat tightly and pulled me into the bedroom. He grabbed a hanger from the closet, loosened it, and began to beat me with it. I still remained silent. I was so numb now until I did not feel the lashes. He stood over me and took off my clothes. This was getting so old the way that he would have sex with me. Somehow, I guess, he told himself that it was necessary to seal a beating with a rough form of sex.

I said in my mind a silent prayer: 'I will lay motionless this night, and I pray not to see the light of day tomorrow. The children are away. Will he kill me tonight? Which night will he go too far? Will I ever find the courage to retaliate? What will happen if I do? Will anybody believe me if I tell them he is not a minister? I am so scared!'

A few days later, Trina came by with the children. This time Mr. Johnson could not pretend that we were not at home, because we were walking down the sidewalk. Mad as fire, she got out of the car. But it was also time for the Social Security checks, and Mr. Johnson had them.

Mr. Johnson told her that she would not get them unless she came inside to discuss my children and to discuss how to stop the checks from coming to me. This was one of the reasons for her first-of-the-month visits. Those damn checks!

❧

Somehow in the discussion, Trina and I were supposed to go to the bank without the Mr. Johnson. This had to be a test by the Old Man. I have no idea how this happened. When I started to leave, he grabbed Junior by the shoulder and said that the children would be alright with him. I was terrified for their safety. Trina was talking nonstop as we climbed into the car. She was calling the Old Man, well, "The Old Man", out loud. It was as if she were trying to insult him away.

Trina was making sneering comments, saying, "Mr. Johnson was old enough to be my father".

'Here we go.' I thought to myself, 'Another nail in our coffin and another life I've got to worry about saving.'

Trina talked as we drove all the way to the bank. I cashed the check and gave it to her. I was nearly in tears, because every minute needed to be accounted for. As we drove up to the house, Junior walked slowly across the street. It was like a scene from a movie. He looked as if he were told how to walk. Terror rose up from the bottom of my feet to the depths of my soul.

I turned to my chatter-box sister and said, "Listen to me! For once in your life, listen to me! If I ever call you to come and take my children, please come and ask no questions!"

Trina stopped, and nodded yes. For the first time in her life, I thought she heard me. The terror in my eyes were real, and I knew that pretty soon I was going to do what was necessary to stop the Old Man from following through on his plans to have sex with my children. I needed desperately to do something, and I was praying that I was not too late.

Mr. Johnson came out of nowhere and jumped in the car. I believe that he came from behind the apartment building. He told Trina that he needed a ride to his apartment to get something. I was afraid of that place, and I knew that he wanted to get the bigger gun. I was surprised when Trina said "OK".

❊

Tisha came down the steps and Trina told her to get into the car too. Trina waved for Junior to come. Junior came, holding his arms close to his sides as if he was trying to find comfort from within. My son was losing his baby-like charm that I adored so much. He did not smile and tell jokes anymore, and that big laughter that I used to call my gift was gone. The pain deep inside him was very evident. Tisha was now silent and resentful, but she was also very much afraid.

As Trina drove us to Mr. Johnson's apartment, she talked constantly about Jim's temper. This fed the Old Man's ego. He was telling her the directions to take and encouraging her to give him more information. He was enjoying the game that he played with Trina. I suppose she thought that this kind of talk about Jim's violent outbursts was scaring the Old Man, but he was planning to use this conversation to his advantage. His conversation with Trina was very calculated, but he somehow made their dialogue seem like it was between buddies. When we got to the apartment, he jumped out of the car like a cat.

Trina had barely finished telling me that I needed a younger man when the Old Man came back holding another case. It was heavy, but Trina assumed that it was clothing, but it was really his bigger gun. She began to tell the Old Man that I did not need anyone to live with me. He replied that he was grown and I was grown. Again, they were having this conversation about me as if I were not there. I was beginning to wonder if this was a little of what Jesus felt at His crucifixion. I said to myself, 'Here I am, set up to be crucified!'

I knew that Trina was concerned about me, but the Old Man was having the time of his life because, the words that she was saying were like adding a few finishing touches to my coffin.

As we drove back to the house, Trina and the Old Man talked as if they were great pals. She didn't know she was playing a game of Russian roulette. As I listened, their voices faded into nothingness; the quiet that my mind created in the car deafened me. I could hear the humming of the engine and the sounds of the outside world beyond the interior of the vehicle, but their voices did not register on my senses anymore. A few days later, the Old Man moved the rest of his belongings into my apartment.

How I longed for the creek back in the country and the endless fields with the lonely tree. I thought I wanted to see beyond the country when I was a child. Now I wish I had not seen this world as it is.

❧

Chapter 8.

♎

Let My Children Go

A few weeks later, Mr. Johnson was terminated from the Marriot. He claimed to have suffered an illness while at work, but actually he was found sound asleep in one of the ballrooms. He was furious with his boss, whom he thought would never fire him. When the Old Man came in that evening, he had me draft a letter to the corporate offices of the hotel chain.

After several days, a response came from the corporate offices to the Atlanta Marriott; the Old Man was rehired. I hated his games, but what else was I suppose to do?

Mr. Johnson was on a mission to get money from the company. Finally, after several meetings and write-ups for being late or calling off work, the Old Man played sick enough one day to be admitted into the hospital. He made a mockery of the doctors when he was placed in a room. He had a previous condition with his sinuses, and he knew how to use this to his advantage. The doctors discovered an unusual rhythm in the Old Man's heart called mitral valve prolapse, and they hooked him to a heart monitor for 24 hours.

The hotel staff sent the Old Man get-well flowers and promised that he could come back to work as soon as he was well. He wanted to celebrate by having sex, but the nurses

❖

kept coming in the room. Although it was a non-smoking room, he went into the bathroom and smoked, because he just did not want to follow the rules. Later that night, he wanted to entertain himself so he made me watch him masturbate. I was disgusted to the point of nausea.

He worked a short time after that, and he never gave up his fight to get some money. We went to an attorney who helped the Old Man get $3,000. He wanted more and continued to fight long after the attorney was released from his duties. With a portion of the money, the Old Man turned on the phone at the apartment and bought an old car.

I was choked so much by now that my throat hurt all the time, and it was very difficult for me to eat. The muscles in my neck were bruised and I began to talk in a hoarse tone. I sat straight up to avoid extra strain on my aching back. One day Trina came over while I was alone. I sat in the apartment afraid to look out the peephole.

"I know you're in there," she said. "Open the door."

I sat at the same spot that I had been told to sit so many times. It was where the Old Man expected to see me if he came home. I was seated at the keyboard with a tape recorder near by. This is where he expected me to be.

I heard Trina take a deep breath and I stood to my feet trembling. I wobbled to the door and looked through the peephole. I saw her getting into her car and closing the door. I hadn't realized how long it took me to get to the door. From the depths of my soul, I wanted to scream for her to come back but I walked back to the keyboard and sat down. I had made up my mind to let the children go, forever.

I had just sat down when the Old Man came in and grabbed me from the chair like an animal. He had seen Trina as she drove off, and he accused me of letting her in. He reached outside the door and got the note she'd left.

Trina wrote that she was going to take the children from me, calling me an unfit mother who had given up her chil-

❧

dren for an old man. This infuriated him. He yanked me by the throat and squeezed. I thought I could hear the roar of the ocean as I began to loose my grip on life. I must have seemed too willing to die, because he slammed me to the floor and started calling out my name in that weird boyish voice. I stayed there on the floor not moving. Once again he grabbed his big gun from the closet and began playing with the most private parts of my body with it. It was some kind of fetish with him to run that gun up my clothes as he was taking them off, then up my vagina with the barrel. Next came the familiar panting and then the sex. I hated this Old Man more than I could ever put into words.

When he'd finished, I was once again forced to stand on his makeshift platform to sing a hymn. "Soon I Will Be Done" was his favorite. Ironically, I sang it each time as if it would be my last song. He would try to direct me as if he were a conductor and pretended that he had an orchestra.

The Old Man looked comical as his big naked body swayed with the movements of his hands and the fat in his face wiggled as he gritted his teeth. I would have to sing all night whenever he was like this. I stood at attention so long until my legs felt like they'd locked in place. The Old Man would literally have to drag me off of my perch. His feet would be swollen, but he still would not sleep.

Two days passed and he became even more irrational. His little boy self would come out, and he would go in the middle of the night to the hospital to see a doctor. Rarely would they ever find anything wrong. Many times they would send him home with placebo pills, which he would take diligently.

As time dragged on, Mr. Johnson created many fake certificates. They were plastered all over the living room wall. He stole books from everywhere. They were stacked about a foot high across the living room floor.

❧

"Peek-a-Boo, I See You!"

It was a very quiet night in March 1988 when I was typing on a script that my daughter had written called *FAILURE.* The children had been sent to bed and the Old Man and I were supposed to finish re-writing the script, and prepare for the Stax stage show at the Civic Center with Rufus Thomas and Isaac Hayes. For some reason, the Old Man decided that he wanted to go over a few pages of the script with Trisha, so he went into her room.

As I listened to them read out loud, I relaxed and focused on my writing. It was always difficult for me to concentrate when he was in the room with me. But for some uncanny reason, the ribbon to the typewriter broke at the end of the script. I started to yell for him to come and look at the script, but I decided to take it into the bedroom instead.

As I walked down the hallway the sounds of their voices echoed in the air, and the script reading sounded a bit forced. I thought that this was due to the fact that my daughter was a writer, not an actress.

I was in no way prepared for what I was about to experience. The shock began when before me, the door was wide open; the Old Man did not know that I was standing in the doorway. To my horror, Trisha was lying on her left side holding the script at an angle so that he could see when it was his time to read. She had her right leg propped up in what seemed to be a very uncomfortable position, and he had his left hand between her legs masturbating my baby. I was in a state of shock. I just stood there a few seconds and backed silently away.

My head was spinning, but I still needed to be sure that my eyes were not playing tricks on me. I held my breath and looked once again. This time he was so involved he had sweat forming on his brow. I was dazed, and as his hand movement became more rhythmic, my daughter was doing

❧

her best to read.

I fought the thought of murder that crossed my mind at that precise moment. I quietly backed into my room, directly across the hall, never taking my eyes off of him.

I had to think fast because I knew that if he thought I saw him, he would kill us all. I knew that he would wonder, when did I leave the living room? And how much did I see?

I sat on the bed and began to pray, Dear Lord, give me the words to say.

Holding back tears, I walked back to the door and spoke as I approached the entrance. He seemed startled when I said, "You two sure are reading that script funny. Why don't you let me read the third person?"

I noticed when he quickly pulled the covers over my daughter's nude body. He gained his composure, but I reached over him and took the script from Tisha. He slyly pushed past me just enough to give a look of his eye for me to follow him.

He did not expect me to keep on talking. "What about the script, Charles?" I said defiantly.

He shook his head and walked briskly down the hallway, saying, "Naw, that's all right. I'm going up front."

I watched the Old Man as he sat on the tattered sofa. "Why don't you read the rest of the script in the typewriter?" I said, coldly.

"I'll read it tomorrow," he angrily said.

"Is it all right for me to go to the restroom?" I asked.

"Go ahead, but hurry back." He said this with great frustration as he looked at me with evil eyes.

As I took this second journey down the hallway I was trembling as I heard him jump up from the sofa, and the sounds of the springs rang in my ears. I heard the clank of

❀

the big machine gun as he retrieved it from the closet. I was terrified, because I did not know what he, or even I, would do next.

I took this rare opportunity to peek into my daughter's room. Tisha was lying there looking so angry and lost. A heavy weight took hold of my heart. I signaled for her to be quiet and walk with me down the hall, but she shook her head no and whispered that she was naked under the bed sheets. Although I already knew that she was naked, I didn't expect her to say it to me.

Deep down inside, I was hoping that this was just a bad nightmare, and soon someone would awaken me, take me in their arms, and say that everything is all right. But this was reality, and no one was coming.

Finally, what she said registered in my mind, and I gasped and covered my mouth to hold back a scream. Tisha lowered her head in disgust as I quietly closed the door. I went back toward the living room, but I knew that I had to make it seem as if I had used the restroom. So I went back and turned on the water in the sink and flushed the toilet.

I had to find some way to explain why I was in my bedroom. So I walked into the living room and forced myself to smile. The Old Man had lit a cigarette, and the gun was across his lap.

"My legs were hurting, so I went to elevate them for a while," I said.

I tried to sound convincing, but he just jeered at me. I knew that he was looking for some kind of signal from me to indicate whether or not I had seen him with Tisha. That night Mr. Johnson did not argue as usual, and he quickly changed the subject from the script. He caressed the gun as he discussed the upcoming Stax show. He told me that I was to secure Carla Thomas, and he was going to talk to the Strikers, a local motorcycle group in Atlanta, about working security. He especially wanted to be security for Isaac Hayes. After a

❈

lengthy discussion, he told me to go to bed.

I could not sleep that night, because I didn't know his intentions. I promised myself that I would not sleep unaware again.

He woke the children early the next morning and sent them to the store before it was to open. The children were not to return empty handed. I lay as still as I possibly could, because I could not begin to imagine what he would do to me if he knew that I was awake. Once he was through giving the children a note for credit to get snacks from a small grocer up the street, I heard him lock the door, and he stormed down the hallway.

As I listened to each of his footsteps, I prayed that he would not force himself on me this time. He opened the door slowly, saying "Barby, Barby" in a sneer, over and over again. I held my eyes closely shut and tried to breathe evenly. My heart pounded as I listened to his breathing as he placed his lips next to my ear. He stepped away and walked suspiciously along the side of the bed. My heart skipped a beat when he put his hand to my throat and began to squeeze.

I knew how strong he was whenever was angry. He actually picked me up by my throat like a maniac. The next thing I knew, he threw me back on the bed, gasping for breath. Then he said, "Get up, bitch, and come into the living room." He yanked me to my feet like a rag doll and called me all kind of names as he pushed me violently down the hallway. It was a journey I had taken many times, and I knew he was going to get his beloved gun.

He Who Walks With Me

The Vineyard

I'm seeing for the first time the face of He . . .
He took hold of my hand when I was an infant

❧

and he caressed me and soothed my fears
from the terrible pains of neglect.
He calmed the terrible hunger that I craved
seeking my Mother's arms...
and He whispered to me in dreams,.
"I love you, in the most Fatherly way!"
I saw Him when I began to talk
and He carried on a conversation with me
when everyone else saw me as a disgrace.
My hair was unkempt and my shoes were raggedy.
He played games with me and taught me songs to sing.
I saw Him when I suffered the loss of a loved one,
when He came to my bedside and said.
"Surely you know your loved one is safe with Me?"
I took a long look at the hand that held mine.
and gave to Him my innocent faith.

I promised myself that this was not going to be another routine day. I made a pact with God that he was never going to see me afraid again. I gained my composure as the Old Man pushed me into the side of the table. He sat on the sofa.

"Go get me some grease," he shouted, while grasping the gun. He pulled back the clip of the machine gun as if trying to make as much noise as possible to frighten me. I did not flinch this time. I was filled with anger. When I did move, I purposely took my time moving to do his bidding. He looked at me with as much evil as he could muster. But no fear struck my heart this time.

I do not know what came over me, but I said, "You have

the gun, and here I am. Go ahead and shoot me."

He could not believe his ears as I defiantly walked away.

I heard him hiss as he said, "Don't forget the grease, bitch!"

"Bitch" rolled off of his tongue as spit rolled down his face in a grotesque way. He wiped it away with his fat arm, and I looked at him sternly. I made my actions speak even more defiantly as I tossed him a container of hair grease. This enraged him so much he trembled.

And you know what? Under my breath, I could hear myself laughing.

"Killing you would not be good enough. I'll kill the kids first in a slow death right before your eyes, and I'll dare you to move!" he screamed as I shuffled down the hallway away from the sound of his voice. And then I realized, I really was laughing.

"You hear me, bitch! I'm going to kill those children of yours, and carry them in the trunk to California. And then I'll kill you so slowly, so slowly."

I walked back down the hall to face this screaming maniac with a menacing grin on my face.

Boldly, I turned my back on him and he said, "I know that you know that I was masturbating Tisha."

All of a sudden, I felt his hot breath on my neck, and he was sliding a large hunting knife down my back. "I told you that if you did not masturbate the children that I would," he hissed. "And you know what? She has a better orgasm than you do."

I was shocked. I did not hear him when he stood up. What he had said was like a bullet in my heart. I felt his heavy hand on my shoulder, his breath hot against my left ear. Then he began to describe to me in detail what he had been doing to my child, and he held his hand up in front of my face showing me his finger in a vulgar manner as he continued to refer to my child as a fucking whore.

"All women are whores! Even that little bitchy daughter of yours," he said.

I must tell you, murder was definitely on my mind at that moment.

As he talked, I kept control of my senses, even as he pulled my gown down and started to fondle me. I felt myself being pushed down the hall to be raped like so many times before, but no tears today. I felt nothing as he kept screaming, "You are my wife, and I'll fuck you whenever I feel like it! Do you hear me, bitch? Do you hear me!?"

I would not let anything he said or did cause me to cry on this day, because I needed to be the strongest that I had ever been in my life. I needed to be strong for my children. As he raped me, he continued insulting me. But it did not matter any more, and I knew that as far as he was concerned, I was dead anyway, I could tell. Just as he had finished, the children knocked at the door. He jumped from the bed cursing, and he strutted down the hall nude. I heard him as he pulled his pants on yelling for the children to hold on. I heard the clank of the gun as he put it back in the closet. He was trying to make the house look presentable.

Since he was preoccupied, I jumped from the bed and went into my daughter's room to look for the four pound dumbbells. I knew to get ready, because soon it was going to be now or never. I visualized his every move while he was attempting to deceive the children. I knew that I needed to think things through. I found the dumbbells, and quickly hid them deep under some clothes in my closet. I jumped back into the bed, just as I heard him tell the children that I was ill. He sent the children to their rooms, and they told me that they hoped I would feel better.

I felt his hand on my shoulder as he leaned close ear and whispered, "Why don't you rest a while and I'll cook dinner. Now you know you need to eat so that people will stop accus-

❧

ing me of doing something to you. I love you, Barby." When he said, "I love you, Barby," it sounded like a child asking for forgiveness.

As he closed the door, I asked in a low voice, "What are you going to cook?" I was sure that he was gone, because there was no response, I decided that this was my time to make my pact with God. I knew pretty soon I was going to die.

DIARY

Today is December 9th, 1996,

It is sunny but cold. I was watching the news and heard that Howard from "In the Heat of The Night" passed away. I was hurt deeply, and I'm truly going to miss him. A few years ago, I had a vision concerning the set, and I shared it with a few chosen friends. I saw a wheat field lit up in a yellow light, and I saw three graves far out with the head-stones touching each other. I saw people gathered in a small crowd away from the field in deep sorrow for the three buried in the field. I now see the vision has come to pass as I looked away from the vision and see the passing of time. In the pass few years, three have passed away – a beautician, Hugh O'Connor, and Howard.

What Do I Do Now?

As I listened to the voice of the Old Man echo down the hall, I began to feel as if I was in a deep dark pit, black on all sides. And when I looked above my head, I could see my family weeping for me. "Why can't my children be free? And how can I set them free without killing this man and without him killing us? Who holds the key to our freedom?" I knew that my only hope was my faith in God.

I laid on my back so that I could meditate, because I didn't want him to catch me praying. I felt like I was hiding

❧

from the boogie man, and soon my mother would awaken me, and it would have all been just a bad dream. But the sounds in the hallway quickly reminded me that it was all too real. So I began to pray what I believed would be my last prayer.

"Oh God, in the name of Jesus, please give me the courage to set my children, my family, and everyone who cares for me, help me to set them free. Even those who crossed our paths just in casual acquaintance are caught up in the demonic force of this ungodly man. There are those in danger, and they do not even know it. Help me to set them free, Lord. Hear me as I call on your name, Lord. Please set us free."

I felt I was losing this raging war where I had no weapons. I had no foxhole. I had no comfort, and I had no peace of mind. I felt as if I was in a huge devastated desert, facing miles of scorching sand and sun, and up above my head was death, waiting for my children and me as we marched through this barren land.

The voices of my children brought me back to reality as I heard them asking about the show at the Civic Center. The Old Man was chasing them through the house; he had the children feeling like it was OK to just play. He had taken them from their beds to play in the house, not with each other, but with him, as if he were a 4-year-old child. He even made his voice sound like that of a child. Tears fell from my eyes as I began to sort out the events of the show that was soon to come.

I was so skinny that I needed to wear layers of clothes because it was impossible for me to look decent anymore. I was several shades darker that my normal skin tone. My every thought seemed to echo back to me, "Where do I go from here?"

Suddenly, Mr. Johnson swung open the door and his shadow filled the room. He looked like a giant standing there, holding a plate of food. He walked to the bed and tossed it at me as if he were feeding an animal.

"When you finish, come up front. I want to talk to you and

❊

the kids." When he spoke, he had a deadly eerie look on his face. He closed the door, leaving me to eat in the dark.

When I was sure that he was gone, I took the food, put it in a sock, and put it under a pile of clothes in the closet. I left a small amount on the plate and headed for the door.

When I walked into the living room, it smelled awful. Cigarette smoke filled the air, and I felt like vomiting. The Old Man nodded at Junior and told him to do 200 pushups; the boy immediately began to cry. Tisha sat motionless because, if we moved, he would accuse us of being hostile or scheming against him somehow. So we weren't allowed to speak to each other unless he told us to do so. Junior had been forced to do pushups for eating too fast. After my son had done about 50 pushups, the Old Man told me to whip him for being disobedient. I was so tired that I believe that he thought that I was dying on him. Even he could see the numb state that I was in. He grabbed Junior by his arm and dragged him into his bedroom, all the time telling him that he was going to beat him because his mommy whipped him like a sissy. When he finished whipping my son, he sat on the sofa to begin his daily discussion about masturbation.

Sexual Satisfaction Must Come From Home

Mr. Johnson told the children that I did not approve of such talk. But he said that the Bible said that a man is the master of his house, and he can do what he wanted to in his own home. He said that he felt that they should be sexually satisfied at home.

I boldly protested this form of conversation and asked him to stop discussing it in the apartment. He had been having these talks for over a year, but tonight it was different. I know that he was trying to brainwash us, and I know that he knew that it wasn't working. He became angry, and his hissing and cussing went on for nearly eight hours. He boasted

❁

of making sure that his other nine children from his other three marriages were sexually satisfied at home. He swore that they were the epitome of society. It was very late when he finally allowed us to go to bed, with the children only having one meal that day. There were many days when we barely got anything to eat at all, listening to him talk for hours. But when he did eat, it would be enough for two.

Early the next morning, April 3, 1988, he was so excited about the STAX show until he could not contain himself. He constantly called people about it, and he didn't even protest when I told him that I needed to clean the house. I watched him as he tried to arrange all of his weapons in a neat order. I asked him to put the large knives away because he did not know who might come over after the show. When I felt that I had a temporary moment of trust, I asked him to go ahead and get into the shower, and I would see to it that the children got dressed.

When I heard the water from the shower I ran to the closet and I rearranged the weapons. The Old Man always wanted things to be in a familiar order. I thought that having the weapons rearranged would give me a little time. He had taken the small gun and placed it in the jacket that he was wearing to the show along with his radio and fake badges. For some reason, I was preparing for my death, because I was going to do everything in my power to save my children, even if it meant giving up my life.

I remembered that he repeatedly said after the Stax show that he was considering getting rid of my children so we could slip away from Atlanta. His desire was to go to California, and start a new life as a minister with the fake ID that he had acquired here.

We had to take a cab to the show because something was wrong with the car. The artists were backstage in their dressing rooms when we arrived. The Old Man was upset because Isaac Hayes was already on stage rehearsing. He wanted to be the only one to walk with the singer everywhere. The

Strikers arrived, ready to help with security. No one knew just how unstable the Old Man was.

He told one of the bikers to take the children to sit in the front row before the crowds arrived. As the show progressed, the Old Man told one of the bikers to walk with me to find the children because he did not see them. When I saw the children, they were crying, because they had been asked to move a couple of rows back. Tisha was terrified because she had gone to the restroom and lost my purse. I told Junior to stop crying, and I told the biker to tell the Old Man that I was going to take Tisha to the restroom.

As Tisha and I walked to the restroom I told her, "The purse is not lost, only misplaced. In my vision, I see it sitting on a counter. As we walk, do not look back, and everything will be alright. This is the moment for you to tell me the truth."

She told me, "Charles has been having sex with me, and I'm tired of it. Mama, I want to kill myself."

"So I did really see what I saw last night?" I asked, and Tisha nodded, yes.

I told her, "I'm going to try to set us free, but I need you and Junior to go to school on Monday, and do not come home. Go get Junior from his classroom and go see Horace Walker with homicide, downtown Atlanta. If you are sent for at school for any reason, do not come home. Remember everything I'm telling you."

Tisha did not speak, but I knew she heard me. The purse was on a counter in the bathroom, and all of the contents were still inside.

When we were walking down the aisle, I saw the Old Man glaring at us with so much anger he could barely control himself. We left the children and stayed backstage until the show was over. When we came from backstage, a couple was with the children. The Old Man was trembling as he put his hand inside his coat to get his gun. The children must have sensed the danger, because Tisha ran to me and grabbed my hand as she held on to Junior. The couple nodded to us and left, saying that they wanted to make sure that the children were safe. Of course, the Old Man was very uncomfortable, because he wondered if Tisha had told anything. He didn't believe her when she told him that she did not say anything to the couple.

The show came and went, and the night to prepare for the end had begun. Mr. Johnson lay on the sofa in the living room deciding our fate, and I was in the bedroom doing the same thing.

As The Shadows Fall:

The Vineyard

While sitting under the Shade Tree of Life
The power of the Son came forth and the
shadows retreated and the brightness caused
my spirit to spring forth.
My spirit stood like a Great Soldier and called out,
"Lord, Lord, Art Thou Almighty?"
The Son stood there in ardent array and with his
gentle voice He said, "I come to call on Thee!"
My Spirit took in a deep breath of strength and said
"Lord I Am At Thy Calling! What Is Thy Will?"
"Go to the people.
First you will endure great peril and sorrow
for Thy Calling
But your reward will be great upon the earth

❖

and in heaven
But you must endure in Great Humility
I am with you
That is My Will
That is that you endure for a little while
So that the people will know and come to you
I will give you great knowledge
Like no knowledge that man can give
Then I will set you among Kings of the great cities,
and among the lowest, and you will be a great
reaper of souls for the building of my great bride,
The Church.
You will fill it with great allegiance in honor of Me,
the Son and Glorify My Father Which Is In Heaven."
When the words were completed
the Son was gone, and my spirit returned
the shadows began to fall once again
and my spirit bowed on its knees within me
until the Calling is to be completed.
I awaken from my sleep fully aware and prepared
as my spirit was preparing for my great
and merciless suffering
for it is the will of the Son that I endure for his sake

Chapter 9.

❦

I Do Not Want To Die

Mr. Johnson had played sick for a long time and had finally found a doctor who had given him some real sleeping pills. He'd made me take one soon after he'd gotten them. I knew that they were not dummy pills, because I had been lethargic for quite some time.

I remember walking down the hallway and listening to him play with the big gun. He was still somewhat excited about the show, and he had a couple of albums from Isaac Hayes that he had placed next to the sofa. I realized by looking at the signature that the Old Man had signed them himself, not the singer. I stood silently for a couple of minutes as he stared at me with that ever-so-menacing grin.

"Charles, can I please go to the bathroom?" I asked in a whisper.

"Go ahead, because we will be leaving by daybreak." His voice was different, and he was not the same. I knew exactly what he meant. The children were sound asleep and I prayed that Tisha would do as I had told her.

We were expecting a producer, Mr. Brody, to come to the house at 7 in the morning, and that was about three hours away. The Old Man was planning to be on his way to Cali-

❀

fornia before Mr. Brody arrived. That meant that my children were to be dead before sunrise.

My knees almost buckled under me because I was so scared. I backed down the hall so that he would know that I had not turned my back to him. As I urinated, I reached into the cabinet and grabbed the bottle of sleeping pills. I heard the Old Man cock the gun.

I poured some of the pills into my bra and quickly placed the bottle back into its exact spot. I flushed the toilet and hollered down the hallway that I was through. He called me into the living room. I prayed silently that on this night, please God, do not let him discover the pills. I walked down the hall obediently, and the Old Man asked me to get him a glass of water. When I handed the water to him, I asked if I could have a glass of water, too. He nodded yes. I poured a glass of water and started back down the hall. I heard him mumble something about bitches.

My mind was void of all thoughts as I pulled the covers back. The tears flowed like the river. They rolled from my eyes, down my face onto my breast. I kept wiping the tears away as fast as I could as I placed the cup under my bed. I had a large picture of the Shroud of Turin over the headboard. I looked up at it and began to pray, looking for a ray of hope.

"Man in the picture, if you are Jesus, I can not even imagine your great suffering and pain. No, I did not walk the road of Golgotha or feel the brutality of the whip across my back. No, I did not carry the heavy cross on my shoulders feeling the splinters tearing into my flesh. No, I did not feel the agony that you endured when they placed you on the cross. No, I did not feel the excruciating pain you must have felt as the soldiers drew back their heavy hammers and pounded the nails, driving them into your flesh. And as the blood spilled from your body and poured onto the ground, they laughed at you on the cross and placed you so that every eye could see. And as the sun seared your flesh, they drove

❧

a spear into your side and ridiculed you. No, I did not see you as you endured this great pain for me. But God I do know great pain. Yes, deep within my heart and deep within myself, I can feel the splinters of the cross tearing into my tormented soul and my tortured soul is screaming. Please set us free! Amen."

Fearing for the safety of my children I had to pray and prepare myself for whatever might occur.

"Please God, do not let me die without knowing that my children are finally safe."

I took the pills all at once and placed the glass under the bed. There were several under there, because the Old Man believed that placing a glass of salt water under the bed would ward off evil spirits. I did not want to die; I wanted my children to live. I hoped that the Old Man would do as he'd always done – sneak up on me to choke me, only to discover that I was already dead or dying. I prayed that he would panic and leave, or call the police, or maybe play the minister's role, or try to leave town while my children were safe at school.

"Barbara Clark ... You're In Grady."

I was walking down a winding dirt road with dark walls that seemed to never end. There was this incredibly bright light that appeared to be a great distance from me. I could feel a kind of warmth around me that was very soothing. I saw what appeared to be other people with me as shadowy images. I heard what appeared to my senses to be a bell and I heard a voice say, "I think we lost him."

I felt lonely in the darkness and then a voice filled the void saying, "Barbara, you're in Grady. You're in Grady."

I was confused. Who was Barbara and what is Grady? I opened my eyes and heard a voice saying, "That's the lady!"

❧

I later found out that the voice was Tisha's. I fought to come out of the tunnel, but it was so far. I wrestled with the thought of coming towards the voices calling out to me, because I did not know where I was going or who they were.

I fell into the darkness, and I saw Tisha crying. She was telling me that she wanted to die. I didn't know if I was dreaming or not, but I needed to save her. I wanted to hold her, but I couldn't move my arms. The voices were like an echo to me. I listened for the calm voice of the lady calling for Barbara. I felt pain in my chest as I opened my eyes. I did not know it was the Old Man, but he was squeezing my rib cage so hard that I could not breathe, and I could not scream.

"You are my wife, bitch, and you are never getting away from me!" he said.

I wondered why was he hurting me, and who was he. He looked evil as he slid his hand to grab mine under the cover. He squeezed my hand until I felt terrible pain. I must have responded because the nurse headed toward my bed and the Old Man turned loose my hand and walked away.

The nurse stood by my bed and held my hand gently. "Did that man do anything to frighten you?" she asked.

I gripped her hand firmly, and she waved for a doctor. I saw the Old Man as a nurse escorted him out. He looked at me with as much evil as he could. This was the person that I needed to save the little girl from, and I realized I was afraid that I was too late.

I wanted to talk, but I couldn't. The nurse told me that a tube was in my throat. She wondered why a woman like me would want to commit suicide. The doctor approached and told me to remember three things. He said the words "ball," "chair," and "the date." I was aware of a light in a window. It reminded me of the light in the road. I wanted to go where I saw the light. Was that for me? I could hear all kinds of sounds. Now, I know that they were from the monitors. The

❧

nurse did not want me to sleep, and so people took turns talking to me. They were all strangers to me. I wondered why they would not leave me alone. I wanted to go back to the place of comfort.

The next thing that I knew, a man who said he was my brother was standing over me. "Barbara, I know everything," James said with tears in his eyes.

A tall white man came over to the bed, a police detective named Mr. Roswell, and said, "Be patient with the Old Man and let him visit your bedside. We will protect you."

I still could not speak. I was terrified of the Old Man, but Mr. Roswell made me feel safe.

A minute later, the Old Man came in with another man dressed like a minister. They both wore collars like those of a priest. They prayed over me and then the unknown man left.

"People in this hospital are trying to kill you," the Old Man said in a whisper.

He grabbed my hand and squeezed it, causing me tremendous pain. But I did what the tall man told me to do. I was strong, and I did not show any emotion to him as he threatened me. He kept telling me that I was his wife, and he was going to kill those bastards. He blamed the children for my being in the hospital. He told me that he was going to hide them in the trunk and bury them in California. The only problem was, I didn't know anything about any children, or who he was. I did not know any of these people. I was concerned about the little girl in my dreams.

Later that day, two nurses removed the tube from my throat. I must have fallen back to sleep, because Mr. Roswell was shaking me. He was talking to me about the little girl. He asked me if I knew where she was. I remembered a closet with a lot of weapons. He asked again about the little girl. He wanted to talk to her, and he wanted her to show him the closet. I must have slept again, because Mr. Roswell

❖

was back with two more men with him. One of them said he was my brother, James. I was comfortable with the one who said he was my brother. The detectives were not dressed like detectives, but as doctors.

James leaned close to my ear and whispered, "I know what's been going on."

He backed away and looked at Mr. Roswell. Mr. Roswell wanted to go into the closet but he needed the little girl to take him there. I nodded yes. They took off in quick steps, and the Old Man came in past them. He leaned next to the bed and began to squeeze my chest. I could not breathe, but I did not flinch from the horrible pain. A nurse asked the Old Man to leave. He walked off in a huff, threatening to sue her and accusing her of doing me harm.

The Old Man was wearing a preacher's collar and a pair of dark pants. He smelled horrible and looked terrible. 'Why was this person hurting me?' was all I could think about.

The Eighth Floor

The doctors came to me early the next day and asked me to recall the three things that I was asked to remember. I knew it was another day, because I saw the light in the window change. I remembered the word ball, a chair and the date. I couldn't speak above a whisper. Although they had taken the tube out of my throat, it hurt terribly, and I couldn't wait to find out who I was.

Mr. Roswell returned with two detectives just as the nurses were deciding what to do with me. The tall detective told me that they had been in the place where the closet was, and they had taken the little girl to the doctor, but they needed to take her to another one. The man claiming he was my brother told me that he would take care of everything. I nodded my head, and they walked away.

❈

The nurse asked me if I wanted to be released to my family. But I was afraid. A few hours later, a team of doctors stood at my bedside and discussed my staying in another area of the hospital. I called the hospital the world, because it was the only place I had come to know as the world. So any area of the hospital that the doctors referred to was another area of the world to me. I was taken to the ward where they kept suicidal patients as well as other patients with mental problems. I was OK in this part of the world. They assured me that my family and the Old Man could not get to me unless I wanted to let them in.

As I was being taken in a wheelchair from the intensive care ward to the mental health ward on the eight floor, James met me at the double doors.

I lit up like a light bulb when James said, "They got him. Don't be afraid, Barbara. We will take care of everything. Barbara, we are all so sorry this happened to y'all".

He stopped in front of the elevator and cried as the orderly pulled me inside. I remembered his tears. I just didn't know what he meant. I didn't understand why he was crying for me. I just wanted to save the little girl in the back seat of that car I saw in my dreams as I came out of the coma. I understood the girl's tears, and I kept asking myself, 'Who is Barbara?'

When I got to the nurse's station, one nurse took my blood pressure and another asked me lots of questions. My head hurt really badly, and I was scared. One of them took me to a private room and handed me a bucket of skin care supplies. She pointed to the restroom and told me where my gowns and some bed sheets were kept. She asked me another battery of questions and left. I laid down in agony, and a few minutes later, the nurse returned to tell me that they were not giving me anything for the headache yet. It might be an after effect from the drugs that I had ingested. She told me that I had to wait a few more hours. I was in so much pain. I just rolled over.

The Letter

A gentle tug awakened me from my stupor. A nurse stood over my bed, and she looked nervous.

"I have an envelope. You do not have to take it. We all know about your case. This is from the Old Man that they had taken to prison. He's downstairs in emergency. He said that he was let out and he sent you this. I didn't believe him, but I want you to decide what you want to do," she said.

Mr. Johnson knew how to trick the doctors. He used his mitral valve prolapse diagnosis to pretend that he was having a heart attack and get medical attention at hospitals. The police had transported the Old Man from the county jail to be treated in the emergency room. He won a nurse's sympathy, wrote a letter to me, and had her deliver it for him.

I was sitting up now, and terrified of the Old Man being in my world. The nurse put the letter in my trembling hands.

"I called your brother. He will have to wait until the morning to see you. Don't worry. You're safe here. Come with me."

She walked me down the corridor. My door was the closest to the exit. She showed me the security guard and a call button that must be used before anyone could enter the area. She took me for a tour of the mental ward. I saw a glass-enclosed area where the nurses worked and administered medicines. I heard a female patient screaming foul language and saw several men tying her to a bed with leather straps. She was so tiny but so very strong. There was a young white man brought in who was screaming about how much he hated niggers and God. He stared at me with eyes that seemed to see nothing. I was an illusion to him. They sat him in a wheelchair and restrained him with cuffs and leg chains. Even in this state, he was powerful, and he kept staring at me. But I was more terrified of the Old Man who had sent me that letter.

I reached into my pocket. The letter was all that I could think about. The nurse came back and gave me a pill and a very small cup of water. I wanted more water, but I was not allowed to have anymore. The nurse told me that I would get more after they checked my blood. I trembled so badly until she had to help me back to my room. The white man never took his eyes off me.

The nurse offered once again to sit with me until I read the letter. I shook my head no. The nurse grabbed my wrist and measured it. She told me that I was so tiny they would need to find some clothes for me to wear. I was falling to pieces and I didn't understand why all of this was happening to me. She walked with me back to my room, and when the door closed behind her, I sat on the floor, curled up as tightly as I could.

A few hours later, I got the courage to read the letter. It was written on a few sheets of toilet paper:

"I am not in jail. You are my wife, and I'm going to kill you if you don't come down here now. I'm going to kill your children, and I'm going to find that sister of yours. She is responsible for me going to jail. I think those doctors tried to kill you with some pills. Don't you trust them. I'm right downstairs. Tell them to send you on down here to me. I am your husband, and you are my wife. If you don't come to me, I'm coming to you. They can't keep me away. Remember, you are my wife!"

I ran to the toilet and vomited. I dropped the letter in the toilet, but I had left the envelope on the bed. I didn't know how to flush it. I wiped my face with toilet tissue, ran down the hall to the nurse, and told her what was in the letter.

The nurse came back to the room with me and cleaned me up. She had found some small clothes and put them in a

❊

drawer for me. Once again, she showed me how to flush the toilet and turn on the water at the sink.

"This is going to be hard for you. I understand. We will walk through your amnesia together. Give us a chance to help you. I promise you that nothing will happen to you. Just focus on remembering what you can to save your two beautiful children," she said.

I was shocked. "I have two children? Where are they? Who are they? What are their names?"

The nurse just kept on cleaning me and babbling about my family and all of the people that loved me. So far, the only love I was aware of came from an Old Man who was threatening to kill me and claiming he loved me in the same breath.

I looked on the floor where the envelope had fallen. The Old Man had the nerve to make it look like an official letter. The nurse was very concerned for me, but all I wanted her to do was leave. I needed time to think. She stopped talking when I sat on the bed and started crying. I was angry at myself for losing the actual letter. I was praying that the "water hole" – this is what I called a toilet back then – had not swallowed the letter up.

The place seemed so dark and lonely when the chatter of the nurse stopped. I watched as the last sliver of light went away as she closed the door behind her. I cried until I could not cry anymore.

I picked my pitiful self up and went to the restroom to look. I did not know how to turn the light on. I ran to the bed and slammed my fist into it. The anger was deep within me. I pulled all the covering off of the bed and pulled the clothes out of the drawers. When I was done, I felt confused and horrified by my actions. I picked up one thing at a time and studied them. I made the bed and folded the clothes all in the dark.

I went back into the bathroom and felt along the wall and

❊

found the light button and pressed it. I gazed at my reflection in the mirror; I looked terrible. Black soot was in my hair and it was plastered to my scalp. My face was black, and I was as skinny as a rail. I looked at my face, trying to remember if I had ever seen it before, but I could not envision my own face. I went to the pile of personal health care products and put them neatly on the little dresser. There was a bottle of lotion and a small bar of soap. I sniffed them; they smelled good to me.

The soot was used to pump my stomach to remove the sleeping pills that may not had been digested. I had not noticed it before and I wondered what I looked like beneath it.

I carried the soap and the lotion to the restroom with me, and I became angry again when I'd forgotten how to turn the water on. I began manipulating all of the parts to the sink until I hit a button and a splash of water came out. I almost jumped out of my skin. I grabbed a nearby washcloth and started washing myself. I soaped myself down from head to toe until I could see no more of the soot. My hair was a tangled mess. I found a small comb. It took some time, but I got rid of the snarls.

I took lotion and put it in my hair and swiped it back. I looked through the clothes and found an outfit. My body was drying out, so I rubbed lotion all over. The smell was nice, and the clothes smelled so good. I looked like a little girl dressed for school. My skin was smooth and very dark. I looked at myself for a long time. I studied this unfamiliar face. I cried out for some kind of recognition. The tears were warm, and I knew that they were mine. I watched them ride down the rise of my cheekbones to the sides of my lips. I licked my lips and savored the taste of salt. I looked deep into those sad eyes, and I saw the image of me staring back. They were as dark as night, and so was the place where my soul was hiding from the terror. I reached for the washcloth, and washed away the tears. I felt strength from deep within when I thought about the crying little girl. It was going to take me to save her, and the courage had to come from with-

❧

in me somehow. I took a deep breath and walked away from
the feeling of doom.

The Struggle to Remember

I turned out the light in the bathroom and stared into
the darkness. I was trying to remember anything. Anything
would do, good or bad. I don't know how long I looked into
the dark mirror, hoping. I knew that having anger fits was
not helping at all. I was shaking, and I wanted control.

I left the room, and as I walked down the halls of the mental ward, I saw some amazing things. A woman was talking
to a door while a young man, hand cuffed to a wheelchair,
was ranting. I saw six strong men trying to hold down a very
small woman who appeared to be possessed. The nurses
walked right by me, and so did the nurse who had helped me
earlier. I walked the corridors undisturbed. I felt free, and I
wondered why. I went to a window and looked out over the
city. I stepped back from the window, terrified. I only knew
the world from the corridors I'd seen in the hospital, but out
that window was a vastness I was uncertain of. I was on the
eight floor, so looking out from it gave me the feeling that I
was falling. I went to a chair and sat down. I don't know
how long I sat there, but it must have been hours.

My nurse came running over to me saying my name cautiously. Her name tag read Melody. She pulled a chair up to
mine and asked me to say my name to her.

I said, "Barbara." Saying the name meant little to me.

She put a sweater over my shoulder and led me back to
my room. We walked quietly all the way back, past all of
the commotion with the other patients. I felt secure with her
beside me. When we entered the room, she noticed how neat
that I had left it.

"We looked for you," she said. "We did not even know

❖

who you were. You're so pretty. If it wasn't for the clothes, I would have walked past you again. I'm going to get you something for that trembling. You should be better by the morning."

Trembling. I was trembling like a reed in the wind. She gave me a pill and sat next to me on the bed.

"I talked to your brother this evening. He went to the police, and he called back about an hour ago. He told them about the letter. They said that there was nothing that they can do. Also, I must tell you this. Your daughter and son will be brought here to see you in the morning. The pill that I gave you will help you sleep."

Sleep! I didn't want to sleep any more. I became frantic and began to tremble again. I couldn't speak. I looked up from my dazed state, but the nurse was closing the door. The room was spinning. What's going on? My mind raced out of control. I went to the door and then back to the bed. I had to think. I must remember the words in the letter. I've got to save those children, but how?

I grabbed the pillow and held it to my stomach as I ran to the bathroom and vomited up the medicine. I don't know why I grabbed the pillow, just like I didn't know a lot of things. I was not going to sleep. I sat balled up in my dark corner of the room all night long. I saw the sliver of light come through the window, and I bolted for the door. The hallway was empty. I could hear my footsteps and the pounding of my heart. I sat on a bench directly in front of the nurses' station. I was calm and ready to see those children. A night nurse came into the station and looked at me with compassion.

"It's only five o'clock. No one else will be up for another hour."

I was unresponsive. Time meant nothing to me. I was waiting. Waiting for whatever might come.

"Barbara Clark, do you hear me in there?"

❧

I was upset with everyone calling me that name. "Why do you keep calling me that name?" I said in a whisper.

The nurse leaned close to me and said, "We must call you the name you were born with. One day you will remember. Don't worry. Maybe the memories are too much. In here, you can take all the time that you need."

She was very comforting, but I wanted to know where this place was. "Where is this place?" I said.

"You are in a place that is a part of all of the world," She said carefully.

She walked with me to the window at the end of the hall and pointed to all of the streets. I asked about everything. But I only knew of this world, this place called Grady.

The Children

I was in the lounge with several patients when the screaming young white man, now docile, sat next to me and said, "Hello. I remember you from the other night."

Tears were streaming down my face, and he took a napkin and wiped them away.

"Why is such a pretty little girl like you crying?" He was so gentle and his voice was very soothing.

Before I could say anything, his mother walked into the lounge and he rushed to her to give her a hug.

Fear went all through me. 'What if the Old Man came in too?' I thought.

Wobbly, I stood up when a smiling nurse approached.

"Your children are at the door," she said.

James came from behind her, eased himself into my line of sight, and he held me, crying.

❀

"I'm going to walk with you to see the children. They are bigger than you think. Also, I wanted to let you know that Mr. Johnson is still in jail, and he did come to the hospital faking as if he was sick. The police said they can't stop him from calling you, or writing to you." James was trying not to frighten me.

I gently pushed him away, and I guess that a questioning look crossed my face as I looked at the nurse.

The nurse said, "A jail is a place where they put bad people."

"Where in the world is this place?" I asked. "I want to know if the jail was in a part of this world or from where the white boy's mother came."

James looked puzzled, so the nurse explained to him about amnesia symptoms, as we walked down the hall. They listened to me ask questions like a 2-year-old all the way down the hall. At the end near my room were the two big doors that I was brought through. Up top was a small window in each door for people to see through.

I could see two faces through the small glass enclosure. I thought, these must be my children. Neither the nurse nor the man mattered to me now as their voices trailed behind me. Unknowingly, my feet picked up speed. In no time, I was at the door.

The children were so sad-looking and so pitiful. They looked at me as if I was pitiful too. The tall man, Mr. Roswell, who had asked me about the crying girl, was there too. He beckoned for the nurse to open the door. She pointed at a button, and when he touched it, a buzzer rang. I almost jumped out of my skin. The nurse put a tag on my arm and they led me outside of the door. Panic was in my eyes.

The nurse whispered to me, "You are going to another part of this world." She told the man that I referred to the hospital as the world.

❦

The man quickly understood. The children appeared afraid, as the little boy took my hand. Two doors opened and two people stepped out. The nurse told me that they were the same elevators that brought me from another part of the world into Grady.

There were two women on the elevator whom I did not expect. One of the two women was my sister, Trina, and the other lady was my aunt, Betty. At this time I responded as if they were strangers, because they were to me.

Trina said, "Barbara, stop playing. You know who we are. You can't forget us."

I walked past her to be as close to the children as possible. I stood between them and Mr. Roswell.

"You remember me? I'm the guy that went to the place to get your children. You remember that, don't you?" He said.

I nodded yes.

We went to an area with rooms where some men were locked up. I stopped.

"The Old Man is not in there," Mr. Roswell said. "He is far away from here, and all of the people in this part of the world are here to protect you. OK?"

I looked around the space. I felt that it was OK and nodded yes.

The little boy hugged me, and then the little girl did too. We stood there hugged together, and everyone else walked away, allowing us the moment.

I heard Trina say, "I can't believe all of this is happening. Barbara and the children are going to be staying with me, and Tisha's going to court soon about what that man did to her."

A moment of anger rose up within me. It wasn't what Trina said that upset me; it was her tone of voice. It was harsh, calculating and sort of controlling. Mr. Roswell took me by the hand and led me to another room. Everybody followed with Trina constantly talking.

Mr. Roswell was reassuring as he talked in a low voice, almost a whisper. "Is there anything that you can tell me that will help your daughter? Do you remember anything?"

'I am trying. Can't they see that I am trying?' I thought. I looked at the men and women and then the children. In my mind, I could hear the child crying in a car. She was scared to death.

"She is crying in a car," I said in a whisper.

"It's a cab," Tisha said.

"Do you remember a cab?" said James.

"I must have been a wise person, because I must have done something to save these children. I just wish that I could remember everything, but I can't," I said with tears in my eyes.

The tall man began to speak in all earnestness: "Barbara, listen to me carefully. We found the weapons in the closet behind the door in the living room. They were exactly where you said they were, and there are a whole lot of them. When I saw them, I almost jumped out of my skin." He looked at Trina, Aunt Betty, and the faces of my children. "May I talk to her alone for a while please?"

The nurse led us to a small office that had all kind of books about mental health. Mr. Roswell sat directly across from me and spoke in that soft voice again: "You and your children must have been living in terror with that old man. We found a bag full of papers with his true identity, and they found a gun on him when we got him to the police station. Whew! I'm glad we handcuffed him in the front. He had a gun stuck in the crack of his ass."

He made me laugh at his remark. His nose turned red, and his face was crimson from laughing so hard.

❀

But his voice turned very serious when he said, "We had to take your daughter to two hospitals to get examined. She has been sexually molested. There will be a trial in a few days. Can you tell me what made you decide to take your life?"

Tisha had to be examined at two hospitals, because she was raped in DeKalb County and it was reported in Fulton County. The crime had been committed across two jurisdictions. I didn't know the law, but this is the way that they treated the case.

It was agonizing for me as I tried to remember things while answering Mr. Roswell's question.

"I remember a hallway and the voices. I saw them when he was touching her in her room. But I do not know how I got there or where I came from. She was scared and I had to save her. She was crying about a pocketbook in the back of a car. I saw him touch her in the car. She wanted to die. Somehow we talked and I told her that I will save her. Only I am in this world, and she is in another world away from me."

I knew that I was speaking, but I felt detached somehow. Mr. Roswell looked deep within my eyes as if he wanted to reach inside of me, and grab the answers that he was seeking. "That will help me a lot. Your daughter said that she saw you watching her as her stepfather touched her in the bed. Did you know about anything else?"

"He wrote me a letter." I reached into my pocket, and I gave him the envelope. I was shaking all over. "I threw away the letter inside, and all I have is this envelope."

"What did it say?" he said in a peculiar whisper.

"The letter said that he was going to kill us, and that he was in this world, Grady, downstairs. Where is downstairs in this world?" I was crying now.

"You can read?" He seemed surprised.

❈

I answered as if I wondered what was so surprising about my being able to read. "That is why I say that I must have been a wise person, because I can read the words. This world is too much, and there are a lot of things that scare me. I've got to go to the children's part of the world to help them."

Mr. Roswell leaned close to me and said in a matter-of-fact tone. "We are in this world with you, and we are going to help you save the children. The children will be saved."

Mr. Roswell led me back to the others. As we rounded the corner, I could hear them whispering. Whispering was beginning to agitate me. When we got into sight of them, they stopped talking. Mr. Roswell went to sit next to Tisha, and Junior came to me and hugged me tightly. I was not sure how to respond. He held my hand as we all left the room. Tisha seemed to be afraid to come near me.

As we walked back past the front desk, a nurse called out to me, "You have a letter!"

I didn't want to get the letter, but the nurse told me that they must give us our mail. James took the letter and gave it to me. When everybody was leaving, Tisha told me that she was scared, because she thought I was going to die. She hugged me and cried as she walked towards the exit. Mr. Roswell held her hand as I watched them get on the elevator. Then the security guard closed the double doors, shutting me into my world.

❀

Chapter 10.

✄

The First Trial

I was still holding the letter when I received a call on the pay phone. A patient was calling out for Barbara. I looked around to see if anyone else was nearby with that name. It was so annoying having all of these people calling me by that name. I shook my head in frustration. At this time, I was still not aware of what a telephone was, so a nurse ran over to me and helped me place the receiver to my ear.

The voice that came from the other end sent a chill through me.

"Barby, listen to me. You have got to come to the court-house tomorrow. That bitch of a daughter of yours is going to tell everybody that I was fucking her. Did you see anything? Barby, did you see anything?"

I backed away from the phone, shaking all over. The nurse pulled me back to the phone against my wishes.

"Don't you dare hang up on me, bitch! I know where every one of them lives, and I'm going to come and get you! You are my wife, and I'm going to kill all of them for inter-fering in our lives!" The Old Man's voice sounded demonic, and it seemed as if he would step through the receiver.

I was crying uncontrollably now, and the nurse realized

❧

that she had made a terrible mistake. This nurse was new, and she did not know about the Old Man. I was taken back to my room where I was given some medicine to relax.

I fell into a deep sleep and began to have a terrible dream. I saw a hallway, and I was naked. I heard a little girl crying, and a little boy was standing far away. She was lying on a bed, and the Old Man was masturbating her. I knew that she was looking at me. I backed away, and I saw myself at a typewriter. I walked into a room, and there was a medicine cabinet. I opened a bottle of pills and counted out precisely ten. They were blue, and I felt each one land in my hand. Next I was drinking a glass of water in a bed, and I hid the glass under it.

I heard the voice of a woman saying, "Barbara, it's time to wake up. Come on now, wake up."

I opened my eyes, and my nurse Melody was standing over me with a sandwich. "I know that you must be starving. You've got to eat if you want to save those children. You need your strength, because this is going to be a hard fight. We will be monitoring the pay phone to make sure that you do not receive any more calls from him."

Of course she was right about me needing my strength to fight, but before she could finish, another call came for me from the nurse's station. This time it was a doctor who wanted to speak to me. The nurse walked with me to the phone.

When I answered the phone, I recognized the voice as the Old Man's.

"Barby, don't hang up. They think that I'm Doctor Wilson, and I've been monitoring your condition. You see I can always get to you, even from jail. I know that you have amnesia, and you don't remember me, but listen to me. You are my wife, and they cannot keep you away from me. Your daughter is a liar, and your sister is a liar. They are accusing me of having sex with a child. Why would I have sex with a child when I had you?"

❧

I believe my silence agitated him. "I'm going to kill your sister for making her lie on me. Remember this, I know where she lives. They can't hold me here forever. Do you hear me, bitch!?" He slammed the phone and it began to buzz.

I slowly put the phone down and turned to the nurses standing around me with shocked looks on their faces. At first, they had not believed my situation to be as serious as it was. Of course, the place was in a stir as a nurse called the main hospital to see if there was a Dr. Wilson in psychology. I began to make my way back to my room. The nurses were not aware that I had left.

When I got to my room, a naked man was standing looking out the window. He was tall, dark, and very muscular. Outside of the dazed stare on his face, you would have thought that you were looking at a god.

Melody appeared in the doorway. She walked over to him and spoke very soft and low.

"I know that you are wondering who is in your room. Look at Barbara. I want you to help her here."

The man who looked like a Mandingo warrior turned to look at me. He was very much a man, but his expressions were very childlike. He walked over to me in all of his glory and stared at me as if he could see my soul. He backed away and pulled back the covers on the bed to lie down. The nurse put her body in front of me and we backed out, keeping our faces towards him as if we were avoiding a very dangerous situation.

As we stepped into the hall, I saw a dolled up white woman who stood looking listlessly ahead. I will call her Marilyn. She gazed at us as if she were lost. She walked over to me and held my hand. Melody let us walk away together. I quickly realized that the woman was also a patient. We walked to the patient sitting area where a window looked out over the ever-growing city. Marilyn pointed out. I was confused.

❊

Marilyn looked at me, and with her soft fingers outlining my face, she pointed again and said, "I want to go there. Can you take me there?"

Tears streamed down my face now, and Marilyn held me in her arms, allowing me cry on her shoulder. I felt safe there. The tall white screaming man from before – I'll call him Bobby – came over. He wanted to join in our hug. It felt wonderful. Bobby was calm, but he walked gaited. His hands were stiff, and his eyes were glassy.

Bobby was about to say something to me when his mother walked into the room, "Isn't that nice?" she said.

Bobby ran to her and hugged her so tight he almost lifted her off of the floor. After he got through hugging his mother, he turned to me and said, "I'm sorry if I hurt you. I didn't mean it."

His mother handed me an apple and walked away with her childlike son. I noticed that she had a basket of beautiful ripe fruit.

Marilyn walked away, and I did not see where she had gone. I was about to go to the nurse's station when Melody walked in, carrying all of my things from the room. I was about to panic because of the uncertainty. "I'm sorry Barbara, but whenever Jack is admitted, he always gets that room."

"Am I going away from this world?" I said fearfully.

"No, just another part of it," Melody answered, handing me a hospital pail with my soap and brush inside.

I was not allowed to have a comb or pencils or any objects that might cause me harm. They were not certain as to whether I was suicidal. I really wanted my comb, but Melody said I couldn't have it. I was led to a room where a medium-built, light-skinned woman was nursing a large wound in her shoulder. I'll call her Jacqueline. She looked at me as Melody laid my things on the bed near the window. Melody knew her, because Jacqueline had been there several

❖

times before, and they carried on a conversation as if I were not there.

Jacqueline turned to me with a big smile on her face and said, "I tried to kill myself many times before this, but this is the closest that I've ever come. I tried pills, but I threw them up. So I decided to try a gun; I couldn't even do that right. So come on in, and keep me company."

I turned to Melody for some kind of reassurance. Melody nodded.

I saw dark clouds forming in the world outside of Grady, and it reminded me of something, but Jacqueline interrupted my thoughts.

"You know they wake us up at 6 in the mornings, and we have to go do exercises before 7. Then we eat breakfast. They will not be bringing you any food over on this side. They won't let you bring combs or anything else that you might use to cause harm."

A tall, slim, dark man stepped into the room holding a Bible; his name was John. Jacqueline beckoned for him to sit on the edge of her bed. He was very soft spoken when he addressed me. "Did you try to commit suicide, too?"

I shook my head no.

He looked at Jacqueline. "She's in denial," she said. "Over here is where they put all of the ones who tried to kill themselves. How did you do it?" Jacqueline asked.

I had no idea what suicide was. He continued to tell us why he decided to kill himself.

"You see, I was raised in the church, and my father didn't approve of me being a homosexual. Also, I am in no shape to go home like this. I felt that I had nowhere to go, so I wanted to kill myself. So, here we are, the suicide pack."

That became the term of endearment that we called ourselves. Soon another young lady came into the room. She

❀

was short and very dark-skinned, with beautiful long black hair. She lost no time telling us how she tried to kill herself. I will call her Felecia.

"I took pills," Felecia she said, as she took a puff from a cigarette that was not lit. She held a lighter to it and never lit it. "Look at how stiff that medicine makes me. You know I'm skinny now, but normally I weigh about 150 pounds. I always gain it back in here. I don't really smoke, but I just like people to think I do. Ain't that weird? Not that I can have matches in this area anyway. I'll see you in the lounge later. Oh yeah, the guitar lady will be here in a few minutes."

Jacqueline and John looked excited. Jacqueline explained to me that after the guitar lady comes, a few days later they get to take a bus ride to the zoo and play games. She was the signal of better things to come.

We got to get treats as the woman played that evening and we also got to play touch-and-feel with different instruments that she brought with her. John sang a song, and we all rejoiced. It was such a beautiful evening that I had forgotten about the events earlier.

That night Jacqueline asked me to help her pull her gown over her arm. I felt some importance there. She groaned as she laid down. "We take turns waking up every one in the mornings by ringing bells and screaming, 'Reveille'! Even though I'm like this, I still must participate. Can you make sure that my bandage is covering all of my scar?"

A male nurse came to the room, and he looked at me still in my regular clothes. "Ready or not, lights are going out. Reveille is at 6:00 sharp!"

Rain began to splash against the window. I started to ask Jacqueline what it was, but she was softly snoring. I fell asleep listening to the melody of her snoring and the pitter patter of the rain.

I was startled out of my deep rest by the sounds of what seemed to me to be machine-gun fire. Terrified, I sat up. I

❄

grabbed my slippers, and ran up to the nurses' station. No one was there, so I sat close by, shivering. A few moments later, Jack, the Mandingo man, came and sat down next to me. He was silent. He took a torn piece of paper from his pajama pocket, wrote the word "thunder" and handed it to me. He pointed at the window that was at the end of the hall to my right. He began to walk to the window, and I followed him, trusting him. I felt like a child being led by a child.

I saw the rain splashing against the window, and I ran to it. Jack took my hand and placed it against the window, and he wrote the word "rain" on another piece of torn paper. We stood at the window for a long time. I knew then that this was going to be my place of solace in this world called Grady. Jack never spoke to anyone else for as long as I was in the world of Grady. He wrote poems and short stories about the war in Vietnam and everyday life. He shared the stories, written on old pieces of notebook paper, only with me. It was our unique world until one morning, after we had gotten through with breakfast.

I had told Jack many times about how the Old Man had been finding all kinds of ways to talk to me, either by phone or mail. My daughter had already gone to the trial, and I was trying to cope in this place.

Jack broke his silence. His voice was deep and soothing. He took time to pace himself to make sure that I understood everything he was saying to me. The story he told me on this morning had to do with a verse in the Bible about the struggle of Job. Then he gave me a piece of paper telling me about his being in the war in Vietnam and why he has to struggle with insanity. When I got through reading it, a nurse had read it over my shoulder. She could not believe it. She turned on her heals and headed to the nurses' station to get his specialist.

Jack turned to me and said, "It's up to you to save them. You must try to remember. I will be leaving you soon. Go to your room and try to remember the world, another world

❀

bigger than this one. You need to go out into that world to save them."

He stood to his feet and walked away.

That night he was irate and walking through the halls naked. The orderlies put him in a cell room. I could see him through the tiny window, but I could tell that he was completely lost now.

Melody came to me and walked with me for a while telling me, "Jack has been a patient for many years, and he knew that he was going into another schizophrenic state. He cannot cope in that condition. He is so strong that it takes seven men to hold him. In that room, he can't harm anyone, and nobody will hurt him. After this episode, he will probably remember you, because he has never communicated with anyone else like he has with you."

Stop the Confusion

My daughter had survived the first of several trials to come, but this one was without her mother. I was determined to try to be there for the next one, and for the rest of my children's lives. There was so much confusion going on. Mr. Johnson was calling constantly and sending mail. He continually claimed to be different doctors checking on my progress.

Mr. Roswell told me to continue to take the calls and the letters, because the Old Man might say something, or do something that might help my daughter and son. He also told me that the trial in Atlanta had gone well, and the Old Man had been found guilty. But there was going to be an appeal, and another trial was being scheduled in DeKalb County.

One morning, the suicide pack went on an outing to Grant Park Zoo. The day was beautiful, and other patients and I got to smell the air of the world away from Grady's world. The other patients taught me how to handle a ball to play catch. It was a wonderful day for me. I believed that I could survive out there.

When we arrived back at the floor, a patient ran up to me. She grabbed my hand, and led me to the wall phone. She put the receiver up to my ear, and the voice on the other end said, "Barby, don't you hang up on me. I heard that you were at the park today. I told them that I was Dr. Wilson."

On this day, I made it a point not to run. Instead as a nurse approached me, I simply handed her the phone, and began to walk toward my room. I heard her saying, "It's against the law to impersonate a doctor. You must not call her again!"

Her voice was like an echo in my mind. I was about to get my guard up for battle with this Old Man. He was not going to continue to cause people harm. I just needed God to help me remember.

A few days later I was asked to attend a meeting, which included the patients as well as the staff. I had a few of the many letters that I had received, and I was receiving them on a daily basis. Melody asked me to bring the letters so I could show everyone how serious the situation with the Old Man was. She also had a list of the different doctors' names that the Old Man had been using when he was calling from prison.

At the meeting, staff members were given a list of all of the doctors licensed to call on patients, and the patients were told that the pay phone was going to be moved. I was not to receive calls from anyone. I could only call out if there was someone that I needed to talk to.

After the meeting, was over a phone call came in. A nurse answered it. The Old Man was asking her about me, thinking she was a patient. She beckoned for me to come to her and listen. She encouraged me to say something.

"Hello," I said.

�֍

The Old Man tried to sound comforting. "Barby, I heard that you went to a meeting today. What was it all about?"

I hung up the phone with intensified anger.

I looked at the nurse as if she had betrayed me.

Diary

Today is November 16, 2000.

Hosea Williams passed away. As my daughter, now an adult, and I watched a news report showing old footage from the march to Forsyth County in 1987, we could see the Old Man in a group of marchers. The newsperson is talking about the march to Forsyth County, and the Old Man and I were there.

Now, an icon was gone, and I am just overwhelmed at the loss of such a great leader, the leader they called the Agitator.

Diary

Today is March 4, 2001.

I had my hopes up to be finished with this book today. But I was in the hospital for a few days with chest pains. I'm almost 45 years old, and I feel in my heart as if I'm just beginning my life. I don't want to wage war with my health right now. I've got too much to do. I need more time to make sure that my children can cope. I fought against great odds to live for them. Why should this be any different for me? I know what part of my problem is. This is another anniversary of my decision to do what was necessary to save my children's lives. Every March through May, we suffer depression and we help each other deal with our feelings. It

❧

was in April when the Old Man invaded our lives. It was in April when I almost died trying to save us. It was in April when Tisha went to her first trial without me. My son always seems to get in trouble, and he cries a lot, even though he is a man. J. Tom Morgan told me that a boy has a hard time dealing with trauma. My son still does not want to talk about the past at all. I have to search for him, because he hides among friends away from home as if he's afraid he would have to confront his fears. It's hard on all of us, even though they are grown with children of their own. My son would not visit me in the hospital for fear of losing me again. My daughter follows me around now like a sick puppy. I want her to feel secure about being in control of her own destiny. I thank the Lord always for allowing me this much time. Though the journey has been hard and many days unbearable, we made it through together. The homelessness and the many days of missed school my children endured. The therapy sessions, and the opinions of others who expected my children to fail, us to fail, because of the abuse. I'm more than happy to say that we are still on the racetrack of living life anyhow. Ironically, I was in the same hospital where the Old Man used to fake illnesses when he was at the Marriott. It was quite a lot to bear. But I'll do what's necessary for my children to be around a little while longer.

❧

Chapter 11.

ℒ

The New World

I needed to begin to take full control now, and I knew it. People were coming to visit me that I did not know. Trina was very opinionated and seemed to have a lot of anger toward me. She wanted to know if I was getting food stamps, and if I was, where were they. I asked James to bring me a bag where I kept a lot of papers. Tisha had gotten it from the dark room that I remembered in a dream. The Old Man had told me to keep up with a whole lot of papers that he was stealing from people as we met them. I had kept the most important ones, including personal papers, in a big black bag and an attaché case.

James brought the bag to me. I went through it and found a lot of business cards and notes. I seemed to have kept a journal of the things that the Old Man and I did together. I had a letter for food stamps and a key to my mailbox. That is where I told Trina and James the stamps would be. I found copies of tickets to concerts and all kinds of important information that I could see and touch that would help me remember more. As I went through the pocketbook, I got a tremendous headache. I went into my room and cried for what felt like hours. At the time I did not think about the fact that I had left my family.

❖

Melody came in after she had given all of the other patients their meds, and gave me a very potent pain medication.

"You might be beginning to remember things," the nurse said. "This medication will help you relax and make it through. If you feel that you need any more to help you, just tell the doctor. We will help you make a smooth transition from here to the world outside of Grady."

"Outside of Grady!" I heard that sound echoing in my own voice.

When I awakened, Jacqueline was sitting on the foot of my bed holding a letter from the Old Man. She looked as if she had seen a ghost. The letter was referring to a settlement from Marriott for millions of dollars. Of course, money had no meaning to me at that time. Jacqueline was excited about the letter and felt that I needed to respond to it. Dazed from the medication, I fell back into a deep sleep. I awakened later, assuming that I was dreaming. But it was real; she had left the letter next to my pillow.

Trembling like a leaf, I took the letter to Melody. I wasn't afraid of the intruder anymore. I was angry. When she finished reading the letter, she walked with me to the nurses' station. A doctor was there, and he read the letter, also.

"This man is a liar," he said. "We need to get in touch with the Marriott and warn them about him. We can stop bringing you the letters if you want us to."

I took the letter and decided that this would no longer be the thing that made me weak. I was going to use his words to help me remember what happened.

I went back to the room and began to read through all of the letters the Old Man had sent to me. The first thing I looked at was the envelope from the initial letter threatening to kill me. The second letter summarized the events of the morning that I was taken to the hospital, with the Old Man was accusing my daughter of trying to murder me. He also

❖

claimed she was having an affair with a bishop from another church. He said she was jealous of me and plotting my demise. He said he would never have sex with a child, and I should know that.

Memories of the two years began to flood my mind, and the horrible headache was back with a vengeance. I cried out, and Jacqueline ran in. She saw all of the letters, and began to take them from me. I grabbed them back, and she ran for the doctor. He came in and gave me a shot. I was beyond myself with grief. I was holding the letters to my chest praying that I would remember in some sort of order. It was so confusing to have someone try to convince you that the child that you are trying to save tried to kill you. I was so angry with the Old Man that I didn't know what to do.

Somewhere during the commotion, I fell into a deep sleep and I dreamed. I dreamed about the night of the concert. I dreamed about the night of my daughter's play. I also dreamed about the night that I caught the Old Man molesting my daughter. And the storefront church that we had shared with the minister who prayed at my bedside. I saw us at the King Center. The Old Man was threatening me and accusing me of not being as good at sex as my daughter was. I saw him putting his middle finger in my face doing gestures relating to sex with my daughter. I saw the spit flinging from his mouth when he talked. I saw myself sitting in darkness terrified.

I woke up screaming and alone. No one came this time. I got up and went down the hallway with tears falling down my face. I was looking for Melody. When she saw me, she knew that it was important to come.

Like so many other times, Melody led me to my room. I babbled about so many memories bombarding me at once. When I got to the room, she wrote in a report that I had retained all of my memory. I hadn't I had lost all of my childhood memories from birth to 5 years old. But, I knew no one by name, and I was in an unsure state of mind. Melody was

❋

not listening to me and I became angry with her. She told me to start writing a journal, because she would not help me anymore; my case was too much for her. She could not imagine being in my position with her children.

'I've lost another familiar face,' I thought, and I couldn't bear it. I could not stand wondering what to do without Melody's help. I went into the lounge and saw an older woman who had been admitted a few days earlier. She had defecated on herself, and a nurse was chastising her. I walked over to the new patient, and without a word, I took hold of her hand and walked her to the nurses' station.

"What do I need to do to help this woman get cleaned up?" I asked the head nurse.

She did not say a word as she handed me an adult diaper and several towels. I took the lady to the restroom, and as we walked, feces dropped to the floor on the way. The nurse said she was not going to clean it up.

After that, I found a purpose that helped me not be too preoccupied by my own situation. Day by day, slowly, I began to help other patients recovering from comas or suicide attempts, patients who were worse off than I. I set up a make-believe office by the first window that I looked out of when I was first admitted to the eighth floor.

The nurses even began to respect my place at the end of the hall. Sometimes the nurses and the patients would come and just sit at the window, and I would jokingly tell them that they knocked over my door. They would get up and pretend as if they were picking it up, then knock on it.

I was beginning to feel whole, and I was anxious to go beyond the walls of the world of Grady. James began to tell me on his visits to call him James, not "that man who says he is my brother." It was getting easier to want to see him coming. He began to go to therapy sessions with my doctor as we planned for me to take leaves of absence from the hospital. They were called LOA. The purpose was to introduce me back into society over a six-week period. James had to give the staff a report on my condition after each LOA.

One day Jim's mother came by to see me. She was very kind, and before she left she gave me three one-dollar bills. I had not handled money yet, and I had to ask her what it was. She tried to tell me what to do with it, but I did not understand.

"You take this with you when you want to buy things in the store," she said.

I had no idea what a store was. That evening I told a nurse about the money. She gathered a few patients, and we went to the store in the other part of Grady world. I was so excited. We rode the elevator down and I asked the nurse what seemed like a thousand questions. She kept explaining to me that I was still in Grady world every time we turned a corner.

When we arrived at the Grady food store, a few people were buying candy, drinks, and sandwiches. The colors of the candy bar wrappers tantalized me. One customer opened a Baby Ruth bar and offered me a taste. It was delicious, so I grabbed a couple and a few of the other beautifully-wrapped candies. When I got to the register, a blind man was responsible for ringing up the purchases. A customer before me received change back and walked away. When it was my turn, I laid all of the candy on the counter, and the man fingered through everything. My nurse told him that I had only one dollar. The man gave me one piece of candy and a few coins back. I was so upset because the customer before me had gotten a whole lot of stuff and got back more bills like paper. I was upset because I did not know what coins were. What was I suppose to do with them? The nurse was aware of the looks from the other people, and she explained to the man that I had amnesia. He told me that I was going to get better in time.

In time? How much time? I thought long and hard about time as we went back to the other part of Grady world. I

✺

had never really considered time. James was waiting for me when we returned. He was with Trina, who said she was my sister. We had to attend a family counseling session. Throughout the meeting, Trina was calculating and mean to me. The counselor was wary of me staying with her if ever I was to be released from the world that I knew. Trina told him that she could look out for me when I got out. The therapist talked to James a little while alone, as Trina and I went into the waiting room. I was very uncomfortable with her and talked very little.

I began to take more LOAs with James; the world was a frightening place for me. He took me to the apartment with the door where the weapons were. Police tape was still visible. I found the key in the big bag that my daughter had brought to me.

We went inside, and the place was mess. It appeared as if the police had gone through almost everything. I found a stack of books that were mostly magazines. As I turned pages, inside were all kinds of papers with our false identities. The Old Man had hidden our identities, for what reasons I did not know. I collected what I found, feeling that these important papers could be helpful for my daughter's case. I also found the case in my son's room with the Old Man's secret identification papers, and I gathered that information also.

James took me to the DeKalb County Courthouse where the second trial was to take place. I had no way of knowing if the information that I was bringing would be necessary to the case. I felt destined to come. James was nervous and unsure. I was anxious, but felt very sure.

We went to see the prosecuting attorney, J. Tom Morgan, the tall man who had talked to me along with Mr. Roswell by my hospital bed. He was shocked to see me. He took us to his office, and I gave him the papers that I'd found. He remembered something important. He jumped from his desk and began to usher James and me down a hallway that led to an outside door. He was anxious because my daughter was coming at any minute and the court session was about to take place. They were preparing for jury selection. Police escorted the Old Man into another area of the courthouse where prisoners were held to await jury selection before the trial.

In a way, our showing up was bad timing, but in another, the information that I brought was necessary. I did see my daughter from afar as she was being led to J Tom's office with a lady assistant DA named Mrs. Roman; Junior was not far behind.

I saw Tisha's downcast face, and it reminded me of the pain she had suffered. I also saw the elevator opening just as J. Tom's door was closing, and out stepped the Old Man with two cops in tow.

Mr. Johnson was handcuffed as he shuffled angrily towards a courtroom door. A state-appointed lawyer was also with him. At this trial, J. Tom Morgan did not want anyone to see me. The Old Man was hoping that I would never recover so that I could not provide evidence that would help my daughter's case. He tried to come across as a caring minister with a crazy, jealous stepdaughter who had tried to kill her mother.

As James and I headed back to Grady world, I asked him all kind of questions about me before the amnesia. He wasn't sure as to how to respond to me in detail. I picked up on how uncomfortable he was. So, I asked him instead about places. He took me by my old home where I had grown up as a teenager. He took me to a grocery store, and I stood there with my mouth hanging wide open. There was too much to see in this food world, away from Grady. I was afraid and began to cry. James took me to so many places that I had totally forgotten where I'd begun. I had no idea where Grady world was anymore, and I wanted to go back.

For a few days after that, I did not want to see anyone. I spent the time contemplating the huge world that was once home before Grady. I stared out at the people working on the streets and at the skyline. I went from window to window, and I always saw something different. I ended up bedridden for two days with a horrible headache. The doctor came in and discussed a way to bring me comfort. They had found my old medical files, and discovered that I had suffered from migraine headaches, although my doctors felt that the headaches might be from my brain being flooded with so many memories. Treatment was started immediately. I remembered a medication called Elavil that I had taken for headaches. I looked in my bag and found in there an information form from a specialist. The doctor was happy to see I had it. So with this information, I began pain management.

I began to get more involved in the activities in the ward. I created some educational positive murals on bulletin boards. One was a design called "The Tree of Life." I asked fellow patients to give me positive and negative words that meant a lot to them. It did not matter how funny it was or how serious the words were. The tree was an effort for all, even nurses and caretakers. They all participated. Everyone watched the effort from start to finish, wondering how it would finally look.

When the wall was finished, it consisted of brown leaves and green ones attached to many branches from a strong tree surrounded by green grass and flying birds. The brown leaves fell to the ground, illustrating bad thoughts falling from grace. The good thoughts clung to the tree as green leaves, illustrating hope, peace, justice and life.

The tree got a lot of praise, and many people from other parts of Grady world came to see it. I had no idea what all of the hoopla was about, but it gave me a reason to look for the rising of the sun and the rising of the moon. I created other walls of inspiration, and I received more leaves of absence.

The Old Man continued sending me many letters, trying to bring terror into my life. The letters came to my mailbox at the apartment and at the hospital. J. Tom encouraged me to continue receiving them. He warned me that it would be difficult but necessary.

The letters only inspired me even more to go into battle for the sake of that little girl whom I had seen in so much pain in my dream. I realized that those children were worth fighting for, and I was living to fight for them. Sometimes I received letters that seemed to be orders for me to appear at court for a trial. James would call the courthouse, only to discover that the letters were lies. J. Tom told me that the Old Man would lie about anything to get out of jail.

A few weeks before my release from the world that I had grown to know and love, the patients and the therapist played a game. The game was to be a reflection on death from the old life into the new. Some patients were upset and cried, including me. To me, crying was a way to deal with the grief of possibly dying and leaving my children alone. Some patients playing the game seemed to wither within and lose themselves, but others thought it was an interesting and fun idea. I decided to join the fun-idea team.

I quickly understood the purpose of the game – to turn lose the past and move forward to the future. We created tombstones that reflected who we were in life and how we died. The doctors told us that we could express ourselves in poems, art, or song. There had to be some words of expression, no matter what method we chose to create. I decided on art and a comical poem. I felt that it needed to be comical, because life brings us so many obstacles in life that we needed to seek a release somewhere. And oh boy, did I need a release from all of the seriousness in my life at that time.

This game was like candy to me, and I wanted all that I could get. I realized that I was creative, and the other patients and I had a good time enjoying our gifts.

My poem on my tombstone read:

Barbara?

6/11/56

❧

1/1/2000

Cause of Death: Stepped on a singing praying mantis
Talks and writes plays for laughter and praise.
She's always joking and makes people happy.
She's thoughtful and considerate of children
family and friends.
She went skipping through Pussy Willow Drive,
And came across a praying mantis singing,
"Crosseyed and blue are you."
She made one skip forward and stepped on
William Wee, the mantis
Only to find herself in
Never, never wake up land.
Cause of Death:
Stepped on a praying mantis.
The Rose Vine Resting Place
0000 Rose Vine Drive
Where no one's crying or dying

My Release from Grady World

Soon I was writing songs and singing them. One of the patients liked one of my songs that I sang about the meadow.

The title was, "I Was Down in the Valley," and the words were:

Don't you believe me?
Don't you believe me?
That yesterday Jesus came

and He set me free.

I was down in the Valley

so low . . . so low . . . so low.

I was down in the Valley

so low . . . so low . . . so low.

I looked out over the meadow

and I saw Jesus standing there.

He said, "My child

don't you cry no more.

'Cause I'm standing in the eye of the know,

'Cause I'm standing in the eye of the know."

I was very cooperative and hoped to reach a point where I could leave Grady world without the feeling of terror. I saw Grady world as a safe haven; outside these walls was an element of chaos. I remembered no one, so I studied everything I could find.

One day while on LOA at my old home, I found a journal and a calendar that started from the day I had met the Old Man. It felt like I was holding a hand grenade. The pin was pulled, and I did not know what to do with all of the information that was blowing up in my head. I did not remember writing the journal that I held so cautiously. I began to frantically flip the pages, hoping to not just remember the days of events, but to know that I know.

James took me back to the Grady world, and I hid my agitation from him. I realized that he was a very sensitive man, so I believed that if I had let him know how much this information was affecting me, he would not come from the big world to the little world of Grady to get me any more. I wanted to be in the big world, because there was so much for me to learn. I arrive at Grady world seeking my nurse, Jennifer. She had become my friend, and we shared special moments together. She encouraged me to do anything that seemed too difficult. She helped me believe that I could succeed in the big world no matter what.

She saw me and approached me with pad in hand. "James, I will take her to her room. She looks as if she has had a long day."

James gave me a big hug, and I watched him as he rang the buzzer to be let out. I saw his shoulders shake as he wept. James stood on the other side of the door, looking through the small window, thinking that I could not see him.

Jennifer took me to my room and asked me to explain the day and what I remembered. I was remembering more details of the two years that my children and I had been held hostage. I remembered the screaming, the guns, the cigarette burns on my hands, and the many hospital visits that the Old Man made trying to win a settlement from the Marriott Hotels. He would laugh, thinking that he had them jumping at his every command. I remembered the old car that he bought with the few dollars that the hotel lawyers had allowed him to have as a settlement of his claim. It had been a mistake to give him anything at all. To him, it was an admittance of guilt. To them, it was a way to get rid of Mr. Charles Johnson, but instead they created a horrible monster. I remembered him bragging about setting people up to sue them. He was disgusting.

In my journal, I had a legal paper with the Marriott's lawyers' numbers on it; Jennifer allowed me to call one of the attorneys. The lawyer requested a copy of one of the letters that the Old Man had written me, claiming that the Marriott had promised to settle for millions of dollars. They were concerned for me, but the attornies still had to consider the legal issues.

I also called an attorney, whom the Old Man and I had met and worked with as caretakers of his office mansion,

❋

up until a week or so prior to my hospitalization. I told him where I was, but he had already spoken to the Old Man. The Old Man was calling everyone he had ever met, and he wrote them letters too. The lawyer told me to come by and see him whenever I was released from Grady world. He told me that if I needed a job, he would have one waiting for me there.

I found the number of the "Good Times" television star whom I had met at the Marriott, but when I called, her husband answered. He was angry because the Old Man had been calling from jail, and he lit into me angrily. I was not surprised, but I told him that I was calling because I had some papers that belonged to her. They were legal documents that the Old Man retained concerning her getting incorporated to have a church in Atlanta. Her husband accused me of helping the Old Man meet his wife. He told me that the papers were public record, and not to ever call back again. For some reason, his blasting me did not hurt me as badly as maybe it should have. Slowly I put the phone down, realizing that there was no information I had in my bag that the Old Man didn't have. I needed to regroup if I was going to save those children's lives.

Jennifer called me to my make-believe office at the end of the hall and gave me another letter from the Old Man. I asked her to read it to me. He had put together a mock trial, trying to prove to me that my daughter had set him up. This was the second such letter on the topic, but this one caused me great discomfort. He also wrote that his sons were coming after my family. He claimed that one of his sons was coming to the hospital to see me, and I was supposed to know what that would mean. He also wrote that he had called Rev. Hosea Williams and Mrs. King; he believed their influence would help get him released. Jennifer knew that this letter was upsetting me, so we found a business card from Rev. Williams and called him at his office. Indeed, the Old Man had been calling Hosea, but Hosea did not want to have anything to do with the case. He wished me well and told me that if I needed anything when I got out of the hos-

❊

pital to come see him.

Jennifer told me not to call anyone else after I tried to call the Martin Luther King Center, because she believed that everything else in the letter was a lie. She gave me a tranquilizer and walked with me to my room.

That night I had a terrible nightmare. I stood naked in a dark hallway, and the Old Man was screaming at me. He was doing painful sexual things to my body. The next thing I knew, I was sitting in a dark room on a big bed, and the Shroud of Turin was above the headboard. I was drinking a glass of water, and when I'd finished it, I put the glass under the bed. The Old Man burst in the door carrying a tray of rotten food. He handed the tray to me and walked out of the room. I got a sock out of a drawer, placed the food in it, and put it in a closet. The dream was interrupted when I heard a voice.

It was Jennifer telling me that James was on his way to take me on another LOA into the big world. I did not speak on this day, because so much was going on in my head. I avoided everyone and only did what was necessary to wait for the man James, whom they called my brother.

When James arrived, I heard Jennifer tell him that I was very quiet today. She wondered if I should stay. I assured her that I could go. I had a plan for this day. I asked James to take me to the place of the guns again. Reluctantly, he agreed.

When we arrived, I focused on the dream. James opened the door, and a foul odor came out. It wasn't very strong, but it was offensive. I headed straight to the back of the apartment. I heard sounds of the hell from the past two years in my mind. I looked under the bed in the master bedroom, and there was the glass with a small amount of water still in it. I looked over the headboard, and there was a large poster of the Shroud of Turin. In a dresser drawer, I found the last poem that I had written before I took the pills. I was retracing steps from the past. I went to the medicine cabinet in the hall bathroom, and there was the small bottle that held the blue pills that I had taken. I ran back to the bedroom, and looked into the closet where a lot of clothes were piled. I searched near the back, and just as I thought I could reach no further, I bumped into a hard bundle. I discovered the sock with the food in it. It seemed to have dried. I found several other socks like it. I ran to my son's room and looked at the walls, and I saw the marks where a leather belt had been used to whip him. I crawled across the bed and touched every single one of them. James did not know what I was doing. He just followed me from room to room. I ran to the typewriter on the table in the living room, and looked at the last sheet of paper that I had been typing. To my surprise, it was still there.

I went to the closet of doom and swung it open. The weapons were gone, but a lot of memories remained. I looked around the living room and saw piles of books that had not matter to me before. As I searched through them, I began to find our social security cards, birth certificates, and my mother's divorce decree from my real father. I found the real estate papers where Trina had bought our old house that had once belonged to the Sergeant Major and my mother, and I found addresses for all of my family members. I found a briefcase in my son's room with information on Mr. Johnson and his true identity. Exhausted, I finally asked James to take me back to J. Tom Morgan's office.

When we arrived, we found that like before, he was expecting my daughter. And again, we had to be ushered out through a back exit. He needed the information that I brought him on this day, too. J. Tom did not want the Old Man – or Tisha – seeing me out of the hospital. It was very important that neither of them knew that I was trying to help, because the Old Man was using my amnesia as part of his defense. He believed that the jury would believe him, a man of the cloth, over Tisha, this pathetic little kid.

I began to believe that the man in the picture of the Shroud of Turin was guiding me. Once again, I saw the Old

176. Annihilator of Innocence

Man step off an elevator, but this time he was carrying a bundle of papers in his handcuffed hands. Looking angry and deep in thought, he walked gaited because of the chains around his ankles. Now I could not wait to get back to Grady world to study the information that I had gotten, including a handful of letters I had grabbed from the mailbox. It was crammed full of letters from prison dating from the day that Mr. Roswell had removed the Old Man from me at Grady.

As James pushed the buzzer to leave Grady world, he turned to me with admiration and spoke matter-of-factly.

"I love you B.B. I know that you don't really remember me, but I'm going to be here with you until this is all over with. I just wanted you to know that."

Preparing For Battle

I was released into the big world to live with Trina. I had to learn how to take the buses and the trains. I had been offered a job to work as a house cleaner for the attorney who had promised me work whenever I was released. On one of my LOAs, I had met with the lawyer; he offered 10 dollars an hour, which he was to pay me at the end of each evening.

Getting to work was a challenge because my sister did not offer me a ride to the train or to the bus stop. Trina's house was about two miles from the bus stop; the road to her house was dirt and not yet paved, because it was being prepared as the entrance into a strip mall. James walked with me down the dirt road to the bus stop once, but after that I endured this ordeal alone each time I had to go to work. But I was determined to learn, and I was kind of stubborn about not failing. Trina would say things to me that made me uncomfortable, but that made me even more determined to excel. My children were my driving force. They needed to see that I would be able to take care of them.

At the end of the first evening working for the lawyer, I

received a handful of those green papers called money. I had no idea how to spend it. Every night, Junior would count out for me exactly what I would need to get on the bus or train. I had learned great cleaning skills in Grady world, and I was proud of my work. The lawyer told me one evening that I had cleaned his place better than anyone else. I was floating on air.

My birthday was coming soon, and the son of a patient whom I had cared for had my sister's telephone number. I told Trina that the young man was coming to take me out for my birthday. Trina had a sleepwear party that day, and I had won quite a few prizes. I was excited and happy. When the young man came to pick me up I assumed that Trina was happy for me.

The next morning, I overheard Trina referring to me as a bitch and a whore. I had no idea what the words meant, but they were said with so much hatred, I thought I was hearing the sounds of the Old Man radiating from her mouth. She told James that she was not going to allow me to date. I had heard those words "not going to allow" too many times in the past few months. No one else was going to decide what I would be allowed to do anymore without my say-so.

I grabbed a bag, stood before her, and said, "I have a home waiting for me." Standing firm and strong, I turned to James and asked, "James will you please take me home?"

I told Trina that as soon as I cleaned up my apartment, I was coming for my children. She screamed obscenities at me as I left. I knew that she was going to make my life hard because I'd defied her authority over me.

As James drove me from Trina's house, he was in tears. He told me how courageous I was. When we arrived at the place of doom – this is what I called the apartment where we were held hostage – I saw the pieces of police tape. I acknowledged the fact that this time I was going to be left there alone. I went inside, and the stench was overwhelming. James began to vomit over the railing.

❧

I pulled open the refrigerator, and it was filled to the brim with rotten food. This is when I realized that all of the utilities were off. I tried all of the switches for the lights. I tried the stove, and the gas was off. I looked in one of the cabinets and found a few cleaning supplies. In apartments in Atlanta, the landlord is responsible for water, and the tenant is responsible for gas and electricity. So the water was on.

James went to the store to get large trash bags and bleach. I found a couple of bags and some Comet, so I sprinkled down the countertops, sinks, and bathtubs.

While James was gone, I began to recall being left in the dark for days. So I began to walk through the place with my eyes closed. I walked into my son's room and felt his bed and touched a few items of clothes in the closet. I left there and went into the first bathroom. I turned on the water on and off, and everything there was just as it was left, including the Old Man's medicines. I went to my daughter's room and bumped into her bed. I fell across it, crying like I had never done before. My own cries sounded like a hurt animal to me, but I could not stop until I had no energy left. I heard children outside playing and the sound of the ice-cream man, and I remembered how much my son loved to go to the ice-cream truck.

I went across the hall to my room with no shame about the tears that were falling. I went to the headboard, touched the picture of the Shroud of Turin, and prayed.

"Oh Man in the picture, I had dreams that you would help me through all of this. Just let me live long enough to see my children grow up. Help me to give them a decent place to live. Help me to remember so that I can save them. What do I need to do to prove to You that I will do everything that You ask of me? I'm just a woman who has no memory, and I'm confused about everything, but I trust in You. I don't even know how to count money. I don't even know how to shop. I don't even know how to get from one place to the other. I'm scared, and I'm not afraid to tell You that. I know

I'm going to make mistakes, because I do not know anyone. Are these people who say they are my brothers and sisters really my brothers and sisters? I hope it's not a joke of some kind, because I really do love James. Help me, please, Man in the picture!"

I heard James calling out to me when he came in the front door. He came into the room, and hugged me because I was crying so hard I couldn't stop. He cried with me; it was a miraculous moment, because I knew then that this must truly be my brother.

I began to bag rotten food as James stood outside, away from the stench. He helped me drag the garbage bags across the street to the dumpster. I cleaned the refrigerator with a bleach solution, then I washed cabinets and scrubbed the bathrooms. I left what was necessary for evidence as it was: the knives in the back door, the clothes, the big gun closet, the leather bag in my son's room with the Old Man's true identity inside, the black leather belt he used for beating my son, hundreds of magazines and books on the floor, the fake certificates of ministry on the walls, the security alarm on the door, etc.

I also left the lanterns out that I had used for light when I was hostage, because I was not allowed to use the regular lights unless the Old Man was home. He allowed the lanterns, because they emitted a very low light. This was one of his ways of having as little light as possible around so that people would not know when we were home. I had learned to do everything as a blind person would. I was very aware of the slightest sound or movements.

When I was satisfied with the cleaning, James and I dragged the last bag to the dumpster. I looked across the apartments and remembered the hours that the Old Man sat on the back porch of my apartment, pointing the big gun at the apartment manager's home. As James tossed in the last bag, I started walking over to the manager's apartment. James followed me, wanting to know where I going. I did

❧

not speak, but I approached the door, praying under my breath that the manager would answer. I knocked. When the manager opened the door, he looked as if he had seen a ghost.

"I thought you were dead, or going to die. I left the apartment as it was because I knew that someone was going in and out of it. I thought it was the policemen looking for more evidence. I'm so glad to see that you're all right. Come on in, both of you. Do you need anything?" the manager said, taking me by the hand.

As we took a seat, I told the manager about my memory loss. I told him that I remembered how Mr. Johnson threatened his life constantly. I explained to him the necessity of staying there, that I believed coming back to this place would help me remember and find evidence that would help the children. I asked him to allow me to stay in the apartment, if only for a little while.

The manager was overjoyed with my courage, as he put it. "I'll do this for you. Come to my office first thing in the morning, and we'll fill out some papers. I'll help you get reinstated on the government program that will allow you to stay a year rent-free until you get on your feet. It'll be up to you to get your utilities on. You will receive a small check from us each month to help with utilities, but you are responsible for anything over the amount of the check. Anything I can do, I will. Barbara, you've been through hell and back, and we'll be glad to help. By the way, Rev. Johnson has been calling me, and I stopped accepting his calls a long time ago. I will definitely not take them now that you are here."

James and I left knowing that I would have a roof over my head. He was so happy for me. He hugged me tightly as we approached the bottom of the steps to my apartment. I did not let him go back up the steps with me. I had a battle to prepare for. Emotions of fear were now being replaced with the will to fight. I had lives to save, and I needed my memory to do it. I watched him as he drove away. I stood

❧

in the big world, now totally alone. It was going to be up to me.

I went into the dreary place. I looked at the raggedy sofa, so torn from where the Old Man had lain smoking cigarettes and plotted people's demise. There were cigarette butts throughout the place. I looked at the small table where papers were strewn about, and remembered the screams of my son, begging me to let him in during the cold winter months before. The Old Man had had a knife to my throat, laughing and threatening me not to let my son know that mommy was there. I was left to wonder, where did my precious son go? I remembered my children and me walking around with downcast eyes, because the Old Man did not want us to look at each other. I sat in front of the typewriter and read the last pages of my daughter's play. I studied all of the musical instruments –the guitar on a stand, a couple of microphones, the keyboard. Everything was covered with dust. The Old Man would have hated that. Surely he would have beaten me.

In the middle of the room was the stool from which I was forced to sing into the wee hours of the night. Bullets were everywhere. I looked at the door again where the knives rested inside the frame, and I looked at a long wooden board wedged beneath the doorknob. The walls were littered with fake certificates and a giant copy of a script that I must have written, "The Eye of The Know."

I must have fallen asleep, because the next thing I knew, I felt as if I could not breathe. I felt as if I were being dragged down the hallway. I wanted to scream but could not. I landed on the floor with a forceful thud, heard a muffled scream, and opened my eyes. I awoke to the sounds of my own screams. I had fallen off the sofa, and papers had fallen on top of me. I got up and found photos that the Old Man had taken of me playing the guitar and the keyboard. There were pictures of the living room and the bedrooms. I held the pictures to my bosom when I came across the one with my children clowning around. I held the photos until darkness fell and I could not see them anymore.

It was night now, and since the electricity was off, I fumbled in the dark. I found the few clothes that I'd brought with me, and I began to undress. I was paranoid now, and I decided to keep my clothes on. I found my way to the bedroom where the picture of the Man of God was, and I touched it for reassurance. I was afraid to go to sleep, so I decided to sing in a low hum about the valley: "I was down in the valley so low, so low, so low."

I stayed awake until I heard my neighbor's alarm clock go off below me. I felt around in the darkness until I found a pack of matches. I lit a candle and went into the bathroom. I washed up with cold water and dressed by candlelight. It was wonderful to be able to do this in my own home and not be afraid. There was no food, but it didn't matter to me. I grabbed my pocketbook, found the keys to the door, and held them as if they were gold. They were mine to control now.

I went outside into the darkness to head for work. I did not know the way to the train or bus, so I just followed a couple of people and did as they did. When I got to the station, I put the money into my hand the way that my son had taught me: "You do it this way, Mama." I could imagine how hard it must have been for him, teaching his own mother.

I'd learned how to ask officers for help. One recognized me and guided me to the bus that I needed to take to get to work. I was exhausted that morning when I arrived, but it was my job to be cheerful and ready to clean. That evening, I got lost going home. When I did arrive, it was very late. This happened for several days after that, but I was determined.

After a few days, Trina came over with her boyfriend, and I was still in darkness. She seemed cheerful at first, but I soon realized that my security as an employee was about to come to an end. Trina asked me how much did I get paid an hour. I told her 10 dollars, and that I got paid at the end of each day. She became silent for a moment, then stood to her feet and told me that she was bringing Junior back home. Trina said she was keeping my daughter, because she needed a babysitter so she could work. I told her that I was saving up to get my lights turned on because I wanted the children to come home to a comfortable place. She became verbally abusive as she threatened to keep my daughter from me. Upset, I asked her why I could not get my daughter. She screamed at me and threatened to fight me. I decided in this moment to trust God and be obedient to His reason for letting me live. I backed away and promised her that I would be all right. She changed in the wink of an eye, and so did I.

"Bring me my son and keep my daughter to care for your children, is that what you're saying? I just got out of the hospital, and I really need her to help me with my son." I said.

Trina did not care as her voice changed to arrogance. "I dare you to try to take her away from me!"

I pointed to the door and with a calm voice said, "Bring me my son, and we will be all right."

Right at that moment, I felt pity for her. I want to say I felt sorry, but this moment was important for things yet unseen. As the door closed behind her, I fell to my knees crying. I made up in my mind that this would be the last time that I was going to cry about Trina's treatment of me. Somehow, I was going to get control of my life and my children. When I finally got it all figured out, no one else would use us or take advantage of us again. I felt my strength return.

Early the next morning, Trina and her boyfriend arrived with Junior in tow. It was the weekend, and I didn't have to go to work. Tisha walked in the door so happy to see me. Trina tried to block her from hugging me, but Tisha pushed past her. We were tangled together, the three of us – Tisha, Junior, and I. I knew that her taking my daughter was not my battle any more, but the Lord's. I let Trina walk out of the door with Tisha, and I began life with Junior. No lights, no

❁

food, no gas, no clothes that fit, my knowing no one – but I was okay with it all.

Junior was 10 years old, but he became my teacher, instructing me how to navigate the neighborhood. He went with me to get my lights turned on with the money that I had saved. He would walk with me everywhere. I put him in the YMCA at the suggestion of a stranger whom we had met on one of our evening walks. At the Y, the people were so nice, and they took me on a tour. Junior seemed to love the place. Every day, early in the morning, we would walk up there, and every day, during lunch, he would leave. I would receive a phone call at work telling me that he had run away from the Y. I'd leave work and find Junior at home, sitting on the steps holding his chubby jaws in his hands. He looked so small. He would say, "Mama, I'm waiting for you!"

I had to quit working for the mansion and focus on my son. One day as I was walking my son to the YMCA, I saw a man go into a building that looked familiar to me. I let my son go with a teacher while I proceeded up the street. I went into the place and sat down in the hallway for a while, watching people walk past me and children lick envelopes. I heard the man on the phone. He seemed so powerful. Kind of like the Wizard of Oz. My knees trembled at the thought of meeting him. I decided to come back another time.

One day I found the nerve to walk into the office and meet the man, Rev. Hosea Williams. I was so small, and I was dressed the way I liked to dress, not the way the Old Man had dressed me. Rev. Williams did not recognize me as the minister's wife. I approached his desk and introduced myself. He was shocked. He had just gotten off of the phone with the Old Man. I told Rev. Williams my predicament, and he asked me to help him at the office.

Junior and I began to help at the office for a while. Practically every day around the same time, the Old Man would call, and I would leave. Finally, Hosea stopped taking his calls.

❅

One evening as I was walking home with Junior, a little boy met us. The two boys were so happy to see each other. Later a woman knocked on the door, and when I opened it, she stood there with two plates of hot food. It was my friend Cindy. She talked to me about the old days and the Old Man calling her from prison. She said that she would not take the calls. She asked me to come over to her house and see her other children. She offered to help me care for mine. She told me that we were a family who helped each other. Some other women from the neighborhood came by later that evening.

Soon, I had helpers who cared for me. They told me tales of all of our accomplishments as single mothers. They were saddened by my relationship with the Old Man. The women were helping me, but there was still a sore in my heart for my daughter.

One day I decided to go over to Trina's unannounced. I saw her children there with no supervision—and no sign of Tisha. So I sat on the sofa and waited for her return. When she did come back, she was followed by Trina's boyfriend carrying some Chinese food. I thought that this was peculiar, and familiar. I asked Tisha where had she been, and why she wasn't there with the children. I saw a worried look cross the boyfriend's face. Before Tisha could answer, I walked up within two inches of the man and said, "This is my daughter, and we have been through enough! You have no business taking her anywhere, wining and dining her. Her responsibility was to watch the children. If I ever think that you touched my child, I will be coming after you!"

He claimed that he was not after my daughter, and said that he was just trying to be nice. I left there angry with myself for not walking out the door with my child. When I arrived at my apartment, I sat on the sofa until dark waiting for Trina to come and curse me out. But she never came. That was my confirmation. I made it a point to stop by every other day for about two weeks.

❀

One evening Trina stopped by with Tisha. She was going to allow her boyfriend to baby-sit the children while she was out of town. Trina claimed that she did not trust Tisha being alone with her boyfriend without her supervision. Trina's boyfriend was with her, so I did not want to tell her then that I did not think it was wise to leave him alone with her children.

A few days later, I heard from Trina, and she was frantic. Her ex-husband had caught her boyfriend in what he believes was an embrace with his daughter. Her ex-husband had taken the children and charged Trina's boyfriend with child molestation. Trina was torn apart and needed my help. She had also discovered through a friend of hers that the boyfriend had a previous conviction for child molestation, and that he was not supposed to be alone with children.

It was sad to sit in court with Trina. We talked a lot about what I had gone through. I was there for my niece, because Trina had a hard time accepting what was happening. I told her that her daughter was going to need her more that ever, and that she needed to be strong to give her motherly support. The trial was quick, and the boyfriend was found guilty. Trina allowed the children to spend some time at my place every now and then, but that lasted a very short time as her wounds began to heal and she got on with her life.

My case, however, never seemed to be over. My children and I began to receive letters from J. Tom Morgan to appear in court. During this time, I saw very little of my family.

Chapter 12.

✄

The Next Battle Begins

It was getting difficult surviving without employment when I had two children to feed. I had to figure out a lot of things on my own, where my children could not help me. Looking through all of my business cards, I found the number of a casting agent. I went to the pay phone in the apartment complex and called her.

She was surprised to hear from me. "My name is Barbara, and I found your number in my pocketbook. I don't know if you remember me, but I thought I could call you to help me remember you. Why do I have your card?"

"Where have you been since *Kids Like These*?" she asked.

I didn't remember *Kids Like These*, so I explained about my amnesia and my hospital experience.

I was surprised when she said, "I need an assistant for a movie called *No Holds Barred*, starring Hulk Hogan and Tiny Lister. Can you help me? I need someone to help me cast ethnic talent."

Now I was really confused, because at that moment I did

✻

not know what ethnic meant. She told me that she needed people like me, people my color. I looked around my neighborhood and saw many people my color, so I agreed to do this job. I told her number to the pay phone and hung up. I was so excited that I started telling everyone I saw about the new job. People reacted to my excitement, and suddenly everybody wanted to be in the movies. I began getting up early in the mornings to go talent hunting.

"A Man Who Represents Himself Has a Fool for an Attorney"

The Old Man's letters from prison kept coming – to family, to associates, to attorneys and to friends – as my children and I were being prepared for the next trial. The team from the attorneys' office would pick us up for the trial and drop us back off.

As the movie *No Holds Barred* came an end, I was asked to help with the production of "In The Heat of The Night," a weekly television series starring Carroll O'Connor and Howard Rawlings. This would become the production that saved my life.

James began to get his own life, and I began to become more independent with my new role in life. Sometimes I would get cussed out on the sets, and I would come home not the least bothered. I would tell Tisha what someone had called me, and she would let me know that some words were meant to be an insult, like "nigger" and "stupid," especially coming from a certain female crew member. Some of my talent was so angry at her one day that, when they overheard her racist remark, they wanted to stage a protest during a scene for football players. I convinced the actors to perform in spite of the way that they felt. At a wrap party, she apologized for insulting me, and I could tell that she sincerely meant it.

※

Other crew members insulted me too, but they never called me names that had to do with my race. I would take the insults, get what I needed, and just move on. When my boss asked me to get something done, I was determined not to take no for an answer, and that carried me a long way. I didn't hear insults; I just saw the results. Soon crew members were teaching me valuable film knowledge, and I also gained long-lasting, wonderful friendships.

During the production of *No Holds Barred*, I had met the friends who supported me, and we learned the film business together. Every time I needed to be on set, I had a ride because they all wanted to be in the movies. Pay was low, but food was free. Hours were long, but it helped to make my days in court bearable. Many days I was able to take my children with me, and that gave us precious make-up time together as a family.

The jury had a real job ahead of them now. I had to sit out most of the beginning of the trial, and the Old Man used the system as a way to intimidate my daughter. I had thought that my family would be there at the courthouse with me. I'm sad to say that this battle was ours alone – mine and the children's – except for James. He had to work, and court days were his work days, but he kept in touch by phoning me through Cindy. He was dedicated, but he needed to make a living. However, I had more "family" through strangers who constantly came to my aid.

The day came when I was to make my presence known in court. J. Tom Morgan was ready to put me on the stand. Mr. Charles Johnson had tried to convince the jury that he was the highlight of our lives. He claimed that we had begun to eat steaks since he had gotten there and that he had brought religion into our lives. Mr. Johnson did not know that I was out of the hospital, or that I'd found all of the information that he had hidden. He didn't know that now I knew he had another name and was wanted for other crimes. He assumed that I was still in the hospital, without any memory of him. He tried to make the jury believe that my daughter had tried to kill me. The state-appointed attorney who was representing the Old Man was finding it difficult to defend someone determined not to follow the law or listen to reason.

On the day that I was to testify, I saw a hallway full of people milling about. I was afraid as I was led into the attorney's office, as the witnesses in the hallway looked at me with such sad eyes.

As I passed the crowd, I looked into the courtroom, just as Tisha was about to take the stand, and I saw the back of the Old Man's head. I went weak in the knees. If I was this nervous, I could only imagine how terrified she was. J. Tom had told us that there were cops all around who had bigger guns than the Old Man did, and that we needed her to make sure that he never hurt any more little children again. I was proud of how alert Tisha seemed.

When I got into the office, J. Tom prepped for my defense. He warned me that the Old Man might lose it when he saw me, but he told me not to worry. The police were ready in the event that he became violent. Soon Tisha came into the room and ran into my arms. They were keeping Junior somewhere else, because he might have been called to testify also. As star witnesses, we were not allowed to talk to each other on this day. Tisha and I just looked at each other. Today, *she* appeared to be *my* mother, sending me hope with her eyes.

It was my time to go. I could hear my heart pounding with each step. I was so ready to do this. I was so ready to face the man who had turned my life upside down. I wanted this battle; I needed it. It was real, but the ultimate reality was the one that I was about to face. I heard my name called, "Barbara Clark." I felt like I was rising from a pit with weapons drawn. My prayers were about to be answered. I knew that I needed confirmation that the battle was finally in a true court of law. J. Tom Morgan had warned me as I was about to go into the courtroom, that now I must learn how to fight within the system. Even if we know he was guilty as sin, we

❋

were still in a court of law where the prosecuting attorney had to convince a jury that he was guilty. I remember to this day J. Tom saying, "Once a victim, always a victim." I was determined to change that.

I had prepared myself through several days of fasting and prayer. My stomach knotted as I looked at the faces of the jury members. The courtroom was silent as I walked down between the aisles of benches. As I approached to take the witness stand, the Old Man began to rise from his seat with a wide-eyed expression on his face.

"I call for a mistrial, Your Honor!"

The Old Man's attorney tried to calm him as two officers took positions near his desk. That demonic look that I had grown accustomed to seeing filled every crevice of the Old Man's soul. I took my place in the stand and was sworn in.

Somewhere during the direct examination, the Old Man decided to fire his attorney. He decided to represent himself. And so it was. I was asked to step down, and Tisha was called back to the stand to answer the Old Man's questions. This went on for many hours, and then several days. But Tisha did not break down; she just kept telling the truth. The Old Man kept questioning Tisha, trying to discover what I might be prepared to say when I took the stand.

Introducing J. Tom Morgan

A few days later, I had to be back on the stand to face the Old Man as he represented himself. My first experience on the stand was gentle compared to what was to come. I had had to watch from afar as J. Tom and his staff escorted my children back and forth. But this time, it was my turn to join them, and there stood J. Tom Morgan. He was in his domain. He looked into my eyes and guided me through the fiery thunder, preparing me for the storm that waited ahead. This was going to be a different kind of battle where the playing field was not going to be fair.

J. Tom Morgan was a calm man, but I could tell that he was a leader and a fighter for what he believed in. For the first time, I was meeting the man with shield and armor, and he was fearless. He knew the law, and he knew that this case was worth fighting.

The case had been a challenge for some time. The courts seemed to give a lot of chances to a man who represents himself. Attorneys are bound to certain rules of conduct in court because of their knowledge of the law. But in this trial, I was not going to face the Old Man's defense attorney, but the Old Man himself.

I was going to have to face the most aggressive assault on the stand by the Old Man. He had the courtroom floor as his playground. He had a public place now to demonstrate his rule over me. I knew I would have to endure his tactics to destroy my image, because the Old Man had gotten plenty of practice for this day – the mock trials we recorded on tapes with me for hours, with himself as judge and jury. In those proceedings, the Old Man had always found himself innocent.

I was sworn in this second time, and J. Tom began the questioning.

It was a tense time for the Old Man, who saw that I was no longer in the state of mind in which he had last seen me. He assumed that I would be somewhat lost, but I was strong, and I was still fasting. I wore a simple outfit and had my hair pulled back in a bun. I saw all of the people who were sitting before me in court; I knew that this was going to be my first opportunity to tell the world what had happened to my children and me. The Old Man stared at me as if he were watching someone he had killed rise from the dead.

For the first time in years, I was able to look someone in the eyes. I made it a point to be certain of the questions that were asked of me. With J. Tom's questioning, I had

❁

been able to correct the lies that the Old Man had told jurors in the previous trial. Yes, we ate steaks, but only because I was receiving government assistance in the form of food stamps. Yes, the rent was low because we lived in subsidized housing. I provided proof that we were not truly ordained ministers. The Old Man had created many false certificates claiming that we were, but he had forged the signatures of ministers whom we had met. No, we were not professional film producers. We had taken a beginner's course in public television, and the Old Man had forged "T.V. Producer" on the little form that they had given us. Yes, we had been terrified of the Old Man because he possessed many weapons, which were then displayed before a shocked jury. No, he was not with the CIA, nor had been a Cleveland police officer. Nor was he a coroner or professional painter. No, Tisha did not have a play produced on Broadway, nor had we done any professional productions of movies or plays. We had lived each day walking the streets of Atlanta, with the Old Man trying to be all of the people he wanted to be. I was told every minute of every day what I should say and do. The jurors looked surprised when I testified that I had to ask his permission to use the restroom.

I answered J. Tom Morgan with all the hope in my heart that this Old Man would not get the opportunity to hurt another living soul again. It took hours to lay out the true story, because the Old Man repeatedly interrupted J. Tom's questioning, with the judge constantly warning him that he was out of order.

And then it was his turn to question me.

Mr. Charles Johnson stood up. He wore pants hanging low, showing the crack of his buttocks, and a pair of glasses that had been taped over and over again where the frame had broken. He did not look so hard now, and I felt that it was just one more of his tricks to have the jury pity him. He adjusted himself as he faced the jury and stated that he had such a beautiful wife. He looked at me with those eyes that would normally have caused me to tremble. I was scared, but there was no trembling today before the Old Man. For the first time, I had support.

Mr. Johnson tried to put on his best behavior as he attempted to tear down the image that I drew of him through my testimony. He was not succeeding, so he focused on his personal items that he thought that I might have in the apartment. He wanted to know where a particular policeman's badge was, and I did not know. He wanted to know about his instruments, and to remind me that I was still his wife, and it was my duty to make sure no one messed with them. He wanted to know about all of his weapons, because he did not feel that they were all there with the evidence that he had seen. Soon he tired of me, and Tisha was called to testify again.

The day proved long, and the trial ran for weeks. Mr. Johnson finally had his stage to try to prove himself as an attorney. No more tape recorders, but a real trial. He even claimed to have earned some kind of degree while incarcerated, to prepare for his own defense. He had been allowed to use the law library, and this was when he had taken the opportunity to copy legal documents and make unmonitored phone calls.

The Old Man had sent out dozens of subpoenas to people whom we had met, and to many from whom he had merely received business cards. These were people whom he hoped would remember him and prove his story that he was truly a man of God and an upstanding citizen.

As I got off of the elevator, I saw teachers, civil rights leaders, and a host of neighbors who were grouped together, protesting. Next, the elevator opened; two police officers and the Old Man stood inside. Mr. Johnson stepped out in chains, pushing a cart loaded with boxes of papers. He looked at all of the people whom he had called and puffed up with pride. He wanted to show to the jury that if he knew all these different kinds of people, then he must not be capable of child abuse. I know that people thought that both the Old Man and I were crazy. I could hear them whispering. Some acted compassionately towards me, while others were angry.

The day was full of theatrics as the Old Man called his witnesses, one by one, to testify. As some people walked out of the courtroom, they did not glance my way. They appeared awkward being involved in a case of child rape.

After the Old Man exhausted his witnesses, he recalled Tisha. This forum would have broken the spirit of some, but not my child. She was both afraid and courageous. The Old Man was at war, and J. Tom Morgan was the angel that protected us all. His staff was always there to comfort us and guide us through the battlefield.

Finally, Junior was called to testify. J. Tom asked him about the meeting that the Old Man had had with us discussing sexual satisfaction. Junior told what he heard in his child-like innocence. The Old Man tried to discredit Junior during cross examination, but the child only stated what he had heard and saw.

"I heard you say that my mama and Tisha belongs to you, and then you pulled at their private parts," Junior testified.

The Old Man became enraged as the judge banged her desk with her gavel to regain control. The jury was asked to leave the courtroom as the judge asked J. Tom Morgan and Mr. Charles Johnson approach the bench. The judge made sure that Junior was OK, and the jury was asked to return to the courtroom. Upon cross-examination, Junior said exactly what he saw and heard again. The Old Man looked defeated and asked no more questions.

A trial was coming to an end and it was time for closing arguments. Everyone, including the witnesses, were allowed to sit in the courtroom. The judge gave instructions to jurors before they listened to closing arguments. I sat and watched as the two men talked to the jury. One spoke the truth, and the other told lies. The jury was patient as they listened to the Old Man's long, rambling and incoherent closing state-

❀

ment.

J. Tom Morgan elaborated on facts, and he led the jury through the evidence to make sure it all made sense. The jury was asked to weigh the evidence, and J. Tom took a seat. After the jurors left, we all went to get some food, and we were asked to return to the courtroom when the jury had reached a verdict. It seemed like an eternity, until this day I do not know how long the jury was out.

The jury came back and found Mr. Charles Johnson guilty of child molestation, aggravated child molestation, and statutory rape. Count 1: 20 years. Count 2: 25 years. Count 3: 20 years. The wave of relief swept the courtroom. But the Old Man rose to his feet and started to run towards me, with fire in his eyes, drool rolling down his face and pants hanging below the crack of his buttocks. Immediately, a female investigator from J. Tom's office stopped him, saying, "Step back! Step back! I have a gun and I *will* use it!" He was within a short distance of me when he stopped. I never moved.

As he turned back toward J. Tom, he said that he would appeal. He screamed "They cannot keep me in jail forever!" Everybody was happy for us as we were leaving. With no less than 20 years per count, I believed he would be in jail for the rest of his life, so I was relieved. However, I later learned that that all the counts were to run concurrently, which meant he was eligible for parole review every six years. And when released on parole, the Old Man was to be under close supervision; he was also recommended to receive psychological counseling. I received a copy of the trial transcript. The verdict came on September 28, 1988.

We were led out of the courtroom, exhausted. I left there that day knowing that my children and I had become strangers to each other. We were all different now. The people we had been before we couldn't possibly be again. The children had lost their innocence, and they had lost the mother they knew.

❧

Strangers to Freedom

Freedom was new to us the first night. We were quiet as we ate. It was difficult to know what to say to each other. We gathered the dishes, and Junior began to cry, and that's when the pain we had locked up in our souls gushed out like water through a broken dam. The next day, I took the kids with me to the movie set. No one there was aware of the events from the previous evening before. Was this truly going to be freedom?

I began to watch all the educational television shows. I read every book I got my hands on, although I forgot every page as soon as I put the book down. I'd even forget the title and why I read it in the first place. I needed to learn, and I needed to remember things. Amnesia is a strange condition most people do not understand. They think you're lying until they spend some time with you. Doing films was safe, and I found that the imaginary world provided a wealth of knowledge. You got practical learning on everything: language, math, art, architecture, interior design, fashion design, hair, lighting, maps, people relations, and contracts. I saw so much in a day until I had trouble sleeping at night. I began to realize that I had a knack for encouraging people to do what they never believed they could do.

On a film set one day, someone asked someone else about me. The person responded, "Oh, she ain't nobody."

I took the response positively and created a saying: "I am the Nobody that helps other Nobodies be somebody special!"

I knew that without the Nobodies, a star is nothing. They are needed to be the extras and the beauticians, drivers, cooks, grips, photographers, publicists, producers, etc. They are the first audiences who show approval if a job is well done. They are the fans who come from all walks of life. These many faceless Nobodies are the ones who help

❅

create that Somebody. Without all of the Nobodies shouting their applause, where would that Somebody be?

Justice to Justice

In the midst of all of this, I got custody of Justice again. My aunt in Rhode Island and her husband were having difficulties with the teenaged girl. Justice was physically very much a woman, but she had the mentality of a 14-month-old baby. With her severe cerebral palsy, Justice simply did not know how to help with her own care. My aunt realized that Justice was never going to mature into a responsible human being, and that she would always be difficult to handle.

My uncle set out on the long drive to bring Justice back to Atlanta. He stayed with his sister, my Aunt Ellen for, a couple of months, and then he was gone, leaving Justice behind with her. Aunt Ellen attempted to keep Justice, but she also found it difficult to care for her. My uncle had done some painting and bought a few pieces of furniture for her apartment while he was living there. I had warned Aunt Ellen that some people live on you and that they fix up your home according to the lifestyle that they are accustomed to. I had told her that no one works that hard on a home that isn't theirs for nothing. I knew she was going to be hurt.

My uncle and his wife felt that Aunt Ellen now owed them for the work he'd done at her house, so they were supposedly taking the money from Justice Social Security check to pay themselves back. They kept the first check, which Aunt Ellen desperately needed. Aunt Ellen was devastated when her brother left her with a special person without financial support. Of course, I wasn't surprised, because I had already walked in those shoes before. After a few months, I received a call from Aunt Ellen saying that Justice was too difficult to care for. I did not have time to think about whether or not I could care for her.

While constantly receiving the Old Man's threatening letters from prison, I was beginning to pull myself out from so deep in the gutter. I had a career in the film industry that accepted my children, and sometimes I could bring them on the set with me. I wasn't making much money, but I was doing a job where, in time, I could. So I was afraid of the responsibility of caring for someone like Justice at this time in my life. But I took her in with no questions asked.

I had to apply for food stamps and welfare to support my children and Justice. I had to stand in food lines sometimes, but it was worth it. For a while, I wasn't receiving all of Justice's financial help from Social Security. I had to call my aunt in Rhode Island and demand all of Justice's money to come to her every month. She initially told me that she would send me 50 dollars a month until I gained custody of Justice. I told her that there is no way that anyone could care for her with that amount. I don't remember everything that I said to her, but I remember having no more problems after that.

I sent Justice to a wonderful school called Margaret Harris High School. It cares only for children and young adults with disabilities. The work that they do at that school is a miracle. I am forever committed to trying to find a way to support the teachers, nurses, and staff. I promised myself that if I ever become successful, I would give a great charitable reward to this marvelous school.

Justice was taking the bus in the morning to school, and my neighbors were there to help me whenever I ran late from the film set. Justice was very happy, but she was still a baby in a grown woman's body, and she could not talk. She was limited to traveling with flash cards to ask for what she wanted at stores. She would walk away with anyone with a smiling face. She had an eating disorder that made it impossible for her to realize when she was full, so she would eat until she threw up. Then she would continue eating as if she'd never eaten before. We had to hide food from her while we ate, even though she would stare you down as if she were

❄

starving to death; she begged constantly. We had to watch her in stores or shopping because she would grab food and eat it. But she was my Justice, and I was just as handicapped as she was.

Caring for Justice naturally limited my aspirations in the film industry. My children and Justice came first, but with that commitment came poverty.

Now, I barely saw the extended family at all, until one day Devon came by to tell me why he had not been over. He had feared that I would ask him to help care for Justice, and he was afraid of her. I told him that surely he should not be afraid, because Justice was his full-blooded sister where she was my half-sister. The two of them shared the same bloodline, and so with that bloodline came the same afflictions. I assured him that life has a way of repeating itself, and he owed it to himself to try to understand why Justice was special, so that he could make sure that it was not something that could be passed down to one of his children. Considering the fact that my stepfather had a sister who was also special, I assured him that I would check into why Justice was born with her condition.

I obtained a copy of my mother's medical records, and I also got a copy of her coroner's report as well. I discovered that my sister's retardation was the result of fetal alcohol syndrome; I realized that my mother had been a hidden alcoholic. I decided to look up some of Justice's old school records from some of her earlier reports given to my mother. It was sad, because the one from 1974 in Atlanta read the same as the one from 1989 prepared by a Rhode Island therapist. She had not advanced at all. I did not hear from Devon for some time after that, and it would be a few years before the subject would come up again. I believe that my larger family felt ashamed of the past treatment of Justice and me, and so the visits were few and far between.

I was having some hard times and some great times. I was so unaware of how people ticked, and I did not believe that there could be other people out there are evil as the Old Man. I was used frequently by some people I met, but because of what I had endured, I learned to walk away from these people before they hurt me. As I was learning how to cope, I had a few dates who tried to use me. I tried to assist some friends, but I quickly found out that they were not truly my friends. I learned very quickly that you can't help everyone. I also learned that every smiling face does not have a smiling heart. That includes associates and family members. Everybody who comes into your life should be carefully tested before allowing them too much freedom in your space, your home, or your heart. I began to withdraw and became a bit eccentric. I preferred to be alone and did not like crowds or meeting new people.

"It Ain't Over Till The Fat Lady Sings!"

I got so many letters from prison, but one from the Old Man stood out – he told me that the parole board was about to let him out of prison. He was telling me that he was coming to get his things, and me. He claimed that he had a son who was going to check on me. I was not afraid until I got home, and received an urgent message from J. Tom Morgan. He said that the trial judge had made a mistake in the sentencing phase, and the system was thinking about letting the Old Man out of prison until a new trial could be established. Now I was scared.

When we talked, J. Tom changed his voice to calm me, and then he said, "Do you have anything that I could use to keep him in jail until the new trial? Now Barbara, I need you to help me!"

I looked at the stack of letters sitting on the table, and I knew that the Old Man's own words would give J. Tom plenty of reasons to keep him in jail. I grabbed as many as I could in my hands and said, "I've been getting threatening letters from the Old Man. He's making threats against many people, including you and others. Also, he sent a frightening letter to my best friend, Cindy!"

J. Tom asked me to bring the letters to his office immediately. I took the children over to Cindy's and told her that I was going to the courthouse to meet with J. Tom Morgan. Once I was there, he read the letters and made copies. The letter to Cindy was most damaging, because the Old Man had shared this threat with a witness. J. Tom was surprised about some of the threats from the Old Man; one in particular threatened the judge herself!

J. Tom asked me to go home and wait for his call. I was really scared to death, because I didn't want my children to endure a trial again. J. Tom was angry with the judge, and he knew that we were going back into the battlefield with the Old Man representing himself again.

About two hours later, I received a call from J. Tom. He told me to prepare for another trial. He was also excited, because the authorities decided to keep the Old Man in prison.

But my knees were like jelly. How was I going to tell my children that we had to go back to court? I fell to my knees and began to cry from somewhere deep inside. Justice heard me and ran to my aid. She got down on her knees beside me and held me; she was just so full of compassion. I had to be strong for four now.

That evening, I sat with the children in the living room and told them that we were going back to court. Junior's biggest fear was eating with the Old Man again. The Old Man had been so hateful towards Junior at meals before, and the Old Man ate so nastily. The thought made my son sick to his stomach. Tisha just sat on the sofa, and I saw all of the pain return. Freedom was gone.

The next day I checked my mail box, and another terrible letter was there. The Old Man had drawn a picture of himself breaking out of prison with a notation: "I will see you soon!"

❧

Also, he wrote a letter reminding me that people had a tendency to believe him because of his gray hair. Then he went on writing, "I can tell a lie long enough to be believed!"

Finally the time came when I had to tell the children that we were headed back to court sooner than expected. Tisha was so hurt and torn until she could not cry. She sat still like a remorseful kitten. She looked so fragile. I went to hold her, but she resisted my touch. I didn't take it personally. Junior looked at me and said, "Will we have to see him eat again?"

"The Old Man will not be coming back here." I replied.

To this day, my son will hide to eat his meal. He is overly conscious of eyes watching him.

We talked about my being in the hospital. When I asked my daughter what she had thought when she saw me lying there, she replied, "I did not know that lady. I only knew you when you lived for me."

I was devastated. I knew then what I needed to fight for. I needed to fight so that my children could understand what it was to have hope for a future. J. Tom Morgan called and asked me if I had talked to the children. I told him that this was very hard for us. He told me to get them ready, because he was sending a car for us. It came to pick us up about an hour later.

We were met by one of the secretaries, who led us to the office, and the work began. We were questioned over and over again. We were instructed not to talk to anyone. The focus was preparation. We were warned that the Old Man was calling everyone again, and he was trying to subpoena them again, although J. Tom knew that many people were requesting not to show for the second trial.

There was no one for me to talk to any more. Nobody could understand the impact that this time had on my life. The children were reluctant to talk, even to me. We went day by day in a lull. We were afraid, but we trusted J. Tom

Morgan and his incredible staff.

Now I was caring for Justice, taking the children to therapy, and trying to mend my torn-up soul. Challenges were coming from everywhere. I was still working on "In the Heat of The Night." I was in the office with J. Tom one day and on the set the next. Some of the talent and crew knew what I was dealing with, and some even went through the painful steps with me. They drove me to the movie sets and acted as principles or extras. One was taking up photography, so he was able to get clients by being on the set showing photos of me. One crew member was white, and he had worked with me on the production of *No Holds Barred*; he never left my side. He was my confidante and best friend. He made me laugh, and he held me when I cried. He kept up a vigil with me as I went through the day-to-day preparations for the trial. Another friend who was reserved and quiet, had an incredible musical talent and was a serious actor. He did whatever it took to be available to my children and me. Before I knew it, I had several great friends who worked closely with my family. When we needed food, a ride, or a smile, someone was always there to provide it for us.

A few days before the trial was to begin, I went to the mailbox, and there were several letters from the Old Man. He had prepared handwritten subpoenas to try to trick me into coming to a prison to see him. I was not about to fall for such trickery, so I saved the letters until I saw J. Tom.

I didn't see James much until just before the trial. I had made it a point not to involve him too much, since we were not allowed to talk to potential witnesses.

Chapter 13.

✍

The Third and Final Battle

I had a terrible nightmare the night before the third trial. Thunder roared, and I saw the Old Man walking through my apartment, threatening my life. I saw my children huddled in a corner terrified, and I had to think quickly about the situation. I decided to confront the Old Man; he pointed a machine gun at me and started shooting. As I fell to the floor, I could not see my children any more.

Before I woke up the children to get dressed, I had flashbacks of the years when were hostages. I peeped in on them and was so happy to see them sleeping contentedly in their own beds. I remembered the first time Tisha told me that the Old Man had taken her to the storefront church to have sex with her before taking her to school. She told me about this after I was released from the hospital. She was afraid to tell me before, because she did not want to make things any more difficult for me. The first trial was hard for her because her mommy was not able to be there to support her.

I remembered all of the mornings that the Old Man took me to her school to prove to me that Tisha was going to school late. Now I knew that he was always the reason why. He was trying to plant in the minds of her teachers the idea

❖

that Tisha was a loose and sexually-active child. I remembered my daughter telling me that the Old Man would walk down the hallway of my apartment, and tell her to go up front room where he would have sex with her near the front door. I walked to the area, and I could not imagine what had been going through my child's head. I remembered her telling me about his sneaking into her room before the alarm went off to have sex with her before she went to school. I remembered walking down the hall and seeing him masturbating her and later describing to me in a vulgar manner his sexual appetite toward my children. I remembered him demonstrating to me how he was using his finger to masturbate her. He would talk repeatedly about having sex with my children.

I thought about the second trial with all of the people watching my children endure hours upon hours of grueling questioning. I remembered the pained faces of the jurors and sensing the fear all around us. I was just beginning to overcome. I wondered if I'd have the strength and the courage to face my second trial and my daughter's third.

I began to scream out in a voice I didn't recognize as my own. I dropped to the floor in a fetal position and cried out until I could hear the sounds no more. It was as if someone else were crying for me now, and finally I could take a break from the pain.

When I recovered, I heard the alarm clock go off. I got up off of the floor, stronger than I had ever been. An unseen force went out with me on that morning as my children and I got into the car with one of J. Tom Morgan's investigators. My situation was different this time. I was different. Girded up through the power of God, I knew that the battle was already won. I believe that the power of the Holy Ghost was apparent, because several times that morning people said that I seemed different.

We prepared for the morning, and as we attempted to get on the elevator, we were stopped because the sheriffs were escorting the Old Man up to the courtroom. He had a dolly brought up carrying several boxes of evidence, while J. Tom Morgan had one box about the size of a shoe box.

We were led into J. Tom's office for a final prep talk. He reminded us that this jury did not know us and that it was our job to help them. The Old Man was representing himself again, and we all knew that this was not going to be easy. It was all right to let our emotions show, and J. Tom Morgan said that he was going to present the weapons at this trial too. I was still terrified of the weapons, and it unnerved me that I would see them again.

J. Tom looked like a man on a mission, and he was going to be our savior.

The Trial That is Called "The Zoo"

This was the second trial in DeKalb County, but the third for Tisha; her first trial was in Fulton County. The judge presiding over this case was only concerned about the trials in the DeKalb County system. Though Mr. Charles Johnson was representing himself again, and he had someone at his desk to help him stay within the rules of the law as an attorney.

In the courtroom, the jury was seated and the trial began.

(Note: I'm quoting directly from the trial transcript, which is a matter of public record. Some sentences do not make grammatical sense, though I have made some minor edits. I will attempt to lead you through the proceedings with as much ease as possible, but much of what the Old Man said was rambling in order to buy time and to purposely cause confusion. He called this form of defense, when he used to practice trials at home, "walking through the back door.")

The judge addressed T. Tom Morgan.

"We would now be ready for opening statements. Mr. Morgan, do you wish to make an opening statement?" she asked.

❧

"Yes Ma'am. Thank you, Judge Workman." He addressed the jurors. "Good afternoon, ladies and gentlemen. Let me introduce myself. My name is J. Tom Morgan, and I am assigned to the Crimes Against Children unit of the District Attorney's Office. Seated at the table with me is Ms. Yvonne Ross. Ms. Ross is an investigator. She has been assigned to the investigation of this case, and she will be in and out of the courtroom assisting us with these proceedings. The defendant in this case is charged with two felony counts: child molestation and aggravated child molestation. We anticipate the evidence will show that the defendant committed both of these crimes, and you need to understand what these crimes involve. Child molestation is defined as any immoral or indecent act done to or in the presence of a child under the age of 14 with the intent to arouse either the sexual desires of the child or the accused. That is child molestation. He is charged in count one of child molestation in that he placed his finger in the vagina of Tisha Clark, his step-daughter. In count two, he is charged with aggravated child molestation. Aggravated child molestation is when someone commits the crime of child molestation, but it also involves the act of sodomy. Sodomy being, in this case, that the defendant placed his mouth on the vagina of his stepdaughter, Tisha Clark. Those are the issues that you will have to deal with in the indictment in this case. As Judge Workman said, opening statements are not evidence. Anything that the attorneys say in a case is not evidence unless the attorney has been subpoenaed and has to take the stand. That is very important that you understand that, in that the defendant is representing himself. So anything that he says, just as an attorney, is not evidence unless it's taken under oath, just like the opening statements."

J. Tom continued.

"The evidence will show that defendant under oath has said that he is an engineer, that he is a reverend, that he is a police officer, that he has worked for the CIA, that he is a musician, that he produces television, that he produces theatres, and many, many different types of things. The evidence will show, we anticipate in this case, that he is none of those, but a con man. The defendant came down from Ohio . . ."

J. Tom Morgan was interrupted by the defendant.

"I object, your honor. The prosecutor is putting my character into reference, which has not been brought into reference as of yet."

"I'll overrule the objection. Your objection is noted for the record. You can proceed, Mr. Morgan," the judge said.

"Thank you. The defendant came down from Ohio a few years back and met Barbara Clark, started calling himself Reverend Johnson. He and Ms. Clark were married. They lived in an apartment over there on Hardee Street with the section 1 housing. Ms. Clark has two children from a prior marriage: Jim and Tisha. Jim is the younger son; Tisha is the older daughter. They lived together in this apartment complex. The evidence will show that during that time that the defendant, on many occasions, would complain of some type of ailment or some reason, and would want to sleep in the front living room of the apartment complex, and that during this time he would go get Tisha, she being around eleven or twelve years old at this time, bring her to that front room, and he would molest her. The molestation began with acts of masturbation. And he being a preacher, and one she was supposed to confide in, explained to her that masturbation was okay. Masturbation was not a sin. Tisha would go to his church over there on Memorial Drive, where he had a small congregation. She even confided in her stepfather one time that some man was working in an office had grabbed her between her legs. This is a person that she at one time trusted. However, evidence will show that this trust was violated in the most reprehensible manner. The molestation continued on and progressed to the point that he would place his mouth on her vagina. She said she was scared of him, and she was scared to tell, that he threatened to kill her if she ever told. And those threats were very real to her, because as the evidence will show, the defendant possessed an Uzi with 80 rounds of ammunition, that he had shot the Uzi in her presence, that he possessed small caliber arms, that he possessed knives and different types of martial arts equipment. And through fear and intimidation, she was scared to tell her mother or anyone else about what was going on. Until one time, around April, 1988, end of March to be exact, the defendant was in her bedroom, under the pretense of reading some type of play. He was, in fact, molesting her vagina area. Barbara Clark happened to walk by the room and see this. She saw it with her own eyes. She will state to you that she was scared and shocked, but that she didn't know what to do. She was under the same fear and intimidation of the defendant, her daughter. She waited a few days until she and her daughter were alone at the Civic Center, where her husband, Reverend Johnson, and herself were working an odd job in security. She is able to get her daughter aside and talk to her and asked her. She asked, 'What was going on that night when I walked by the room? It looked like he was fondling you.' The child said, 'Yes, he was.' The kid then told her mother for the first time some of the acts that had been transgressing between her and the defendant. Ms. Clark didn't know what to do. She didn't know how to get out of this situation. She was scared of the man. She didn't know how to report it. She was scared for her safety, and she was scared for the safety of her children. The evidence will show that she told Tisha, 'Look, if anything happens to me, I want you to call a friend of mine who is a policeman with the Atlanta Police Department. His name is Lieutenant Walker. Remember that, Tisha. If anything ever happens to me, I want you to call Lieutenant Walker and explain to him what you just told me.' Tisha didn't realize what her mother was trying to say to her."

J. Tom continued. "A few days later, Ms. Clark took an overdose of sleeping pills, and had to be rushed to Grady

Hospital as an apparent suicide. They were able to pump her stomach out. And during that time, she made some comments to her brother James, who will also testify, as to some of the things that Tisha had told him. And James will testify that he went back and talked to his niece. He said, 'Your momma just tried to kill herself. She has come out of her coma. She is telling me that I need to ask you some things about what is going on with your stepfather.' Then Tisha, realizing now, putting it all in place what her mother was talking about, told her uncle James what the defendant was doing to her. An arrest warrant was made, and they found the defendant about to see his wife. And he had concealed in his pocket some brass knuckles. Lieutenant Kelley, who made the arrest of the defendant, will testify that, concealed in the defendant's pocket at Grady hospital, were a pair of brass knuckles."

J. Tom continues, "As I said, also, after his arrest was made, you'll see evidence that the defendant has, even being away from the home, has tried to put fear and intimidation in both Ms. Clark and the victim in this case, Tisha Clark. The evidence will also show – I anticipate the evidence will show – that these witnesses have testified regarding these acts almost two years ago. And it's particularly Tisha, now 15, who has tried to put all of this out of her mind. So, I anticipate that there will be inconsistencies in her statements and that we will have to try to refresh her memory with a transcript that she made over two years ago. I ask you to understand that and take that into consideration, that we're talking about acts that have been some time ago and now these witnesses must come in here and testify again about these acts, and how difficult it must be for them. I also anticipate that the evidence in this case will show that the defendant may put up the man that worked in Hosea William's office, and who will probably come in, I'm sure, and deny that he would ever touch a 12-year-old in an inappropriate fashion, and he barely remembers her."

J. Tom continued. "At that time, after the defense has

closed, we will rebut that evidence, and put in evidence of Tisha's truthfulness. Her teachers will come in, and her friends will come in and testify that they know Tisha. They know her reputation, and they would believe her under oath. I submit to you, ladies and gentlemen, that after you have heard all of the evidence in this case, you'll have more than sufficient evidence that you need to find the defendant guilty of both count one and count two in the indictment of child molestation. Thank you very much."

The judge called on the defendant. "Mr. Johnson, do you wish to make a statement?"

"Yes, I do, your honor," Mr. Charles Johnson said.

"All right," the judge said.

"Number one, good afternoon, ladies and gentlemen. The prosecutor has given you a great idea of what he says happened, but I'm not guilty of any of the crimes that he says. There are not things in this case that I will be able to tell you, due to certain things that have happened before in this case."

"Objection! Ask for a mistrial!" J. Tom Morgan said.

The judge spoke, looking toward the jury. "Let me send the jury out, please. Let me let you go into the jury room, please."

The jury retired from the courtroom.

"Mr. Morgan?" the judge said.

"Your honor, you instructed the defendant as to what he can and cannot say. And as to come in and say, I can't tell you things that otherwise you would hear would impress upon the jury that this court has kept out evidence as to his innocence. We went through this every time in the last trial. You know, it cannot happen again, your honor. I'm going to ask for a mistrial each and every time that is inappropriate. That is, if an attorney had said it, it would be grounds for a mistrial, and ask that it be done without prejudice so as not to hamper anything to do with the speedy trial demand. I know Ms. Tinkler is doing the best job she can to instruct the defendant as to how to be an attorney in this case, but this cannot happen again."

"Okay. I missed the last part of your request that it be done without prejudice?" the judge asked.

"Yes, so it would be done, that it does not interfere, that the court finds that the defendant by his own doing caused grounds for the mistrial," J. Tom Morgan said.

The Old Man spoke. "Well, your honor, Number One, I don't think I made any reference to what was said; so it would automatically, the jury would have no idea what I was saying. But I agree with the mistrial, because I'm not getting a fair trial, and I would like to start all over again right after motions. I agree with him. And I also would like, as I asked before, to see Judge Tillman."

"I assume you would have to write Judge Tillman about that," Judge Workman said.

"Yes, I will. Thank you," Mr. Charles Johnson said.

J. Tom Morgan said, "Your honor, the only thing, if the court wishes to give some type of curative instruction at this time, but I promise I can't go through another trial of time and time and time again making statements that an attorney would be held in contempt for, your honor!"

"Your honor, he asked for the mistrial!" said Mr. Charles Johnson.

"Contempt is not much of a sanction in this situation," Judge Workman said.

I know, Judge. We're all in a bind. But I do not know how to – to be honest with you – know how to work our way out of it," J. Tom Morgan said.

"Your honor, Mr. Morgan asked for the mistrial. The jury has been sent out, and I have agreed to the mistrial without prejudice. I would like to start over again!" Mr. Charles Johnson said.

"You won't start over tomorrow. Don't you understand? I mean, a mistrial is going to waive the speedy trial demand," Judge Workman said.

"Well I'll put in another one. There is nothing else I can do. He asked for it. I made a mistake. Like I told you!" Mr. Charles Johnson said.

"But you make that mistake constantly. You made it all during the last trial. The problem is, the contempt citation, at least in your situation right this second, is not very much of a sanction, because you are already in jail while this case is going on. And last time you continually violated Judge Fuller's instructions not to bring up the fact that there is evidence out there. What you're trying to let the jury know is there is stuff out there that if they knew, you know, it would make a lot of difference to them." Judge Workman said.

"Right. That is what I'm saying," the Old Man said.

"That's not what you can say to these people!" the judge said.

"Well, I see, I didn't know that," the Old Man said.

"Well, I don't know how you can learn it better than going through two thousand pages of a trial before listening to me a day and a half. If you can't understand it in that period of time, the concept must be beyond you. Let me take a recess and think about this," the judge said.

The judge turned toward the bailiff. "Do you want to remove him before I let the jurors out? I'm going to let them take a short recess, but do you want to take him somewhere, or do you want to let them go first, or what?"

"How long are you going to take a recess for?" the bailiff asked.

"Probably ten minutes or so, until I can figure out what

❀

I'm doing," the judge said.

"He can sit here," said the bailiff.

"All right then. Bring the jury back out, and I'll give them a 10 minute recess," the judge said.

The jury then returned to the courtroom.

"Ladies and gentlemen of the jury, there are going to be some matters that I have to take up outside your presence for awhile. And rather than keep you in this room, I'm going to give you about 15 minutes. If you wish, you can remain in the room, or if you wish, go other places in the courthouse or outside, you may. But I'm giving you the option at this point of either staying in there for the next 15 minutes or excusing yourselves outside the courtroom and coming back in that period of time. So whichever you want to do, if you will select it by heading in that direction," said Judge Workman.

"Do you want us to remain?" J. Tom Morgan asked.

"Yes," the judge said.

The jury then retired from the courtroom.

"Would you read back to me exactly the exact wording he used when he spoke to them, please?" the judge asked.

The court reporter read back the pertinent material.

"All right. I'll go back and think about this for a while. I'll be back. You are in recess for the 15 minutes I have described," said the judge.

Fifteen minutes later, court resumed. Everybody stood to their feet as the judge entered the room, "Thank you. You may be seated, please. Enormous time and expense has gone into the first trial of this case, and this far into the second trial of this case. And the court would, if there is any way possible, the court would rather give some sort of curative instruction and go forward. And so, I'm going to attempt to give them a curative instruction which just basically explains the rules of evidence designed to, with the most prominent purpose of the purest evidence from the purest sources."

Judge Workman continued, "The statement he made doesn't actually refer to any specific kind of thing that he is saying. And so I think that I will try to just issue a curative instruction, and tell them that the rules of evidence are being applied in this case, as in any other case, and that they will have all available and admissible information to make their decision."

Judge Workman's next statements were directed at the defendant. "Mr. Johnson, let me point out to you that if you make any other reference – OK, understand this is the last time that I'm going over this – if you make any other reference to the fact that there is evidence out there they're not hearing, or any kind of information of any kind that you, that there is information that they should have; otherwise, they are going to make a terrible mistake. If there is any inference, intimidation, any kind of suggestion in any way that there is a sexual history on this child that you're prevented from telling them, that there is any kind of sexual predilection on her part or preoccupation with sex, anything that I have ruled out, and that Judge Fuller continually ruled out, if you make mention of that, then I assume the District Attorney is going to move for a mistrial and I will grant it immediately."

Judge Workman continued. "Let me explain what that means to you. You have filed a speedy trial demand in this case. If, by your own actions, you cause this trial to mistry, then your trial demand is waived, and you will have to get in line to get tried with everyone else out there."

"Oh, OK," Mr. Charles Johnson replied. "So that means I would be here maybe for another five or six months?"

"You know how many felony people are out there awaiting trial," Judge Workman answered. "So I'm just pointing out that it's in your hands whether you get tried this week or way down the line, because you get the speedy trial demand, but you don't get to keep filing them, and filing them, and filing them. So you need to understand what this means to you."

❧

"Okay. Thank you," said Mr. Charles Johnson.

"Now is there any way that you are not clear about my instructions?" asked the judge.

"No, I'm quite clear, your honor. I think it was sufficient as it was told to me, and I understand it," Mr. Charles Johnson answered.

"All right. Now you're proceeding at your own peril. You understand that if you make any kind of reference to any of these things I have ruled out?" the judged asked the Old Man.

"Yes, I do, your honor. I don't think I'll need to. I think what was needed to be done has been done. Thank you," said Mr. Charles Johnson.

"All right. Mr. Morgan, if you want to put your objection further on the record. That is fine. Go ahead," said the judge

"No, your honor. I believe the court's curative instruction will cure the problem this time. However, as the court stated, if there is anything else that comes up, we will make the proper motion at that time," said J. Tom Morgan.

The judge instructed the bailiff, "All right, If you'll bring the jury back, please."

The jury returned to the courtroom.

"Ladies and gentlemen, out of an abundance of caution, I want to just give one more instruction or to remind you of an instruction that you have already had," the judge said. "I'm instructing you that you are to completely disregard any mention made as to things you will not be able to hear."

Judge Workman continued. "As the court has instructed you earlier, the rules of evidence are designed with one prominent purpose in mind and that purpose is the discovery of the truth. Consequently, the rules of evidence seek the highest evidence from the purest sources. The rules of evidence are going to be applied in this case as they are in any other case in this court. You will hear all available admissible testimony upon which you will have to make your decision in this case. Now, if that is clearly understood, if you would like to continue, Mr. Johnson."

"Yes. Ladies and gentlemen of the jury, I would try to prove it by the evidence. Thank you," Mr. Charles Johnson said.

"Thank you, Mr. Johnson," said the judge. "Are you ready to present your first witness, Mr. Morgan?"

"Yes, Your Honor. The state calls Tisha Clark."

J. Tom Morgan began direct examination.

"State your name, please."

"Tisha Clark."

"Tisha, how old are you?"

"Fifteen."

"Where do you go to school?"

"Northside High School."

"And what grade are you in?"

"Ninth."

"Okay. Tisha, who do you live with?"

"My mother, Barbara Clark, and my brother, Jim Clark."

"And how old is your brother?"

"Twelve."

"Okay, Tisha, do you know the defendant in this case, Randall Lester, also known to you as Reverend Charles Johnson?"

"Yes."

"How do you know him?"

"He is my stepfather."

"Do you recall when he married your mother? How old were you?"

"Yes."

"How old were you, Tisha?"

"Eleven or twelve."

"Okay. Where were you living then, Tisha?"

"1572 Hardee Street, apartment 38-D."

"And where were you going to school?"

"Cohen Middle School."

"Who lived in the house with you and Reverend Johnson?"

"My mother and my brother."

"Did anyone else live in that residence?"

"No."

"Tisha, calling your attention back to 1987 and 1988, what, if anything, happened between you and your stepfather that either made you feel uncomfortable or you did not feel was appropriate? Would you please tell the court and jury?"

"He started touching me in ways I didn't like."

"Okay."

The judge spoke then, "I think she needs to speak up. I'm having difficulty hearing her. I don't know about the jurors."

J. Tom Morgan continued the examination, "Tisha, I'm going to stand back here. I want you to speak loud enough so that all of the jurors back here can hear you, okay?"

❊

"Okay."

"You said he was touching you in ways that you didn't like?"

"Yes."

"Where did this touching take place?"

"In the house, in my home."

"Where in the house?"

"In the living room."

"Was anyone else present in the living room?"

"No."

"Was this daytime or nighttime, or do you recall?"

"It was nighttime."

"Explain to us how this would come about. What would happen, and where you would be when he touched you?"

"I was, I usually be in the living room when he touched me."

"Okay. Why were you in the living room?"

"That particular night, when it first started, I was in the living room watching wrestling with my brother. And he sent my brother to bed and said I could stay up a little bit later."

"And no one else was in the living room?"

"No."

"Where did y'all sleep in the apartment? Tell me who slept in what rooms?"

"My brother slept in the first room. I slept in the bedroom on the right-hand side, and my mother slept in the bedroom on the left-hand side, and Charles slept in the living room."

"In the living room?"

"Uh-huh."

❧

"Why did Charles sleep in the living room?"

"Excuse me?"

"Do you know why Charles, or Reverend Johnson, slept in the living room?"

"He said he wanted to protect us."

"When he first started touching you, Tisha, where did he touch you?"

"In my vagina area."

"Were your clothes on or off?"

"Off."

"Did anything happen, Tisha?"

"He stuck his tongue in me."

"Where did he stick his tongue in you?"

"In my vagina area."

"Where did this take place, Tisha?"

"In the living room."

"Did this happen on one occasion or on more than one occasion?

"More than one occasion."

"I know it has been several years, but can you recall about how many times this may have happened?"

"No. It was always too many to count."

"Do you recall how old you were when this started?"

"I was eleven. It was two days before my birthday."

"When he put his finger inside of you, were you under the age of fourteen?"

"Yes."

"When he put his tongue on your vagina, were you under

the age of fourteen?"

"Yes."

"Tisha, did he at anytime—Why didn't you tell? Tell us why you didn't tell what was going on."

"I was afraid. He had a lot of guns and things, and that scared me."

"What exactly scared you?"

"The guns."

"Why did they scare you?"

"Because he threatened to hurt us, my family, and my daddy."

"Did he ever threaten to hurt you?"

"No, not straight off. He always threatened to hurt the whole family."

"Were you scared of these guns?"

"Yes."

"Tisha, where were the guns kept?"

"In the living room closet."

"And is this also where the molestation took place, in the living room?"

"Yes."

"Where he touched you?"

"Yes."

"One second. I'll ask the deputies to examine state's evidence No. 1. They brought out a large gun and the jurors visibly reacted.

Mr. Charles Johnson interrupted, "Objection, your honor. You said you will make a ruling on this motion when it came about. You said that when he entered it . . ."

"I have already made a ruling on what was retrieved pursuant to the consent," the judge said.

Mr. Charles Johnson persisted, "I remember you saying to let you know at the time and you would make a ruling!"

"All right," said the judge. "Well, let me ask Mr. Morgan if my assumption is correct. I assume that this is evidence, which was retrieved by Detective Kelley pursuant to the consent given by Ms. Barbara Clark Johnson?"

"That's correct, your honor," J. Tom Morgan said.

"Yes, your honor, but that's – can we ask the jury to go out for a minute?" Mr. Charles Johnson asked. "I think we need to look at this again. Also, we have to look at the fact that – what the warrant said – this is what I wanted to get into before, and you didn't allow me."

"Well, we have ruled out that area of it, but let me send the jury out just long enough to get it clear on the record that that has been ruled out," said the judge.

The jury retired from the courtroom.

"Mr. Morgan, get out whatever it is that you intend to introduce through that theory, and let's do that now so we won't have to do it piecemeal. Does one of the deputies want to come over and check these guns first?"

The deputies walked over to a table where the evidence was and checked all of the weapons to see if there were the ones they confiscated from the apartment, and then they give the OK to proceed.

"Your honor, the search warrant only called for one, a certain type of item, to be taken at the top of the search warrant, which was notes and papers. These guns were not in DeKalb County. They were in Fulton County. The property sits directly on the line. The back bedroom is in Dekalb County. The front is in Fulton County. Fulton County had jurisdiction over them, and the venue. This is what I was trying to say before, but you would not allow me," said Mr.

❖

Charles Johnson.

Mr. Charles Johnson continued, "Fulton County was the one that issued the warrant. Fulton County was the one that suppressed the warrant. At the same time, it only asked for one thing – those papers. These weapons were taken illegally out of the house without reason!"

"But they're not proceeding under the warrant being the basis for the retrieval of these items. They're proceeding under the consent given by your wife at the time," said the judge.

"That is true, but my wife cannot give consent to take my weapons and my handcuffs and my badge out of the house!" said Mr. Charles Johnson.

"Yes she can, Mr. Johnson, and that's what she did," said the Judge.

But he replied, "She gave consent for them to search, from what the search warrant said, was for notes. That is the only thing that is on it. You can look in the transcript. There is a copy of it in there."

"Her testimony on the stand was she told them they could take anything they wanted in the house," said the judge.

"She doesn't have the right, though, your honor!" said Mr. Charles Johnson.

"I understand . . ." said the judge.

"What I understand to say is that as the search warrant reads, the only thing the officers had a right to look for was the notes or the papers, or whatever they were looking for. They had, from the way they had me charged, with no weapons whatsoever," said Mr. Charles Johnson.

"I have repeated this as often as I know how. They are proceeding under the consent. I have authorized them to proceed under the consent. You waived your objection after my ruling to them proceeding under the consent. It has noth-

❧

ing to do with the search warrant, and it's admissible," said the judge.

"But I want to understand something. In the transcript here as I was trying to show you on Page 3, these weapons were dismissed as unlawful possession of weapons, and was supposedly to go back. It's in here!" Mr. Charles Johnson said.

"Well, the City of Atlanta court can do whatever they want with their charges. You are not charged with having weapons here!" The judge said.

"What am I being charged with then?" Mr. Charles Johnson asked.

"You are not being charged with the crime of having weapons. They're introducing these weapons to show that they were kept in the house. They were your weapons, and that they were available to you," the judge answered.

"That's true, but…" said Mr. Charles Johnson.

"And I assume these are the ones they claim she was afraid of," said the judge.

"…but what I'm saying, your honor, is there is a suppression notice in DeKalb County, I mean Fulton County. And what I can't understand . . .," Mr. Charles Johnson said, continuing his objections.

"That may be true . . ." said the judge.

" . . . is that, if these are part of Fulton County, what are they doing in DeKalb County?" Mr. Charles Johnson asked.

"Because you live in the City of Atlanta's part of DeKalb, and that is why you're here," the judge answered.

"Live in…Ma'am…?" Mr. Charles Johnson asked.

"You live in the City of Atlanta part of DeKalb and that's why you're here!" the judge answered again.

"I live in the city — would you repeat?" asked Mr. Charles

❊

Johnson.

"The city limits of DeKalb—No, city limits of Atlanta, DeKalb County," the judge answered again.

"No!" Mr. Charles Johnson responded. "I mean where 1572 was, Hardee. As I explained to you, the front end of Hardee is Atlanta, where these were located, and the back end of Hardee of the same apartment is DeKalb, which would not allow DeKalb to have jurisdiction, would it?"

The judge answered patiently, "I'm overruling your objection. I have over ruled it before. I'm over ruling it again."

"Exception, your honor!" Mr. Charles Johnson shouted.

"Fine," the judge said as she turned towards to J. Tom Morgan. "Identify which items that you're attempting to introduce at this time."

"Yes Ma'am," said J. Tom Morgan, "State's Exhibit Number. 1: a semi-automatic machine gun and two clips that the rounds of ammunition have been emptied from."

" State's Exhibit Number 2: martial arts throwing star."

"State's Exhibit Number 3 is a 7-inch-blade knife."

"State's Exhibit Number 4: 8-inch-blade knife."

"State's Exhibit Number 5: nunchukas."

"State's Exhibit Number 6 is some martial arts weapon to be worn on the wrist."

"State's Exhibit Number 7: handcuffs."

"State's Exhibit Number 8: approximately 80 rounds of ammunition, different calibers."

Mr. Charles Johnson interrupted. "Your honor, may I say one other thing?"

"Not until he finishes," the judge said.

Mr. Morgan continued to add to the evidence.

❧

"State's Exhibit Number 9 is another martial arts type of weapon, 8-inch spears."

"And Exhibit Number 10: a pair of brass knuckles."

Mr. Charles Johnson interrupted again. "Your honor, for a stipulation of the court, again, those are not brass knuckles. They have been proven in four courts. On the back of it, proves again. I'm tired of the belt buckle being called brass knuckles. If this court won't allow it, I want it in record what they are, and I have the papers from Fulton County to prove it, and also the trial transcript, that those are not brass knuckles, but a belt buckle."

"I believe in the last trial, the detective admitted that it did look like a belt buckle, too," the judge said.

"No, it's written on the back of the belt buckle!" said Mr. Charles Johnson.

"So it could serve a dual purpose. But in any event, now she can identify them as the ones, you're going to have to tie them up with Detective Kelley," said the judge.

J. Tom Morgan turns his attention back to Tisha.

"Tisha, is there anything that I have just shown the court that you cannot identify, that you have not seen in your house?"

"No."

"Have you seen all of these things?"

"Yes."

Mr. Charles Johnson interrupted again, "Your honor, now I would like to say something. There are things missing here. I have pictures of the originals from the police department. The ones that are stolen before by Mr. Morgan showed a lot of difference!"

"These are the ones that he is introducing," the judge said. "If you have other problems with items that are missing, that has to be taken up in a separate court in a separate issue."

"What I'm saying is, it was part of this case. And there is a badge case, and the badge missing, and there it is on the big thing!" Mr. Charles Johnson shouted.

"But I assume that is part of your civil suit against him in a federal court?" said the judge.

"No, this is part of this case here. These are the pictures from the case that was submitted by Mr. Morgan to me, through Mr. Netherly, then stolen back by Mr. Morgan, but only with the number 6998, my old badge number on the back, and he had to return it to them," said Mr. Charles Johnson.

"You ask the detective at some point if he knows where those items are. But what is being introduced at this point are these items," the judge said.

"Thank you, your honor," said Mr. Charles Johnson.

Mr. Morgan turned his attention to the judge. "Your honor we finished with State's Exhibit Number 10, correct? We're on 11."

"We're on 11 now. State's Exhibit Number 11 is a photograph of a small caliber weapon."

J. Tom turned his attention to question Tisha.

"I'll ask Tisha if she can identify or has she ever seen that weapon before, pearl-handle revolver? Can you identify that, Tisha?"

"Yes."

"Was that also present in your home?"

"Yes."

Mr. Charles Johnson interrupted again. "Your Honor, may I see that?"

The exhibit was given to the defendant.

❀

"Your honor, I would like to ask where this weapon is?" asked Mr. Charles Johnson.

"This witness is not going to be able to tell you that," answered the judge.

Mr. Charles Johnson responded, "It tells me one thing, your honor. If you look very closely, or if you want to get a ballistics expert, if you look at the way the picture is made here, if you look alongside of the thing, I was just saying again, here's a badge case, showing the badge case. Here are two police officers. I think they know what a badge case looks like. And each photograph . . . "

The judge interrupted. "You can ask Detective Kelley those questions."

Mr. Charles Johnson continued, "No, you don't understand what I'm saying, your honor. Is it not, that pictures are supposed to be factual?"

"Pictures are supposed to be," said the judge.

"Pictures presented to a witness?" asked Mr. Charles Johnson.

"Pictures are supposed to truly represent the item that they are portraying. So the picture of the gun should be representative of the gun," said the judge.

"Right, for authenticity, am I correct?" asked Mr. Charles Johnson.

"Yes," the judge answered.

"Well then, why should you put .357 shells in front of a .22, which I never owned a .357?" asked Mr. Charles Johnson.

"You'll have to ask Detective Kelley about that," the judge answered.

"Thank you. I would like, could I have a copy of this picture?" asked Mr. Charles Johnson.

❧

"No. You can look at the original once it goes into evidence. I am not going to have a copy of it made," the judge answered. "I am not a photographer. I don't have a studio inside here to do that for you in the middle of trial."

"I thought maybe somebody could get a copy of it?" asked Mr. Charles Johnson.

"I doubt it, and we're going to be here all during working hours," the judge answered.

"Thank you, your honor," Mr. Charles Johnson said.

The judge turned her attention to the bailiff. "If you'll bring the jury back in ?"

The jury returned to the courtroom.

"Proceed, Mr. Morgan," said the judge.

"May I have the deputies check the clips to see if they are empty of rounds as well?" asked J. Tom Morgan.

The bailiff crossed the room to the display table and checked the clips and nodded his head in the affirmative.

J. Tom Morgan resumed questioning of Tisha.

"Tisha, I ask you what has been marked State's Exhibit Number 1, and ask if you can identify this."

"Yes."

"What is this, Tisha?"

"A gun."

"Have you ever seen this gun before?"

"Yes."

"Where have you seen it?"

"In the living room."

"Was that on Hardee Street?"

"Yes."

❧

"Whose gun is this?"

"Charles'."

"You're talking about Reverend Johnson?"

"Yes."

"Did you call him Charles, Tisha?"

"Yes."

"Have you ever heard this weapon fired?"

"One time on New Year's, New Year's Eve. New Year's and another party."

"Okay. Who fired the weapon?"

"Charles."

"So he was actually holding it and you heard the bullets come out?"

"Yes."

"Heard the bullets fired? Where was the weapon kept?"

"In the living room closet."

"Did he ever show you that weapon?"

"Yes."

"Where did he show it to you, do you recall?"

"Lots of times."

"Did he ever tell you anything about that weapon?"

"He used to brag about it all the time."

"Were you ever frightened of that weapon?"

"Yes."

"Tisha, I'm going to show you what has previously been marked as exhibit Number 11 and ask if you can identify the pearl-handle revolver in this, and is this photograph a true and accurate representation of what it represents, which

❀

is the gun? I'm just talking about the gun. OK. Have you ever seen that gun before?"

"Yes."

"Where have you seen that gun?"

"In the living room."

"Where in the living room?"

"On top of the TV."

"Do you know whose gun it was?"

"Charles'."

"Okay. This gun was kept on the television?"

"Yes."

"Was this gun there at any time when any of these acts occurred between you and your stepfather?"

"Yes."

"I show you what has been marked as State's Exhibit Number 2, Tisha, and ask have you ever seen this before? Can you identify it?"

"Yes. It's a star."

"Okay. Whose star is this?"

"Charles'."

"Do you know what kind of star this is?"

"It's used for karate."

"Has Reverend Johnson ever told you anything about this star, mentioned it to you?"

"No. He had it on the wall."

"What do you mean, on the wall?"

"He had it on the wall. He had it on the wall, like decoration."

❧

"OK. Was it hanging up on the wall, or sticking into the wall?"

"Hanging up on the wall."

"Which wall is that?"

"In the living room."

"I show you what has been marked as State's Exhibit Number 5, Tisha, and ask if you have ever seen this before? Can you identify it and tell us what it is?"

"Nunchakus, and yes, I have seen them."

"Whose nunchakus are they?"

"Charles'."

"Where were there nunchakus kept, Tisha?"

"The living room."

"The living room, as well?"

"Uh-huh."

"Did he ever show you these nunchakus?"

"Yes."

"What, if anything, did he tell you about the nunchakus?"

"That they were used for karate."

"Did these scare you?"

"Yes."

"I show you what has been previously marked, Tisha, as State's Exhibit Number 3, a sheath knife inside. Have you ever seen this knife?"

"Yes."

"Have you ever seen the blade open?"

"No."

❧

"Never seen the blade open? Where was it kept?"

"On the TV in the living room."

"Where the pearl-handle revolver was kept as well? Did this weapon scare you?"

"Yes."

"I show you what has been marked as State's Exhibit Number 4, and it has been taped, Tisha. If you cannot identify it, I'll take the tape off, but can you identify it without us removing the tape?"

"It's a knife."

"It's a knife. There is a blade under here; is that correct?"

"Yes."

"Have you ever seen this blade before?"

"It was in the case with the big gun."

J. Tom Morgan picked up the gun case. "This case?"

"Yes."

"How was it in this case, Tisha?"

"I don't know."

"Okay. And which gun are you talking about, the big gun, the Uzi?"

"That one, yes."

"The knife and the Uzi were kept in this?"

"Yes."

"Where was this—you said in the living room closet?"

"Yes."

"Did this weapon frighten you?"

"Yes."

❧

"State's Exhibit Number 6, Tisha, I'll ask if you can identify this?"

"Spikes."

"What kind of spikes?"

Mr. Charles Johnson interrupted again, "Objection, your honor. I do not believe that the witness could automatically be any type of weapons expert!"

"Well, if she doesn't know, she can say she doesn't know," the judge said.

"It's calling for a conclusion," said Mr. Charles Johnson.

J. Tom Morgan continued with his questioning, "Do you know what these are used for?"

"You put it on your hand."

"What do you do with it on your hand?"

"Hit people."

"Okay. Whose spikes are these, Tisha?"

"Charles'."

"Where did Mr. Johnson keep these?"

"In the living room."

"With all of these weapons?"

"Yes."

"Tisha, I'll show you what has been marked as State's Exhibit Number 12 and ask if you can identify these?"

"Yes."

"What are they?"

"I don't know."

"Do you know who they belong to?"

❧

"Charles."

"Did he ever take whatever is in this pouch out?"

"Yes."

"Okay.   What did Mr. Johnson say these were used for?"

"I don't know."

"Okay. Where were they kept?"

"In the living room."

"Did you ever see him use these?"

"He would play with it with my brother."

"State's Exhibit Number 7. I ask if you can identify these?"

"Yes, handcuffs."

"And where were they kept?"

"In the living room."

"Who do the handcuffs belong to?"

"Charles."

Mr. Charles Johnson interrupted again, "Your honor, I'll make an objection right now on this assumption: Number One is that everything has been showed to the jury except the rest of the evidence, and I would like for it to be shown— if he has it. There is a badge that goes with the handcuffs, and a lot more!"

"I'm overruling your objection," the judge said.

J. Tom Morgan continued questioning the witness as the Old Man sat down.

"Tisha, these weapons were all kept in the living room. Is that correct?"

"Yes."

"I want to show you another – State's Exhibit Number 10. Can you identify that?"

"Brass knuckles."

"Have you ever seen brass knuckles like these before?"

"Yes."

"Who owned brass knuckles like these?"

"Charles."

"Mr. Johnson?"

"Yes."

"Tisha, these weapons were kept in the living room, is that correct?"

"Yes."

"And you said these acts involving Mr. Reverend Johnson – putting his finger inside of you, and putting his mouth in your vagina – also occurred in the living room as well, is this correct?"

"Yes."

"Tisha, what, if anything, did Mr. Johnson say to you when he was putting his fingers in your vagina?"

"That it was only masturbation; it wasn't a sin."

"He said, 'It was only masturbation; it wasn't a sin.' Did you believe him or understand him?"

"I felt guilty. I didn't believe him. I thought it was my fault."

"You thought it was your fault? Are you and your mother close?"

"Yes."

"Y'all have a close relationship? Why didn't you tell your mom about what her husband was doing to you?"

❧

"I was scared, and he wouldn't let us stay together. We were always apart!"

"Where did you go to church?"

"I don't know the name of that church. I went to a lot of churches. I went to three different churches during that time."

"Was Reverend Johnson ever a preacher at any of those churches?"

"Yes."

"Where was this church located?"

"On Memorial. Memorial Drive."

"How many of y'all would attend services at that church? About how many people did you ever see there?"

"No more than 12."

"And that included your family?"

"Yes."

"Tisha, you have always known him as Charles Johnson, is that right?"

"Yes."

"And was he always a preacher at the church when you knew him?"

"Yes."

"Tisha, I want to call your attention back to late March, 1988, when you and the defendant were reading a play in your bedroom. Do you recall that day?"

"Yes."

"Approximately about what time of the day or night was that?"

"One o'clock in the morning."

❄

"Who was in your room?"

"Charles."

"Anyone else?"

"No."

"What happened that night?"

"He stuck, he came into my room, asked me to read a play. And then he put his hand up under my cover, told me to take off my shorts, put his hand under the cover, and stuck his finger in me."

"Did you take off your shorts?"

"Yes."

"What did you have on that night?"

"A t-shirt, and some shorts, and underwear."

"Did you take your underwear off as well?"

"Yes."

"Can you remember what the defendant had on that night?"

"No."

"Did you see your mom that night?"

"No."

"After that incident, when you were reading the play, did you have an opportunity to talk with your mom?"

"Yes."

"Where did this take place?"

"I talked to her that night. She asked me to get up, and I didn't have any clothes on. And I talked to her the next day, and I talked to her that Sunday at the Stax Show."

"Where was the Stax Show?"

❧

"At the Civic Center."

"Did you tell your mom at that show what had been happening to you?"

"Yes."

"Had you told her at any other time?"

"No."

"Why did you tell your mom then?"

"Because I was afraid he was going to kill me."

"Okay, who, who started talking about what was going on, you or your mom?"

"My mom."

"What? She started questioning you?"

"Yes."

"So, your mom began questioning, and not you, is that correct?"

"Yes."

"Did you tell your mom what had been happening?"

"Yes."

"And then what happened after that?"

"She told me don't worry about it, to go on to school, don't come back, and to call Mr. Walker."

"Who is Mr. Walker?"

"He was a Lieutenant in Fulton County courthouse."

"Why were you supposed to call Mr. Walker?"

"So I could tell him everything that was happening, because she was scared that she might do something she didn't want to, or she might get killed."

"Tisha, what happened after that conversation about Mr.

Walker?"

"We went home."

"Did anything unusual happen after that?"

"We went to school, and they called me at my school, and told me I had to come to the hospital, because my mom had taken some pills that night."

"Did you talk to your mom at the hospital?"

"Yes, but she wasn't awake at the time that I talked to her."

"She wasn't awake, so she could not hear what you were saying?"

Tisha shook her head in affirmative.

The judge spoke to Tisha, "You need to answer out loud, not just shake or nod your head."

"Okay," Tisha said.

J. Tom Morgan resumed. "Did anyone else question you about what happened?"

"Yes, my Uncle James."

"And how is he your uncle?"

"He's my mother's brother."

"Where did this take place?"

"At my aunt's house."

"And when did Uncle James question you again?"

"The night that Charles got arrested."

"Okay. What happened after you told? Did you tell your uncle what had happened?"

"Yes."

"And what happened after you told your uncle?"

❧

"They took me to, they took me to the police station, and at the police station I was told to meet Detective Kelley at Grady Hospital, and I got a test."

"Did you talk to Detective Kelley?"

"Yes."

"Did Detective Kelley also question you about what had happened?"

"Yes."

"Did you tell Detective Kelley, if you remember, Tisha, about the incident in your bedroom?"

"Yes."

"Tisha, you say you cannot remember about how many times this happened. Did it happen more than three times?"

"Yes."

"More than four times."

"Yes."

"Now, you said the defendant said that when he put his fingers on you, it was OK, because masturbation wasn't a sin. Did he ever say anything to you about putting his tongue on you?"

"No."

"Do you know about how many times that that happened?"

"No."

"Tisha, before all of this happened with Mr. Johnson, what kind of a relationship did you have?"

"We didn't have a relationship. I did not like him."

"OK. What made you scared of him?"

"He was constantly threatening us with weapons."

❧

"Let me make sure I understand this. You didn't tell any grownups about what was happening to you until your mother questioned you about it. Is that correct?"

"Yes."

"Had you told anybody about what was happening to you?"

"No."

"So no one knew about it, and then your Mama started questioning you at the Civic Center, at this show, is that correct?"

"Yes."

"Was anyone around when this was happening?"

"Just my brother."

"I didn't make myself clear. Was anyone around when your mother questioned you about what was happening at the Civic Center?"

"My brother."

"Your brother? Was he present there? Could he hear everything that was being said?"

"Yes."

"Okay. That's Jim?"

"Yes."

"Tisha, you testified that you were scared that he might kill your family?"

"Yes."

"Why were you scared? What did he say?"

"He constantly threatened about killing my father, saying that he'd make me turn against my father, and make me think my daddy was bad."

"Did he ever hear you threaten anyone else or hurt any-

❧

one else?"

(The reason that J. Tom asked this question was because the Old Man had tried to portray Tisha as being violent and jealous towards me, and because of that, she may have tried to kill me. But Tisha answered only what she had always heard.)

"He threatened my aunt, and my grandmother, and my mother, and he used to always make my mother beat my brother," Tisha answered

"And your mother is Barbara Clark. Is that right?"

"Yes."

"Tisha, realizing that it has been a long time, is everything that you remembered today true, as best as you can remember it?"

"Yes."

"OK. And you have given testimony before regarding these matters. Is that correct?"

"Yes."

"And as far as you can remember, your testimony today is the way it was then. Is that correct?"

"Yes."

"Tisha, going back, you were 11 or 12, and that was in 1987 and spring of 1988 when this started?"

"Yes."

"OK, it was the spring of 1988 when your mother questioned you about it?"

"Yes."

Mr. Morgan faced the jury and then the judge, "No more questions at this time your honor."

Just as the Old Man began his cross-examination of Tisha, her father, Jim, walked into the courtroom. His presence

❈

overwhelmed the Old Man, and he screamed for a mistrial. And then, he wanted to try to subpoena Jim. J. Tom came to me and asked if Jim was violent, or if he was high. Jim was a big, muscular man, and when he got angry, he was very angry. But I assured J. Tom that he was there to show support for his daughter; he would cause no interference or harm. Several friends from the film industry were sitting outside the courtroom on a bench with me. J. Tom Morgan assured the judge that Jim would cause no problems in the courtroom. The Old Man was told that Jim could stay, and so the cross-examination continued.

"Mr. Johnson, cross-examination?" asked the judge.

The Old Man rose and positioned his body in a way to intimidate Tisha. J. Tom Morgan closely watched the questioning for a short time.

"Tisha, you say that this molestation took place on what date?" Mr. Charles Johnson asked.

"Excuse me," said Tisha.

"On what day did you say the molestation took place?"

"Which one?"

"The last one you said took place. Let's start with that one and work backwards."

"The end of March of 1988."

"End of March, 1988. Am I correct?"

"Yes."

"And when was the end of March, 1988? Can you remember back or would you want me to remind you? Can you remember back that far? What time March ended?"

J. Tom Morgan interrupted, "Excuse me, your honor. Can I ask that the podium be moved? I can hear the witness better if I can see her"

Mr. Charles Johnson screamed. "Now, your honor! I

would ask that the prosecutor would stay down so he could not – as I said before – prompt the witness. This happened before!"

"It hasn't happened in my presence, Mr. Johnson. Now I'm going to have the podium moved!" said the judge.

"I'll move this out of the way," said Mr. Charles Johnson, as he moved the podium where he believed that J. Tom couldn't see Tisha. "Would this be all right, Mr. Morgan?"

"He has a right to see the witness the same as you do!" said the judge.

The Old Man maneuvered the podium until both the judge and J. Tom were satisfied, and he angrily resumed questioning Tisha.

"Tisha, you made the statement that this happened when? Now, in March, the end of March?"

"Yes."

"What part of March? March the 31?"

"Last day of March."

"Last day of March would have been the 31. Am I correct?"

"Yes."

The Old Man pulled out a paper report from a previous trial involving an officer not present to testify. He approached the podium and spoke to Tisha, "Can you tell me why the report you gave the police officer . . . ?"

J. Tom Morgan rose to his feet and sternly said, "Objection!"

The Old Man looked at J. Tom Morgan with a familiar, sly smile that we had all grown accustomed to, and he spoke in a very snide tone, "On what grounds, Mr. Morgan?"

"That is not the report that was given to the police officer!" J. Tom Morgan shouted. "I have a copy of the report!"

"This is a report that was given to the police officer, signed by Mr. Kelley, and we can bring him here to recognize his own writing!" said Mr. Charles Johnson.

"I'm sorry your honor," J. Tom Morgan said. "May we approach?"

"Let me ask you to approach the bench," the judge said.

They approached and held an off-the-record discussion about permissions. The judge looked at the form that the Old Man had.

"This is an incident report," said the judge. "This is filled out by the police officer. This is different from her filling it out. This form here is the statement she should have given."

Mr. Charles Johnson responded, "Right, but that is still admissible, because of the fact of what was said on it that led to the probable cause hearing. I'm correct, your honor!"

"Well, they are all a part of the case file, but this is not her report," said the judge.

"I didn't say that. I asked her what she gave to the police officer. Would you read that back, Ma'am? I don't think that is what I said. I didn't say anything about the statement. I said report," said Mr. Charles Johnson.

"All right if you're going to characterize this, it has to be the initial report taken by the police officer," said the judge.

"OK, I'll do it like that!" said Mr. Charles Johnson.

"Your honor!" J. Tom Morgan shouted, with anger in his voice towards the Old Man. "I would object to that being – that is not – that is the officer's report. That is what she told the officer. She cannot be impeached with the police officer's report. She can be impeached as to what she told him!"

"Your honor!" shouted Mr. Charles Johnson.

❦

The judge replied, "She can be asked if she gave that information, if she knows. I mean, he can ask her what she told the police officer, but it wouldn't have to be limited just to this statement. But that's the police officer's report, and he would have to be questioned about where those statements came from . . ."

"Your honor!" Mr. Charles Johnson shouted again.

The judge continued: " . . . or where the facts contained in that report came from . . ."

"Your honor!" the Old Man interrupted a third time.

" . . . the allegations contained in the report came from . . ."

"May I speak, Your Honor?" The Old Man said, interrupting yet again.

But the judge did not take kindly to these interruptions. "When I am through!" she said sternly.

Yet the Old Man continued to speak, saying "Yes, Ma'am. This is the first report that led to this report, which is the primary hearing – preliminary hearing."

The judge addressed the jury, "Let me send the jury out so we can try to get this on the record, and get this resolved."

The jury retired from the courtroom.

"All right Mr. Johnson, what is it you intend to do, show her this form and say –what?" the judge asked.

"This was a part of the last trial hearing. You said I could use it at the hearing. It's part of the record. It's part of the police report that we'll be showing the policeman, because it's two different stories in that report compared to what she says, and also in here, and also in the transcript, and also in the hearing transcript. I have got four different stories from Tisha Clark," Mr. Charles Johnson said.

"You would be able to ask her if she told him this offense

occurred on whatever date you want to ask, but this is not, you cannot use this report to show this is what she said. You would have to ask the detective where she got this information," the judge said.

"That's what I know. But I was asking her did she make the report, and take it to the police officer," Mr. Charles Johnson said.

"Well, she is not the reporting person on this. James, her uncle, is the reporting person. So your incorrect terminology is what Mr. Morgan is objecting to," said the judge.

"Well, from what I understood from the last time now, and in the last hearing that we held, Tisha Clark was the reporting victim with James," Mr. Charles Johnson said. "That's what I have in here, also. I'm wondering who reported what to whom."

"If you look on the form, the reporting officer is Investigator Kelley," said the judge. "Who discovered the crime is James. I mean, that is what the form says. But this is just by virtue of putting it on the form. It's a uniform form that everyone uses in police work, at least around here. You cannot try to impeach her with information that is on this form, 'So therefore, you must be lying.' You can't do that. Now, you can ask about your statement . . ."

Mr. Charles Johnson interrupted again. "Yes, that is what I was going to do."

" . . . that they signed," the judge continued. "But that is different from this report that you're talking about on top."

Mr. Charles Johnson defiantly interrupted again: "Right. I just was bringing that in, to bring in the preliminary hearing. I was laying a foundation. Your honor, that led to the preliminary hearing. Here is the preliminary transcript here. I have to lay a foundation to get it in, I would think."

"Well, the charge led to the preliminary – the arrest led to the warrant, which led to the preliminary hearing," said

※

the judge.

"I never got a copy of that, neither," Mr. Charles Johnson said.

"Well, you don't get a copy of the arrest warrant," said the judge.

"Well, what I'm saying , though, I can't lay a foundation if I have nothing to lay it with. If I had to use that, which is the preliminary offense, and then bring this in as what I want to bring in out of here – I have to lay a foundation!" Mr. Charles Johnson said.

"You can ask her if she made a statement to the police that was reduced to writing. You can ask her if she testified at a preliminary hearing, and then ask her if she testified to so and so, at a preliminary hearing after she is given a chance to look at the transcript to see what you're talking about. But you can't just – his objection is that you can't just hand her this report, because it is not her report," said the judge.

Again, the Old Man interrupted, "Right, I didn't hand it to her, your honor. I was asking, was this a report that she made to the police. That is what I said. I said nothing about what she had written in a report. I already knew DeKalb County had written the report."

"She would not know. She wouldn't have ever seen this piece of paper unless she was shown it in court!" the judge said with angry frustration.

The Old Man grew more defiant as he interrupted yet again, "Yeah! But, she was the one!"

This time, the judge interrupted the Old Man, and, turning to the court reporter, gave her this order: "If he talks over me, then his words just don't get taken down, and the court of appeals will miss it. But if both of us are talking, you take down what I say, and Reverend Johnson can wait, or it just can be missed. He has been instructed that he can't talk over me."

❖

J. Tom Morgan finally got a chance to speak. "Your honor, may I be heard on this issue? It's a rehash of what we had at the last trial. He kept trying to impeach her with that police report. Detective Kelley came in, and said that was the synopsis that he made after taking down Tisha's written statement, and that he made a mistake . . ."

The judge understood and helped him finish the sentence, " . . . and got the wrong date."

" . . . in his report and got the wrong date," continued J. Tom Morgan. "Tisha came out to Detective Kelley, gave one statement to him. He put it into writing. He made an error when he took her statement and made the incident report."

Mr. Charles Johnson interrupted, "Yes, your honor. And there is also something else on there. Here is the statement written by Detective Kelley in the preliminary hearing. I also have statements by Detective Kelley again before Judge Fuller, which shows beyond a reasonable doubt that she was impeached on certain things that she said prior . . ."

"The jury is the one who has to make a determination of whether she is impeached or not," said the judge.

"That's what I'm saying. Mr. Morgan is saying that she isn't impeached on it. But I'm trying to impeach her right now. What I'm trying to do is lay a foundation to present the jury my case," Mr. Charles Johnson said.

"Well, the only foundation you should be laying with this witness is to show her the statement that she made, not the report that was written by Officer Kelley," the judge said.

"In order to get into this, I have to lay this-that-that particular report because that came before that!" Mr. Charles Johnson shouted.

"No! No! Because this is her statement, you can ask her about this without asking about the initial report!" said the judge.

"All right, your honor, I'll accept that with exception!"

❊

Mr. Charles Johnson said.

And so the trial continued throughout the day with constant objections, and explaining of court rules over and over again.

A few days into the trial, a representative from the television series "Matlock" came by to inquire about the trial. It had been a tough few days, and the Old Man's theatrics were memorable, but not for a show like this one. J. Tom turned to the pretty blond rep and said, "Welcome to the zoo!"

She only stayed a few minutes and left. I thought it was ironic. Why was she there at this trial on that day? For a split second, I felt as if I were back on a movie set, and that in a few hours, this trial would be all over, and my life would just return to normal.

The days came and went at the trial. It was very much like the second trial, with all of the theatrics and confusion. The Old Man was found guilty on two counts, and was sentenced to 20 years for child molestation and 20 years for aggravated child molestation.

Chapter 14.

𝒮

Final Phase

I remained very confused when it came to meeting new people and trying to start a new life. I met some good people and some people who took advantage of me. But after all that I'd been through, I learned to distinguish right from wrong very quickly.

The children and I were sent to a therapist, but I barely made any of my appointments, because Justice was sick so often and I was just trying to survive. The children missed many appointments and many days out of school, because we were homeless on three occasions.

In 1990, we moved to an apartment in Stone Mountain, and James stayed with me after moving out of Trina's house. Times were tough, even though James had a job. I could not find stable employment with having to care for Justice. It was then that Tisha recorded gospel music over many of the tapes that the Old Man had made of me when we were hostages. The fake trials – gone. The story of my childhood told over and over again – gone. But a couple of tapes were saved.

Finally, James got a new apartment just as I lost the one I had. We all stayed with him for three months. Because we were considered homeless, I had a tough time getting my children back in school.

On movie projects that I was able to get, I made very little money. Junior was always getting kicked out of school for fighting or not participating in programs. He had a hard time sitting in one place for long, and he had a short attention span. No one really cared to know what was going on in his life.

My time on the set of "In the Heat of the Night" as assistant casting director came to an end after two years. A new director replaced the director who had hired me. But throughout all of the seasons of the show, I continued to have the opportunity to provide talent. At my last wrap party for the show, I met Senator Max Cleland through an introduction by Carroll O'Connor. He sent me a copy of his book, *Strong at the Broken Places*, a couple of years later. I read his book and I felt inspired. Senator Cleland had been a victim of war; there was an explosion and he lost his legs and an arm. But he endured and became a great political figure.

By the time that I received the book, I began living with what appeared to be a very nice gentleman named Ricky. I had met Ricky when I was about to be evicted from another apartment in Clarkston. I quickly realized that something dark lurked deep within him. First, Ricky began to find excuses to interfere with my friends and family coming around. I noticed that he was somewhat possessive. Although he had never said anything nasty to me, not even a curse word, I perceived something evil about him. One day he got his brother released from a mental institution, and immediately he began taking his brother's money and verbally abuse him. A month later, Ricky's son, who was about 7 years old, came to live with us and Ricky began to physically beat the child, abusing him mercilessly. He also called his ex-wife horrible names. Yet during all of this, he never said a harsh word to me.

One evening, Ricky beat his brother severely, took him to the bus station in the middle of the night in the rain, and left him there without knowing when a bus would come. I protested the way he treated his brother and his son. I called his ex-wife and asked her to send for her son, and Ricky began to say under his breath, "I will deal with you after your son leaves." That was my clue to leave. A few family members came to Atlanta to get the boy, and I made it clear to them all that I was leaving that night. One of the relatives told me that it was better that I did leave, because Ricky had a history of being very possessive. On that night, while my son was away, I noticed that the phones were missing.

Ricky began to verbally abuse me, and he had locked all of the iron doors, which could not opened from the inside or outside without a key. This went on for hours. Finally, Ricky said that he was leaving to get cigarettes. He slammed out of the door and locked it. I looked all over the house until I found a phone hidden in the sofa. I connected it to the wall and dialed 911. I told the operator that I had a handicapped person (Justice) in the house who could not run. I also told her that Ricky had not hit me yet, but I knew it was coming, because I had told him I was leaving.

The operator told me that help was on the way. I hung up the phone and waited. I heard the key in the door, and I ran and got Justice. Just as Ricky walked in, four police cars pulled up. I was only dressed in a black slip and a pair of jeans that I found in the confusion. Ricky began to scream at the police as they escorted me past him. One of the policemen grabbed Justice and told Ricky that I would return with an officer to get my things. They took me to the home of a friend who knew me since childhood. The phone began to ring immediately, because Ricky had my personal phone book. The next day, I went to James' apartment.

A few days later, I went to get my things. Ricky had taken all of my furniture, and cut up every piece of clothing I had left. As soon as I got back to the apartment, Ricky called, threatening me. I filed a police report and began another battle with a crazed man. After that, I was terrified to date.

Somewhere amid all of this confusion, the Old Man continued to call people and write letters. I lived my life with my children missing close to 90 days out of school during the two years we were held hostage and for each year of the trials. I could not maintain a real job with Justice needing so much care. We lived off of welfare, food stamps, and the money that Justice received from Social Security.

Many months, her check would not come, and on a few occasions, her check was stolen from the post office box. On those occasions, I had to prove that I had not received the money. I had to go to apply for assistance with rent and utilities, and that only meant a little help at a time.

I had to stand in food lines sometimes and shop at places like the Salvation Army and Goodwill for clothes. Whenever I was homeless, it was hard for me to keep my children in school, so I had to climb what felt like a muddy hill to keep them in, some of the year. I had to face the torture of telling my story repeatedly to school officials when they asked me why had the children missed so many school days. My children were judged by the school system, because they were the victims of abuse. Whenever a new school discovered that my children survived a heinous crime, the attitude of teachers and staff changed negatively towards them. That is when I would remember J. Tom's words, "Once a victim, always a victim!"

A few teachers were our champions, bending over backwards to help me get my children through school. One school especially, Margaret Harris High School for Special Children, kept Justice in school and provided her a bus no matter what my situation was.

I had to endure a lot of strife, and I prayed constantly for relief. Just when I was adjusting to freedom again, I had to struggle another hurdle. I received a call, letting me know that the Old Man was coming up for a parole review. It was 1994.

I had to warn anyone who would be affected by his release. I had to gather evidence to show that he was still a threat. I went down to the record division and made copies of transcripts and also gave the parole board copies of hand-written documents where the Old Man had forged signatures of judges, trying to trick me to come visit him at the prison. I also took letters he had continued to write to me and cop-ies of telephone records where the Old Man tricked other prisoners to call me. He was still representing himself as a minister, and some of the prisoners trusted him. Every time an inmate called, I would describe the Old Man and tell them why he was imprisoned. The apologetic prisoner would as-sure me that they would not call for him again.

The last call from the Old Man came when I received a booklet advertising police officers' weapons. He had found a magazine that a sheriff had put down in the prison library, and he stole it. He submitted a subscription card with my name and address. I immediately understood the message the Old Man was sending to me through the magazine. I called the magazine publisher in Covington, Georgia, who told me that they issued those books only to police officers. I asked him to cancel the subscription.

Two days after receiving the first book, I received anoth-er call from a prisoner. He sounded as if he were very young and nervous. I took the call so that the prison's phone num-ber would show up on my bill. When I explained my story to the young man, he was angry with the Old Man for tricking him. He talked to me in a reassuring tone, and apologized. I could hear the Old Man yelling in the background.

When I got the phone bill, I called the prison number. A kind male voice answered on the other side. I told him about the Old Man and the magazine; he remembered it well. He told me that he and the Old Man had been in the prison li-brary. He wondered what had happened to the book. He told me that he was going to do a cell search, and promised that the Old Man would not be calling again. When I hung up the phone, I felt reassured.

❈

At the parole board hearing, I told the officer all I knew. He said the Old Man would have to submit to mental evaluations and therapy to qualify for parole. These conditions for parole were part of his sentencing, but the Old Man refused to abide by them. Officials informed me that the Old Man would come up again for parole review in 2007. It wouldn't be likely that he could reside in Georgia, even if he did get out.

I live with amnesia every day. I keep records of everything, because I forget things all the time. I get lost almost every day. I relearned how to drive on my own. I taught myself a lot by watching educational channels. Gas pumps were the worst, and now, it's computers! Friends make my condition livable with their patience and understanding.

I hope and pray that this book will help someone who has been victimized realize that life goes on. Get on with life, and set an example by being a true survivor. I'm not saying that there will not be bad days. The pain will return. Pick up the pieces of your soul and carry on for the next victim that you can help save.

My daughter graduated from high school, but my son did not. She went into the Navy, and my son got into a few problems hanging with gangs. But he has grown up a lot, now that he is the father of two sons. He still cares for me like he did when he was my little boy who had to become a man too quickly.

My sister Trina and I get along very well, now that time has brought her through tribulations of her own. She has found God and is doing all she can to change her life and her ways. My children's father, Jim, had a heart attack; and he survived to say 'I'm sorry,' and to become a great father and grandfather. He married a wonderful woman who has worked closely with my children to bring them all closer. Jim's mother is now one of my best friends. With so much sad history between us all, we have had to learn to love one another despite the painful past.

❧

The last poem in this book demonstrates how I always had a song humming in the corner of my mind, even in my darkest days as a hostage. Although there were no chains – just guns and knives – my spirit was chained up and bound until I could be set free.

"I Sing In Spite Of The Chains!"
(Because I am)
by Tahiera Monique (formerly Barbara Clark)

"I sing in spite of the chains!"
I sing to the blue skies
as the trees whisk the breezes,
as a tune of grace brushes the seas.
I sing to the infinite elements
to reach out above all eternity,
to say, "Lord, I love you!"
because I know you see,
and one day you will set me free.
"I sing in spite of the chains!"
I sing to the melody of the harps
that the angels play
as they salute the coming of the Lord.
I maintain a hope.
I maintain a peace.
I know His name is Jesus.
I know His voice.
He is as free as the wind.
"I sing in spite of the chains!"
I sing until the melody torches the soul.
I sing until it sears the light of day,
to bring hope of a well-lit way.
I sing until tears of joy fall
from the clouds above.
I sing to the ears a tune
that the angels play day and night.
I sing until the hands of children
release the doves of peace.
Until then I will sing,
Sing,
Sing!

❧

Diary

My dearest diary,

It is April 23, 2002, and I am at the Marriott Long Wharf at the Boston Harbor. My husband is at a meeting, and I've just completed the last line of my memoir. I feel so isolated from my life at this moment. Every single word of this book is the truth. I searched records and many hours pondering the right way to tell this life story. I figured the best way to do that was to tell the truth as best I knew how. Isn't it ironic that, of all places to finish my book, is in a Marriott hotel, and J. Tom Morgan is handling the Derwin Brown case in my home town of Albany, Georgia. It was not planned at all. It dawned on me when a hotel employee said, "It's a pleasure watching you write your book at the Marriott here in Boston." After the employee left, I could not hold back the dam that was keeping my tears at bay. I paced the room feeling the pain from the past and, at the same time, releasing it. With four grandchildren and a wonderful compassionate husband by my side, I am ready to share my survival story with the world. My children survived to adulthood, and I pray that they survive the rest of the journey.

Diary (part 2)

Tonight I finally found the words to tell my husband that I had finished writing. At this moment, he is in a deep sleep. I can not sleep, because so much is going on in my mind. Tomorrow, we will be going back home, and we will begin the process of getting this book published. I'm a member of a great church called, Shades Mountain Baptist Church, in Alabama where I have an extended caring and supportive family. Only a couple of people know about me in this new city. It is wonderful to have new friends. Alabama, the place of great controversy, has become the place of peace and comfort for me.

THE END

❊

ACKNOWLEDGEMENTS

I would like to recognize the following people, institutions, and companies, for their support and encouragement over the years, and throughout this project. Some are family. Some are clients. Some are acquaintances. All are friends. To Hattie Sibley, my cousin, and my greatest supporter (Hattie, you are like a mother to me), to Sarah Clark, my mother-in-law, (Sarah, you are like a sister to me). To Attorney Anne Wheeler, Attorney Bruce Ely, and his wife (my friend), Karen Ely. To Attorney John Strohm, and Fernando & Karen Valentin and family. To Mike & Teresa Hawkins. To Attorney Darryl Cohen. To Myrt Turner and Deanna Cartledge of the Shades Mountain Baptist Church Encouragement Team, (thank you for allowing me to share my testimony with you). To my friends at The Mexican Center of Atlanta and The Mexican Consulate. Thanks to the staff at Crowne Suites at Lenox in Atlanta, Georgia and to HQ Global Workplaces in Birmingham, Alabama. Thanks to Christian Ray, Darryl Lassiter, and Howie and Beth Hodges (Beth, thanks for convincing us to produce this book now!). To Regina Lynch Hudson, "The Write Publicist". To the Alabama Film Office, (thanks for your unwavering support and encouragement). To Artist Wendy Lovoy (I'll be back soon to buy another painting!). To my dear Sunday School class at Shades Mountain Baptist Church (Graham Walters; Nancy Mitchell; Iona Luttrell; Jo Ann Mann; and Mary Collins), you are truly family to me, and I love you. To my friend Maggie Poteau, to my Uncle M.P. McCleave, and his sister, my mother-in-law Wilma Brown, and to my brother-in-law and sister-in-law Charles & Suzette Brown. To Kelvin & Yvette Maddox. To my banker, Jennifer Cousins, at First Commercial Bank (thanks for always being there for me). Norman Saia, Jr., (Norman, thanks for building my dream home, and a safe house for me! You are the greatest builder in Alabama!!). To Norman Saia, Sr. and B.J. To Bert Siegal, my dear friend and Real Estate Agent (the book is finally done Bert!). To Dr. Vance Blackburn (thank you for being a praying Doctor).

❧

To Marie Jones Sutton of The Sword Magazine, and her husband, Minister James Sutton. To the Georgia Film, Video and Music Office To Mark Stricklin of the Birmingham/Jefferson Film Office. To Ed Fields of the Birmingham Regional Chamber of Commerce, and to his lovely wife Cherie Fields of Catalyst. To Jerry "Smokin B"!, and to Durea Rupert. To Vickii Howell of The Birmingham View Magazine. To my cousin Robert West (where are you?), and to Martha and Rachel Hilley. To Margaret Harris High School for the Handicapped in Decatur, Georgia (Gussie Grant is still a hoot!). To the Marriott Marquis Hotel in Atlanta, Georgia. To Samford University Library (thanks for providing a quiet place for me to work on my book!), to Marriott Long Wharf Hotel in Boston, Massachusetts (thanks for providing a quiet hotel room for me to finish my book!!). To my dear cousin and Albany High School Principal, Sheila Chatmon, and to Albany High School coaches Archie and Charles Chatmon. To Gina McAllister (your support and friendship helped to build the foundation for where we are, and where we are going—you will always be a part of this girl!). To Tony and Teresa Mack (you pulled off the surprise wedding of the century!), and to Geraldine and Anthony Shannon (my surprise maid of honor and her husband!) and their family. To Gene Keller, Peggy Hayes, Steve Johnson, and Virgo Williams. To the National Coalition Against Domestic Violence (our journey together has just begun). To India.Arie, "Reen" Nalli, Hoagie, Dionne Farris, Carol O'Connor (deceased) & Nancy O'Connor (Nancy, thank you for the moments that we shared on the set of "In the Heat of the Night"). To the Pastors and Ministry Staff at Shades Mountain Baptist Church (special thanks to Michael Adler, Music Minister, Pastor Danny Wood, Rick Swing, and Steve Killough). To my dear friends Dick & Carolyn Clark and the boys (let's meet for Thanksgiving dinner again!), to Lewis & Debbie Burks (Debbie, thanks for helping me navigate Birmingham. I still have a lot to learn!), to Gwen De Ru of The Birmingham Times, (thanks for the press!). To The Kiwanis Club of the Magic City (my first speaking engagement in Birmingham, Alabama!). To Dan

& Karen Weinrib, Kelvin Knight, and Gary & Michelle Watkins. To Coke and Molly Clark, and Sid and Joanne Lanier, and everyone in the Alabama District of Kiwanis International. To Phil Reddick and Frank Woodson of Young Business Leaders, and to the following prayer warriors: Deborah and Howard Brown; Kerry & Wendy Lok, Rick & Sheri Burgess; Tim & Kimberly Howe; Jim & Deanna Cartledge; Randy & Daina Pittman, Larry & Phyllis Crocker, Kerry & Peggy Kline, Bruce & Karen Ely, and Dave & Connie Matthews. Special thanks to Robin Greenlee, Gail Vaughn, and my favorite caterer, Virginia Crenshaw, on the occasion of my 50th birthday (thank you for what you did for me on that day. I will never forget it). To Ann McMillan and Lajuana Bradford (you are two of the best mentors a girl could ever have). To the Chatmon's, the Idlett's, the Grant's, and the Carter's. You are most certainly my family! Thanks to Jordy Henson, my Sunday School teacher at Shades Mountain Baptist Church, and one of the first to read my "raw" manuscript. Jordy, it's finally done! To his beautiful wife Kim Henson, thank you for embracing our family with love, when we hardly knew anyone here in Birmingham. Special thanks to Kemberly English and Myra Hunter for helping us to put the finishing touches on this work!

It would take all of the pages in this book to thank everyone that I would like to thank. If I have left anyone's name out, please forgive me, and know that you mean everything to me. Without your support, this book would never have been completed.

Tahiera Monique Brown

❧

❈

RESOURCES

✄

National Coalition Against Domestic Violence (NCADV)
1120 Lincoln Street, Suite 1603
Denver, CO 80203
Phone: 303-839-1852
Fax: 303-831-9251
TTY – 303-839-1681
www.ncadv.org

If you need immediate assistance, dial 911.

The National Domestic Violence Hotline: 1-800-799-SAFE (7233).
Operated by the Texas Council on Family Violence.

Appriss
Provider of the VINE ® Service ™
10401 Linn Station Road
Louisville, KY 40223-3842
866-Appriss

www.appriss.com

❤VINE®

VINE, the National Victim Notification Network, allows crime
victims across the country to obtain timely and reliable information
about criminal cases and the custody status of offenders 24 hours a
day - over the telephone, through the Internet, or by e-mail.

✿

Future books by Tahiera Monique Brown

Lord, Please Don't Take My Picture from the Mantel

The Reaching Vine

The Shade Tree of Life

Beyond the Picket Fence

Wisdom Cometh as a Child

Happy Dead Day!

Living True and Truly Living

For information on release dates, please visit our website at:

www.tragedytovictory.com

or

Write to us at

Tavine'ra Publishing, LLC
Suite 700 – 316
270 Doug Baker Blvd.
Birmingham, AL 35242

or

Call our toll free number at

(877) 771-4433

ORDER FORM

Fax orders: 205-678-7453. Send this form.

Telephone orders: 877-771-4433. Toll free. Have your credit card ready.

Email orders: tahiera.316east@earthlink.net

Postal orders: Tavine'ra Publishing, Suite 700 – 316, 270 Doug Baker Blvd., Birmingham, AL 35242. Telephone 205-678-0400

Please send FREE information on products/services available from Tahiera Monique Brown, such as:

___ Audio books   ___ Speaking/Seminars   ___ Mailing Lists
___ Event Calendar   ___ Other books

Name: _____

Address:_____

City:_____   State:_____ Zip:_____

Telephone:_____

Email address: _____

Sales tax: Please add 9.0% for products shipped to Alabama addresses.

Shipping Charges: US: $4 for standard shipping (3 – 5 business days); $10 for 2 day shipping; $17 for 1 day shipping

Payment: ___ Check: ___ Credit Card:
___ VISA   ___ Master Card   ___ Optima
___ Discover   ___ AMEX

Card number: _____

Name on card:_____ Exp. Date: /

ORDER FORM

Fax orders: 205-678-7453. Send this form.

Telephone orders: 877-771-4433. Toll free. Have your credit card ready.

Email orders: tahiera.316east@earthlink.net

Postal orders: Tavine'ra Publishing, Suite 700 – 316, 270 Doug Baker Blvd., Birmingham, AL 35242. Telephone 205-678-0400

Please send FREE information on products/services available from Tahiera Monique Brown, such as:
___ Audio books   ___ Speaking/Seminars   ___ Mailing Lists
___ Event Calendar   ___ Other books

Name: _____

Address:_____

City:_____   State:_____ Zip:_____

Telephone:_____

Email address: _____

Sales tax: Please add 9.0% for products shipped to Alabama addresses.

Shipping Charges: US: $4 for standard shipping (3 – 5 business days); $10 for 2 day shipping; $17 for 1 day shipping

Payment: ___ Check: ___ Credit Card:
___ VISA   ___ Master Card   ___ Optima
___ Discover   ___ AMEX

Card number: _____

Name on card:_____ Exp. Date: /

ABOUT THE AUTHOR

๙

Tahiera Monique Brown is an Author, Speaker, and Consultant. She has dedicated her life to people that are often neglected within our society. Her background as an Assistant Casting Director and Casting Director in Atlanta, Georgia gave Tahiera an opportunity to become a tireless advocate for the homeless, battered women and sexually abused children and adults. Her passion for finding talent to cast in movies and commercials from this segment of the population was undeterred. This burden for "the least of these" awakened a call within her that she can remember from the time that she was a young child. Her constant concern for those in need provides countless numbers of people with hope. She is the founder of The Gussie Grant Foundation, named for her sister. This foundation will "PAUSE...FOR THE CAUSE" of providing funds to support organizations that provide sanctuary for caretakers of handicapped individuals, as well as organizations that provide support and respite for those in our society who need help getting on their feet. Tahiera resides in Shelby County, Alabama, with her husband, daughter, and two granddaughters.

❖

❉